MECHANICS-
MERCANTILE
LIBRARY.

Arthur F Mathews '61

BRAIN GAIN

BRAIN GAIN

TECHNOLOGY AND THE QUEST
FOR DIGITAL WISDOM

MARC PRENSKY

palgrave
macmillan

First published in 2012 by PALGRAVE MACMILLAN® in the U.S.—a division
of St. Martin's Press LLC, 175 Fifth Avenue, New York, NY 10010.

Where this book is distributed in the UK, Europe and the rest of the world, this
is by Palgrave Macmillan, a division of Macmillan Publishers Limited, registered
in England, company number 785998, of Houndmills, Basingstoke, Hampshire
RG21 6XS.

Palgrave Macmillan is the global academic imprint of the above companies and
has companies and representatives throughout the world.

Palgrave® and Macmillan® are registered trademarks in the United States, the
United Kingdom, Europe and other countries.

ISBN: 978-0-230-33809-8

Library of Congress Cataloging-in-Publication Data
Prensky, Marc.
    Brain gain : technology and the quest for digital wisdom / by Marc Prensky.
        p.   cm.
    ISBN 978-0-230-33809-8
    1. Technological innovations—Psychological aspects. 2. Technological
innovations—Social aspects. 3. Human-computer interaction—Social aspects.
4. Cognition. 5. Intellect. I. Title.
HM846.P74   2012
303.48'3—dc23

                                                                    2012011358

A catalogue record of the book is available from the British Library.

Design by Letra Libre

First edition: August 2012

10 9 8 7 6 5 4 3 2 1

Printed in the United States of America.

We actually live today in our dreams of yesterday;
and, living in those dreams, we dream again.

—Charles Lindburgh

For Rie and Sky

CONTENTS

ACKNOWLEDGMENTS

This book would not have been possible without the help of a number of generous, thoughtful people. My involvement with Palgrave began with Michael Thomas, whose Deconstructing Digital Natives and Digital Education and Learning projects set up the relationships that eventually brought this book to fruition. Karen Wolny, my editor at Palgrave, was incredibly helpful in helping me focus my thinking and in spurring my writing along. Jim Levine, my agent, gave me helpful advice at crucial moments. Another of my editors, Deb Stollenwerk, read the manuscript at an early stage and made many helpful comments.

I especially want to thank those who generously gave of their time and ideas in interviews, including Mark Anderson, Bruce Bueno de Mesquita, David Brin, Greg Bear, Ralph Chatham, Andy Clark, Dexter Fletcher, Hank Greely, Christopher James, Bill Jenkins, Shaun Jones, Michael Merzenich, Ramez Naam, Doug Rushkoff, Adam Russell, Vernor Vinge, David Warner, Kevin Warwick, Conrad Wolfram, Stephen Wolfram, and Michael Zyda (and any others whom I may have inadvertently omitted). I also learned enormous amounts from the many speakers at the two Singularity Summits I attended and thank all of them for their work and sharing.

I want to acknowledge as well the authors of several books I have read that had relevance to this project, including Greg Bear, David Brin, Jaron Lanier, Kevin Kelly, Daniel Kahneman, Doug Rushkoff, Nassim Taleb, and Vernor Vinge (among many others) for their excellent ideas which helped shape my thinking. And I also want to thank those people with whom I fundamentally disagree, for raising important issues and highlighting their own perspectives.

Most of all, I want to thank my wife Rie and my son Sky for their continual love and support, and particularly for putting up with both my old-fashioned piles of reference materials and my modern need for time alone with my brain-enhancing digital technology.

Marc Prensky
New York, May 2012

MIND EVOLUTION
IN OUR TIME

I n the twenty-first century, humans need better minds—and we are getting them.

Contrary to what you may have heard, the gains are not just
coming—or even mostly coming—from the rapid advances we are making
in neuroscience in understanding the brain's physical workings. We *are,* of
course, learning many wonderful things from neuroscientists. We are now certain, for example, that human brains change physically in response to their
environment. In fact, in the twenty-first century that is no longer "new" news,
although we are still learning how and where it happens.

What is new news—and much bigger news for humanity—is that our
brain's power is growing *externally,* though a new symbiosis with our technology. Because of this new symbiosis, the human mind, that is, the brain we use
every day, is gaining rapidly in power and ability.

What I try to show in this book is that if both "brain" and "mind" are
taken in a bigger (and perhaps more metaphorical) sense than just the phys-
ical-biological-chemical-electrical structure in our bodies—that is, if we take
them as the interaction of what is in our heads with the technologies that sur-
round us—then what is expanding our brains in the early twenty-first century
is, essentially, *technology.* Technology's evolution and rapid advance is tightly
linked to brain and mind evolution; it is the symbiotic integration of technology with our minds that is producing "brain gain."

To state this book's thesis as simply as possible: Human culture and context is exponentially changing for almost everyone. To adapt to and thrive in that context, we all need to extend our abilities. Today's technology is making this happen, and it is extending and "liberating" our minds in many helpful and valuable ways. Our technology will continue to make us freer and better—but only if we develop and use it wisely.

Because we do not know exactly how the brain works, or how it generates our expanding mind,[1] "brain gain," as I use it in this book, is something of a metaphor. Most of the technologies that produce the gain are not, for the moment, physically wired to or implanted in our heads (although some, as we shall see, are already moving in that direction). Nor are the mechanisms by which the physical brain adapts to connect us to these technologies completely understood. You can, if you wish, think about "brain gain" as a more alliterative term for "mind gain." It is the human mind—our brain in action—that is quickly and vastly expanding to meet the challenges of the twenty-first century as a result of the great advances of technology. Since mind and brain are of a whole, any gain in one is a gain in the other—in extending our minds, technology extends our brains.

TECHNOLOGY?

The technology I am talking about here is pretty much all of it—I see technology as everything that humans have invented or appropriated from the external world to help us. Technology comes in many forms—physical, electrical, digital, even pharmacological—and covers a wide spectrum of human activity, from speech, to writing, to clothing, to tools, to modern digital tools.

Technology has *always* improved humans in the long run, despite occasional setbacks; it is how we have come to where we are, and to be who we are. And technology has always done this by enhancing our human capabilities. Today, more and more of the capabilities that technology enhances are in our minds.

What is happening with increasing speed in the twenty-first century is that a large number of new technologies *external* to our physical brain—technologies invented not by nature's evolution but by humans—are now able to work with the human brain and enhance its power. This is happening in a great many areas and far more quickly than most people realize. Humans can now concentrate more, calculate more, analyze more, connect more, communicate more, and create more than ever before—all because of technology. And it is this phenomenon of connecting ourselves to technology—and not old-fashioned evolution—that is making the huge positive difference in our lives today.

By incorporating these external technologies into our brains and minds, we have entered a period of intense "brain gain." Rather than harming humans, as many fear, the power of technology is already enhancing our entire species in ways that I believe are *almost entirely* positive. A host of technologies are freeing our minds to know more, to do more, and to interact with more of the people that we want to in more and more ways. In Chapter 3, I offer 50 examples of how human minds are being enhanced, leveraged, and improved by technology. Even more importantly, I show that people, on their own, are recognizing these new capabilities and adopting them.

We are now, as a result, far better humans than ever before. This book is about all the ways these many technological changes are improving our minds, and about people's attempts—and urgent need—to harness and use them wisely.

THE GERM THAT GOT ME THINKING

The journey that led to this volume, and to my own clearly positive attitudes toward the possibilities and power of enhancing our minds through technology, began almost 25 years ago. I can even remember the exact moment, although I couldn't give you an exact date. But it all started one day when, while driving to work, I heard on my 1985 Volvo's radio a conundrum posed by a computer scientist working with intensive care units in hospitals.

The speaker (his name now long forgotten by me) explained that the number of beds in most intensive care units is limited by design, because such units are expensive. The number of beds is therefore often smaller than the number of patients whose doctors suggest they go or remain there. So in order to assure that the available beds are filled by those patients most likely to be helped by those facilities, decisions must continually be made about which patients enter or stay in the ICU and which leave.

Up until then, the speaker explained, such decisions were made only by individual doctors (or groups of doctors), based entirely on their own accumulated experience and judgment about each individual ICU patient. That seemed reasonable to most. But that approach, the computer scientist argued, often led to bad results. He therefore concluded it was not the wisest way to make those decisions. I shall never forget his explanation of why.

Doctors, this scientist said, tend to focus, by their nature as humans, on two kinds of data: the recent and the unusual. For many things in medicine, this works well and is an acceptable way to decide. But in cases like the ICU decision, in order to make the decisions wisely and correctly, the focus needs to be on what occurred *statistically* to *all* patients *ever* to have been in an ICU with the same presentations as the current patients. This is something, the scientist pointed out, that human brains, on their own, are just incapable of doing. They just cannot collect, store, or analyze all of that data.

But machines, of course, can—and can do it very well. Given even massive amounts of data, computers, with proper programming, can easily compute the statistics and calculate the probabilities of each patient's recovery. So this scientist and his colleagues had created a so-called "expert system" called Acute Physiology & Chronic Health Evaluation (APACHE) to help make these decisions. APACHE retrieved all the historical data on similar patients, performed the necessary statistical analysis, and provided a ranking of the patients' likelihood of getting well.

It turned out that the *combination* of this statistical ranking with the doctors' judgment provided the wisest solution. The doctors' judgment was enhanced by the addition of the machine. The APACHE system, revised and improved over time, is still in use.[2]

APACHE was a harbinger of enormous changes to come. There are now more ways to use technology to extend human capabilities to achieve wiser solutions and make better judgments than ever before. Not only have our "old" mental capabilities been extended and amplified in the twenty-first century, but entirely new human capabilities have been created and new intellectual paths have opened up. Taking those paths, which are based on a wide range of new technologies, some physical, some virtual, some biological—and some on new combinations of all of those—is enhancing all human minds positively in a growing number of ways that were never before possible (and, in many cases, never *thought* possible).

And this is only the beginning.

In February 2009, Bruce Bueno de Mesquita gave a talk that I attended at the annual TED conference in Long Beach, California. In the presentation he recounted how he has, for years, been using computer modeling to predict the behaviors of the world's political and economic leaders. He has predicted—with over 90 percent accuracy—many important figures' behavior in critical situations. His predictions, he told the audience, have been extremely helpful to the U.S. government, to companies, and to other organizations in the world, mostly in ways that are mostly still too secret and sensitive to talk about.

The audience—a very sophisticated group, many from technology backgrounds, who had paid $6,000 each to be there—greeted Bueno de Mesquita's talk mostly with skepticism. They essentially didn't believe him and rejected the notion that such accuracy of prediction via technology was possible. Many thought both he, and computers in general, had a too-rational view of human behavior to allow such predictions to be accurate.

But they were mistaken. It turns out that, independent of one's view of human rationality, such accurate prediction is possible, thanks to technology. A few months later those skeptics could see Bueno de Mesquita's picture on the cover of the *New York Times Magazine*.[3] They could read that similar technology helped predict Hosni Mubarak's downfall in Egypt and Moammar Gadhafi's downfall in Libya and help find where Saddam Hussein and Osama bin Laden had been hiding.[4] Today, others are using these kinds of technology to make never-before-possible predictions in other fields, with equal accuracy.

Because of the rapid advances in technology, notions of what is possible and, more importantly, "wise" in many situations are undergoing profound change. What causes our old, non-digitally enhanced wisdom to no longer apply, in more and more cases, is not just the sheer volume of the changes in so many areas of our lives. It is also the speed at which the changes are accelerating and will continue to accelerate in our lifetimes and the lifetimes of our children. This combination presents us with more and more new situations where new wisdom is required—and, at the same time, with new solutions for finding it. If wisdom lies in reaching and implementing useful and beneficial conclusions, those conclusions are rapidly changing.

It used to be wise, for example, to memorize a great deal of information when you were young that would stand you in good stead for the rest of your life. Today's wisdom is that it's far better to learn how to acquire new information.

It used to be wise to find a job, or an employer, you could hold onto for life. Today's wisdom is that the skills you will need will come from many jobs and employers.

It used to be wise for an employer to retain those employees who had "learned the ropes" for as long as possible. Today the wisdom for many employers is to unleash capable employees to startups and even to competitors, and to hire new employees who are even more in tune with current technology.

It used to be wise to keep your strongest ties local. Today it may be wiser to have your strongest ties be around the world.

It used to be wise to hold onto an expensive device until it literally stopped working or fell apart. Today's wisdom is often to upgrade to a new device every year—or less.

It used to be wise to get as much work experience as possible before starting a business. Today many find it wiser to just create a company.

It used to be wise to "pay your dues."

It used to be wise to postpone rewards.

It used to be wise not to take drugs to improve ourselves.

It used to be wise for every kid to stay in school, rather than leave to join a startup.

It used to be wise to do all schoolwork independently, and to not allow calculators or computers on exams.

I'm sure you already see, feel, and are aware of many of the changes that have taken place in our "received wisdom," although you certainly might not agree with all of them. It once was considered unwise (i.e., rude and impolite) to have an answering machine on your phone. Now it's unwise not to. It was once considered unwise to spend extra for the maximum computer memory or the fastest Internet connection you could afford. Now it's unwise not to. It was once considered unwise to have a cell phone. Now two-thirds of the planet's people do. It was once considered unwise to send personal notes by email. Now it's expected. It was once considered unwise to give up your landline. Now over 26 percent of U.S. phone users have only a cell phone.[5] It was once considered unwise to answer a request before reflecting for weeks. Now a far quicker response is expected. It was once considered unwise to learn something from TV, a video, a movie, or a game, rather than from a book. Now those media have become the primary way many people learn. It was once considered unwise to read books on screens. Now I see as many Kindles as books on airplanes.

Today, our young people—and many older folks as well—see that much of our "received" wisdom no longer applies in life. We see school dropouts and kids straight out of college, such as Bill Gates of Microsoft and Mark

Zuckerberg of Facebook, becoming some of the richest people in the world. We see highly successful people like Sean Combs and Steve Jobs changing jobs, and even industries, with high frequency. We see expensive purchases, such as TVs, computers, and cell phones, become totally obsolete long before they wear out. We see TV game contestants being told they can "phone a friend" or "poll the audience" to get answers. Much of the world can watch computers beating chess grandmasters and quiz champions. Our kids are being told to expect to have 10–15 different jobs in their working lives.[6]

While many of us feel uncomfortable with all these changes, often wishing we could just go back to the "good old" or "wise old" days before all this technology arrived, we can't and we won't.

So we need new guidance on what is wise in our times—a "new" kind of wisdom, wisdom that takes all this technology into account: "digital wisdom." Not that "old" wisdom never counts or applies—it often does. But we need to figure out where and when the "old" wisdom still works, and where and when it doesn't. And, in the latter case, we need to put something new in its place. This is what I call "the quest for digital wisdom."

I call it a "quest" because it is a difficult journey. There is no fixed destination and no "right" answer. We are all learning about the new technologies and feeling their power to affect us as they insinuate themselves, willy-nilly, into our lives. We are all surprised, at times, by the power of technology, and are all, at times, disconcerted by it. We all struggle to find what is best and wise in the various aspects of our life: home, work, recreation, relationships. We all find that many of the roads technology takes us down lead to new places, some of which we find frightening and disorienting. As part of our quest we conduct a great deal of research, but we have to be careful not to be too definitive in our conclusions, because the meaning of the findings often gets re-interpreted as our understanding grows.

Ultimately, though, the search for digital wisdom is a quest because it is worthwhile—the goal of becoming wiser is hugely important to humanity. Wisdom is an ill-defined term; it involves, I believe, considering the largest possible number of factors, analyzing them appropriately and well, and reaching and implementing useful and beneficial conclusions. *Digital* wisdom resides in doing this for both the technologies we use and the way that we use them.

I certainly do not know everything that is digitally wise. I have my own ideas, but I will try as much as possible to avoid giving definitive answers or preaching a "technology gospel" to you. My preferred methodology, rather, is to present a large number of examples, and to invite you to think about these issues and decide for yourself what you think is (or is not) brain gain and digital wisdom. I do this in Chapter 3, which is the heart of this book.

The good news is that our quest for digital wisdom is already well under way. The goal of this volume is to expand your knowledge of this journey and exploration, and of the many places in which it is happening. My goal is to make you think in new ways about how your life is changing because of technology—changing mostly in a positive direction—and how you and all people are becoming freer and better because of this.

Ultimately, my goal is to change your mind—about your mind, about technology, and about wisdom in the twenty-first century.

A NEW MADELEINE

Just as a product of French cooking technology—a madeleine—was the key to unlocking Marcel Proust's childhood memories in *Remembrance of Things Past*, the products of today's and tomorrow's technologies are the keys to unlocking humanity's capabilities and hopes for the future. Everyone now lives in a very special age for humankind: an age when human capabilities are expanding explosively. Certainly, if you live in the developed world, you are very aware of many of these changes. You probably could not do your job, or run your life, without the help of a great many of them. But even people who live in the developed world are mostly unaware of how much technological changes are affecting their minds. They ignore, in many cases, how technology is changing—in a positive way—the ways they think and the things their minds can now do. To the extent they are aware, they often view these changes as negative. I believe this is both unfortunate and wrong.

Brain science has advanced tremendously in recent years and gotten wide press. We are now finally beginning to understand some of the neurophysical correlates of our human behavior, that is, the mechanisms by which some things occur, particularly at the single neuron and chemical levels. More people are aware today that every change in our environment and behavior (and even thinking) affects our physical brains and bodies, through mechanisms such as neuroplasticity and epigenetics. But neuroscience is not yet providing all the answers we need. Even the experts view current research findings in a variety of ways.

Yet even so, we have all entered a new age of mind change so profound that I characterize it, metaphorically, as a kind of "mind evolution." Today's humans, when enabled by today's latest technologies, can do more, think faster, plan better, analyze more deeply, solve more difficult problems, make better decisions, and even know their own bodies far better than ever before. This, to me, is clearly brain gain.

This brain gain is clearly not happening to everyone on the planet at once or at the same speed. But we are all affected. All humans are on our way to becoming wiser people. That includes the 92-year-old mom in Ohio who uses her computer daily for games, Internet searches, email, and Skype.[7] It includes the many kids in Africa and other developing countries now getting laptops through the One Laptop per Child program. It includes whole villages in India that are learning to use and share a single smartphone.

We are all experiencing brain gain, and we owe all of these expanding human capabilities to the advance of technology—and, of course, to the science that produces it. Around the world, human minds are being augmented, expanded, amplified, and enhanced at a furious pace.

So much so that I argue in this book that a great many of us are already becoming, metaphorically, "new" humans and the rest of us will soon catch up. I call those of us who are already headed down this road *Homo sapiens digital,* that is, digital humans. We are people who are *both human and digital,* and whose minds, as a result, are both expanded and wise. (As we will see in the last chapter, some researchers are already looking even further down the evolution path.[8])

If this idea makes you uncomfortable, I hope you will read on. If you disagree with some of my ideas—and particularly if you disagree strongly—I hope you won't stop listening: I provide a great many examples to back up what I am saying, and the book might even change your mind about some things.

If you are a person who welcomes all the changes I am talking about, and you find them amazing and thrilling, as I do, I hope you will read on as well. I will endeavor to give you additional arguments to help bring those who disagree with you around to a different point of view.

A great deal of what is being discussed and written about technology today is negative. Technology and its consequences often appear frightening. I agree that some aspects of today's digital technology are scary and even dangerous. I discuss them in Chapters 4 and 7.

But too many voices today are suggesting that digital technology is making us *worse* humans: dumber, less able to think, less able to concentrate, less able to reflect, too dependent on machines, less deep, more shallow, or all of the above at once. Those critics suggest that what technology has provided us is not brain gain but rather brain loss. In their view, technology is making us less able people, making our lives less "human" and less worthwhile. And this is happening, they say, even as—and in some cases because—those technologies make many things easier.

Some claim our minds are being taken over and are affected only negatively by our modern technologies. Others worry that human intelligence is about to be, or is already being, superseded by artificial intelligence, to our detriment. Some even fear that carbon-based life is on the way out, and that silicon-based life (or something even stranger) is on the way in.

They tell us to be very afraid. The dystopian takeover will happen soon—if not in our lifetimes, certainly in the lifetimes of our kids. Because of our advances in technology, claim the most extreme of these critics, life as we have enjoyed it for millennia is just about over.

Perhaps you believe this, or some of it. But it is time to also hear the other side.

A CHANGE OF PERSPECTIVE

This book is a counter-argument to those critics and worriers. I do not claim that what they feel is entirely wrong, rather that it is myopic. I hope to bring thinking about technology back into a wider focus.

The book is not intended to blindly praise today's technology, but rather to help you put that technology into a new and more useful perspective. I'd like to help you fully appreciate—despite the critics—that those of us who have the opportunity and decide to let modern, digital technology fully into our lives are better off.

We are not just better off because our lives are safer, easier, and more comfortable—although they certainly are that. Far more importantly, those of us who choose to fully engage with technology are becoming freer, more productive, more creative, and more capable people, and, I believe, *wiser* people. But I will let you decide.

BRAIN GAIN AND "MIND EVOLUTION"

The human brain, and the mind it produces, is seen by many people—probably most people—as nature's greatest achievement. It is certainly the most complex thing on earth. Our minds have allowed humans to become everything we are; to understand, to the extent that we do, ourselves and the world; to create our cultural and artistic heritage and masterpieces; and to experience the emotions, joys, pleasures, and sorrows that make up our everyday lives. And today, if we include all the external technologies that enhance our minds and brains, humans can create even more. We can solve more difficult problems. We can modify our looks, behavior, and the planet. We can make better predictions (of weather, behavior, and politics), take better care of our bodies, and make life-enhancing choices of many kinds, such as helping modify our behavior and bad habits.

But can our minds be even better? You bet!

The "natural" or Darwinian evolution of human minds, that is, the kind in which nature, over time, adds more and more components, capabilities, and complexity to our brains (and, in the process, creates and improves our minds), is now happening in new ways—not just through natural selection but aided by man himself. Some call this "directed" evolution. Whatever you call it, it is speeding up.

Really? you might ask. *Are we evolving that fast?*

We are. Faster, I'm sure, than most of us think.

Are all humans going through this new evolution? Is it happening to everyone?

It is universal, although, clearly, not everyone today receives all of technology's benefits equally or at the same time. But no matter who you are in the twenty-first century—whether a mobile-phone-using tribesperson in the developing world, or a wealthy luddite in the developed world—mind enhancement is coming to you. It has now become impossible to escape many of technology's mind-enhancing benefits—even if you try.

But is this good or bad?

That question is well worth asking, and that is what this book is about. My view about this is different from many observers', and this is, I believe, because it looks at a bigger picture. Overall, and on balance, technological enhancement is extremely positive for all of humankind.

If technology is enhancing our minds so much, as you claim, then why is the world in such a mess? Why doesn't every person have a job? Why am I, and so many people, so befuddled by everything that's happening? If we're now so wise, why isn't everything perfect?

"Better" and "positive" are relative terms. They don't mean perfect—nothing is. Unfortunately, in some cases, better and positive don't even equate to very good. It is important to remember that we can always do more.

But isn't it true, as Marshall McLuhan suggested, that once we invent and start using a technology it starts changing us in ways we can't control?

McLuhan was very wise to observe and write about many effects of technology that had not been widely noticed before him. But I am not—and I don't think McLuhan was—a determinist. I believe that while effects and biases come with certain technologies (and I discuss a great many of them in this book), humans also have the power to shape technology and how we use it to our will—and toward positive outcomes. That is, in fact, what has always happened with our technology.

Will technology become wiser than humans? Will machines replace us?

The fear of this happening underlies, I believe, a great many people's objections to technology. And of course we never know. But for the foreseeable future, at least, my belief is that the symbiotic combination of what humans do well and what technology does well will produce the wisest outcomes and the outcomes we need.

If our minds are expanding so much, why does the world often seem so difficult to understand? Why do so many things feel like they're speeding up and getting out of control?

Unfortunately, as our minds are expanding, the context we live in is also changing, and changing even faster. And as it does, the variability, uncertainty, chaos, and ambiguity of our world increases.[9] We are always, to some extent, playing catch-up. Under these conditions, it is terribly important that our minds do expand, because, to paraphrase Einstein, "The problems of tomorrow cannot be solved with the minds of yesterday."[10]

A POSITIVE POINT OF VIEW

It's time for some perspective.

It's not, I expect, the same "perspective" you have probably been hearing or reading about in the press, or perhaps even feeling the need for. These days "getting perspective" on technology is too often a coded term for focusing on, and worrying about, technology's negative effects and aspects. People have many concerns, both valid and invalid. I will discuss these—and put them into proper perspective—later in this book. But consider this: If the press and popular writers reported on sports such as football or hockey in the same way they do about technologies like videogames or Facebook (i.e., only—and daily—negative reports of injuries, broken teeth and bones, etc.), no parent would allow their kids to play those sports. And yet we do let them play, and even encourage them to, because we also see another side.

The overall perspective I offer, therefore, is of technology as part of the larger human picture. And that is a picture of trade-offs: the trade-offs we all make as humans for overall positive results. It is a perspective of how, despite many issues, the world and people's lives are continually improving. I do not ignore or deny that there are pockets where the world is not currently improving or is even slipping backward—but I believe those are temporary. Mine is a picture of how all people can do more, live better, and most of all be wiser as we advance into man's new millennium.

LOSSES?

I do recognize that as things change many things will be lost, some of them things that were treasured. Some of this is inevitable as human civilization and technology march on—every generation mourns such losses. Rarely, though, do things that were once loved and important disappear entirely; they just become the province of smaller and smaller niches, or—like clipper ships—remain only in pictures on our walls.

But I believe an objective observer will agree that, when one looks at human beings on this planet, those people with the latest and best technology are, and have always been, far, far better off—in ways most of us consider important—than those without it. And I don't just mean in terms of material possessions. What person would want to face issues like cancer, sanitation, or climate change as a caveman, or even as a person from the nineteenth century, rather than as a twenty-first-century citizen?

Although all the positive changes being wrought by modern, digital technology are not happening everywhere at once (and forgive me for repeating this, but far too many technology critics write "we" as if everyone in the world sees too many screens or gets too many emails), the positive effects of technology are clear for all humans. Given all the issues in the world, it is now time for all of us to accept the benefits of today's technology. We have entered a new human-machine age. Our job now, as humans, is to make it the best world we can.

Our quest, in other words, is to find digital wisdom.

HOW FAST?

I am an optimist, and this is an optimistic book. But I am by no means a Pollyanna. I see, hear, and read the same reports that everyone else does. Lots of things about technology are promised and predicted, and many of them don't come true—either as quickly as we expect or at all. Many of today's technology critics enjoy pointing out that we are not (yet) driving flying cars or living forever, as some twentieth-century visionaries claimed we would be by now.

But very few, if any, of the negative predictions for society have come true. And we hear and think a lot less about the positive things that have come true—such as better sanitation for so many and instant news and connectivity around the globe—because they are now a basic part of our lives. Our most useful technologies get quickly taken for granted. And, if we look, we can all observe that the process of technology moving from someone's dream to a worldwide reality is speeding up (see Table 1).

It took Mark Zuckerberg, founder of Facebook, only six years to go from trying out an idea in his dorm room to being one of the most successful and richest people in the world. Zynga.com went from startup to public offering in only four years.[11]

And they are only the visible tip of the iceberg. Every field has been enhanced by technology, often in ways we don't see. For many of us born in America in the first half of the twentieth century (I was born in 1946), much

ACCELERATED SPEED OF ADOPTION
(RACE TO THE BILLIONS)*

Cell Phone	40 yrs	4.0 billion users
www	20 yrs	1.5 billion users
Texting	15 yrs	8 billion messages/day
Google	10 yrs	3 billion searches/day
Facebook	6 yrs	1 billion views/day
YouTube	5 yrs	1 billion views/day
Twitter	3 yrs	1 billion tweets/year
Apps	1 yr	1 billion downloads

*Rough Approximations. Souce: Wikipedia
© Marc Prensky 2012

Table 1

of life today is already science-fictional. Not only are we now almost universally and instantaneously connected around the globe, but scientists are able to map and manipulate our genes. We have people and machines out exploring the universe.

Much or all of this, of course, you already know. But here's what you may not know.

Our mind—that essence of humanity that we all prize so much—is becoming more capable at just as fast a pace. Not because of advances in neuroscience—although those are many and valuable—but because of technology in a much broader sense.

The breadth and depth of this, I believe, will surprise and amaze you—it did me. Once I started looking, I spotted brain gain all around me, with examples of it in papers and magazines almost every day. Our minds are expanding, and rapidly. We are not becoming stupid, or slaves to our machines, as many fear—on the contrary. No matter who you are, your mind is already changing daily for the better—or could and should be.

Sadly, many—or most—people are not availing themselves of all their options, either out of ignorance, fear of negative consequences, or a combination of both. Our education system is, unfortunately, a prime example of this. I discuss why this is our schools'—and our children's—great loss in Chapter 6. But a growing number of people have begun to avail themselves of these opportunities, and those people are becoming the wise among us. I will introduce you to some of them in these pages.

My hope is that you will leave the book convinced by—or if not fully convinced by, at least open to—the argument that the symbiosis of human and machine is better, and wiser, than the human (or the machine) alone. I will not argue that every use of technology is wise—people using machines can too easily be just digitally clever, or even digitally dumb (see Chapter 4). But my key point is that the unenhanced human—and the unenhanced mind—can no longer be considered the wisest thing on the planet. And if that is true, we'd better learn to make the best use of the new combination. Because it is also true that people who have the option to engage with and use technology, and choose *not* to—even selectively—are diminished as human beings by that choice, and lesser in their wisdom and in their humanity. The wise and human decision is no longer whether to engage with technology, but how.

Does your head hurt from today's technology? Is it spinning? Here's why.

ONE

THE HUMAN MIND

Improved, Extended, Enhanced, Amplified
(and Liberated) by Technology

Technology.

You may be a fan or a foe. A believer or a skeptic. You may be a "crackberry" addict, a person who can't live without your iPhone or iPad (or whatever those technologies have become by the time you read this), or you may be someone with a huge desire to turn it all off. You may be a constant upgrader of every gadget or a reluctant user of any.

But whether you are personally for or against modern digital technology (or have, as most of us do, a view somewhere in between), today's technology is *changing your mind*—and all of our minds—for the better. Modern technology is, in the terms of different writers, "extending our minds," "cognitively enhancing" us, "amplifying" our consciousness, creating a "cognitive surplus," offering us "mental prostheses," "extending our thinking powers," and "improving our thought processes and concentration."[1]

As a result of technology, we are all becoming, at different speeds, better thinkers, and better, wiser *people.*

Why can I say this and claim it is true with such certainty? I can make this assertion with confidence because humans today who both have access to modern technology and are willing to use it can:

- sift through terabytes of information, quickly sorting the wanted from the unwanted, the good from the bad in ways they couldn't do before

- accurately and rapidly find and compare old and new thoughts and ideas that they couldn't find in the past
- discover links and influences that no one knew existed
- produce much more than previously of what they can imagine
- liberate far more of their creativity than people used to
- understand their own biases and overcome them better than before
- make more accurate predictions than ever
- perform much deeper, more accurate analyses, foreseeing unintended consequences of actions
- plan and prioritize better
- understand their body far more accurately and forestall or prevent disease
- make better medical decisions than they ever could
- remember much about our lives (including what we read) that we used to forget
- communicate their thoughts and emotions directly, even at long distances.

And that is just a sampling of what technology-enhanced humans can now do that people couldn't do in the past.

ATTITUDE MATTERS

Many of these enormous technological benefits come to us today more or less automatically, without our having to take any action at all, and often in ways over which we have little or no control. We all benefit, for example, without really doing anything special, from technology's increasing ability to help us predict the weather, to make our transactions secure, to provide us with communications networks, and to offer us up-to-date information.

Awareness of other benefits of technology depends on our particular situation. Farmers may have a special appreciation of the kinds of agricultural help that technology can provide in their area of the world. People with disabilities may have a greater awareness than others of technology's ability to create better prostheses.

But there are a great many benefits that technology offers us that depend heavily on our *attitude* toward that technology and our willingness to accept and use it. People certainly can, as many do, regard technology with a very skeptical eye and not adopt anything unless they are absolutely forced to. But my belief is that if people, rather than resist or reject the technical changes that come at them, maintain a positive—though critical—attitude toward technology, and if people take positive, proactive steps to integrate technology with their minds and their lives, they will all be far better off.

Of course, in today's world, keeping a positive attitude toward technology is not always easy. Pretty much everyone in the world—rich or poor—has problems and issues with whatever technology they use, often on a daily basis. Parts break down. Components go missing. Power gets interrupted. Signals are weak. No one is immune to this.

Even the great *New York Times* technology writer David Pogue, author of countless books on technology's benefits and host of several TV shows on that topic, and certainly no technophobe, recently worried on his blog about the fact that his son did not want to part from his iPad no matter where he went. "I think my six-year-old is addicted to the iPad," he wrote on his blog, soliciting help from other parents, who responded in droves.[2] If Pogue, one of the world's great technology advocates, is concerned about technology's effects, where does that leave the rest of us?

Not to worry.

We should, of course, all be concerned about technology's problems, for multiple reasons. There are, we all know, people who misuse technology, some deliberately. There are people who become addicted to practically anything, technology included (and I hope Pogue's son, who, Pogue says, has now moved on to writing on the iPad, is not among these). No one wants to be inconvenienced unduly by a breakdown in technology, without a "backup" way of getting what they need done.

But in my experience, when it comes to technology, far too many people confuse the specific "I was inconvenienced this morning" with the general "technology can't be relied on." Far too many conflate someone's—particularly a child's—heavy use and enjoyment of technology with the type of clinical addiction that actually ruins people's lives.

It takes only a few obvious counter-examples to quickly expose the flaws in this type of thinking. Does the fact that most of us carry watches (or cell phones) make us addicted to them, in the clinical sense that they ruin our lives? Few would answer yes (although some might want to change "ruin" to "run"). Does the fact that the activities of "rabid" sports fans, devout religious practitioners, or even avid readers often interfere with things they have to do make those people addicts? Very infrequently. People rarely cross that line.

A favorite example of mine is air travel, which is a complex combination of many technologies. We often hear people complaining about it, citing problems with lost luggage, or telling stories about being trapped for long periods in planes on the ground. Yet as a frequent traveler around the globe, I can attest to the fact that commercial airline technology, taken as a whole, is one of the very *best* and most reliable technologies in the world. I *always* get to where I am going, I am rarely late, and the chance of an accident is miniscule. This despite the enormous technological complexity of all the equipment. But one bad flight can form your attitude about the whole industry.

And that is what too often happens with all technology: People's bad experience with some aspect of technology overwhelms their sense of the whole. For the vast majority, technology, taken as a whole, greatly helps and enables us—it often helps us do more of whatever we really enjoy and improves our lives.

In general, most people, at some level, know this.

But even with this knowledge, when many of those same individuals look around and see people's noses buried in cell phones, or see children spending huge amounts of their time on their computer or Xbox, they start to get concerned. That's somehow *different*. Now the technology is somehow affecting our *minds*.

Yes, it is. *Everything* we do affects our minds. And, at the same time it affects our brains. It has always been thus.

But it doesn't have to be—or even for the most part—negatively. In fact, I believe what's happening is just the opposite: our minds are being enhanced and freed. What I hope to show you in this book is why and how.

BRAIN, MIND, AND THE STATE OF NEUROSCIENCE

Given this book's title, you could be forgiven for thinking it is yet another book on neuroscience, one of the vast number being published these days. But it is not.

Neuroscience is doing some wonderful and deeply revealing things. I am a big fan of brain research and try to follow it closely. Some recent experiments, for example, suggest that one long-standing science fiction dream, the ability to read minds, may not be far off. Scientists have recorded brain signals that they think are associated with specific images.[3] They have recorded signals they believe correspond to specific spatial locations in a virtual world.[4] They have caused specific events to happen by playing previously recorded signals back.[5] Compared to what we could do only a few years ago, these results are extraordinary.

But we have to be very careful.

The human brain is the most complex thing on earth, and we are still very far from fully understanding it. Today, we know a great deal about how individual neurons work, how they communicate, and how they build additional structures in response to learning. We know a lot about the chemical communication that occurs at synapses, and we know more about how the strength of these connections gets reinforced or inhibited. We know more about the chemicals—neurotransmitters, such as dopamine, serotonin, norepinephrine, and many others—that wash around various areas of the brain in response to outside stimuli, creating pleasure rewards, elation, depression, and other feelings.

What we know much less about, however, is how groups of neurons work together to produce results and, ultimately, our thoughts. We know that the various areas of the brain are massively interconnected, and that communication and feedback are continuously going on. We can identify some of the "superhighways" of our brains' neuron pathways, but we are just beginning to understand the smaller paths and how they work. This complex, often two-way interconnection is known as the "connectome" of the brain, the web of all the interconnections between neurons and areas. As we begin to better understand and map this web, we will still need to discover how it functions, in a similar way that just looking at the map of a place provides little information about traffic patterns or what happens there.

We are also learning more about the brain as an electrical machine, producing effects and fields that we are just beginning to measure and understand. "The brain is best understood as an energy landscape," says Dr. Shaun Jones.[6]

What this means is that we currently only understand *parts* of how the brain works—not the full picture. You might read in the popular press, for example, that some particular activity produces a "dopamine squirt," but the full picture is, almost certainly, a set of far more complex interactions. There are several systems that involve dopamine and at least five types of dopamine receptors. A similar level of complexity exists everywhere in the brain. Although we learn more every day, there are whole parts of the brain the function of which is not completely understood, such as the glial cells, and many areas where neuroscientists' thinking is currently undergoing revision. Theories abound. Some hypothesize that there may be structures called tubules, which we haven't even seen yet and don't understand at all, inside which quantum calculation takes place.[7] We are just at the beginning of exploring the brain's electrical micro-fields.[8]

In addition, some of the knowledge to come out of the neuroscience research is not very widely shared, partly because "relatively few people have the [required level] of understanding," says neuroscientist Dr. Michael Merzenich. And much of what *is* shared is disputed—I was surprised and appalled (as I'm sure you would be) by some of the adjectives very prominent neuroscientists apply to each other's work—and to each other.

One reason we still have such an incomplete knowledge of the brain, particularly the functioning brain, is that our tools, although highly sophisticated compared to what we had in the past, are still blunt and primitive relative to the sophistication level of the object they are studying. Several neuroscientists I spoke with used the word "crude" in characterizing their tools. For example, functional magnetic resonance induction (fMRI), a technique that allows us to see some of the brain's functioning, provides far less resolution than we require. It also requires that the patient lay flat in a huge, very noisy machine, which is hardly representative of the way we perform tasks in life. Some scientists try to do better by combining fMRI with other techniques such as transcranial magnetic imaging (TMI), electroencephalograms (EEG), and other techniques such as diffusion tensor imaging. But major disagreements occur. Some neuroscientists think, for example, that the many studies we have on animal brains are highly relevant to human brains, while others think the human brain is different enough in its organization that comparisons are difficult.[9]

As a result, although we have collected a great deal of data, many of the "conclusions" based on that data are just inferences and hypotheses—educated, intelligent guesses, really—that attempt to put the data into a coherent picture. It's not that our scientists are not smart or clever in their guesswork—they are. Some of their hypotheses will no doubt turn out to be right or on the right track. But many of the theories conflict or differ. And some recent studies have indicated that some researchers need to be more careful in their analysis.[10] So, we do more experiments.

We are very early in the process of understanding the human brain's full functioning. "There are a great many blanks . . . huge gaps remain," says famed linguist Noam Chomsky.[11] Some of the most interesting developments are only just starting, with new tools to detect them just now being created.[12] Many ideas are still controversial. Many neuroscientists think new knowledge, yet to come, will change much of our current understanding of how the brain works.

Which is why this is *not,* despite its title, a book about neuroscience. But it *is* a book about our brains and minds getting better.

The brain gain I am concerned about in this volume is not an increase in our understanding about how the brain's components and structures work internally to produce ideas and wisdom—because we don't yet know much of this. This book is concerned, rather, with the ways that our brain interacts with external technologies and with the products that those technologies produce (e.g., such as new software or new drugs). It is brain gain in a less technical, and more metaphorical, sense than a neuroscientist using the term might wish. But it is brain gain (and mind gain) nonetheless.

The brain gain I am talking about here is also enormously subjective. It cannot be easily quantified. We cannot say today (and may never be able to say) that "because of this technology our brain is enhanced by x amount or by y percent." But the brain gain is, nonetheless, happening and can be recognized by almost all of us. Scientists already observe some physical brain gains, such when the hippocampi of London cab drivers expand to "contain" the "knowledge" of London's streets[13] or when the cerebellum grows in professional musicians.[14] But mostly the gains show up as expanded human capabilities.

One thing everyone *does* know is that the mind can change. As we learn and acquire experience, we frequently "change our minds" (as we say)—some of us more often than others. We all know that people can learn new things and produce new thoughts and insights over the course of an entire lifetime, which is why we humans make the effort to create and provide education for both young and old—we believe it is important to help people's minds change in ways that are positive. We also know that much of the mind develops as we grow, with some parts of the brain continuing to develop long after we are born—that is one reason we often associate wisdom with older people whose minds have been influenced by a lifetime of experience.

OUR BRAIN'S AND MIND'S STRENGTHS (AND WEAKNESSES)

It is important to underscore that while the human brain, and the mind it creates, are in many ways amazing, they are far from being perfect. Everything in life has both strengths and weaknesses, and this is certainly true of the human mind and brain.

Despite our well-deserved place at the top of the pyramid of creatures, the limits of man's capabilities are many. We are born helpless. Our bodies can tolerate, without assistance from clothes and shelter, a pretty narrow range of conditions. Disease can ravage and kill us, often suddenly. Our physical attributes are often less capable than those of other animals. Mentally, we are born prematurely—in order to be able to pass, some think, through the birth canal.

Still, there are clearly things the human mind can do brilliantly. Among the many things the human mind is known for doing especially well are

- reasoning,
- reflecting and contemplating,
- combining reason and emotion,
- solving problems,
- learning from experience,
- working with other people,
- creating,
- storing and retrieving,
- building up expertise,
- having empathy,
- having a sense of context,
- having a sense of humor,
- telling stories,

and I should also mention

- lying.

I won't go into these, since all of these strengths are widely known and expressed continually by people in millions of ways, from our normal lives to humankind's great stories, accomplishments, and works of art.

But, wonderful and powerful as it is, the human mind also has severe limitations. And these do require some explanation.

For example:

- **Limitation:** The human mind makes decisions based on only a portion of the available data.

It is well known that the human brain has severe limitations on what it can store and process. In short-term memory the brain can retain as few as seven (plus or minus two) digits at a time. Although with prompting we can often recall many long-forgotten things, we do know that even the best minds, with the best training (with which people can remember surprising amounts), are limited.

In previous eras, when the volume of information in the world was much more restricted, the limitations in the capacity of our memories were rarely much of a problem—people were able to keep most of what they needed in life in their heads. Yet even then we created reference books of logarithms and other information that was considered a useless taking up of mental space. Now the volume of information has increased by many orders of magnitude. Almost unimaginable amounts of data are collected every day about the world's environment and about its inhabitants—collectively and individually. The total data are now measured in exabytes (i.e., 10 with 16 zeros), zettabytes (10 with 21 zeros), and soon yottabytes (10 with 24 zeros). With today's collection capabilities, the amount of information in the world, even on relatively narrow topics, is beyond the capacity of all the humans on earth put together to remember. Humans' inability to store even a tiny percentage of the useful available data in our heads is now a much more debilitating limitation.

There are also severe restrictions on human brains' ability to *process* information—that is, to keep it all in some kind of an array and manipulate it in useful ways. Scientists often equate a person's ability to process information to their amount of "working memory." At the current time there is still great debate as to exactly what working memory is and how much of it individuals have. Some suspect that the amount of working memory a person has is closely related to his or her intelligence—and may, in fact, be that intelligence. Although people can often perceive patterns in large data sets, particularly if presented visually, the limit on what human minds can take in and think about all at once, compared to the amount of data now available, is quite low.

Wouldn't it be brain gain if we could handle more?

- **Limitation:** The human mind fills in, and makes up, what it doesn't know.

In his book *Thinking Fast and Slow,* Nobel Prize winner Daniel Kahneman points out that part of the mind will automatically make up a story to fit whatever facts it sees.[15] It matters little whether or not that story has any basis in truth—it just has to fit the facts as the people perceive them. That is one reason eyewitnesses are often so unreliable—their brains have filled in pieces that were missing to create a believable narrative. Even scientists make up the parts of their story they don't know—it is called theorizing. The problem with this situation, and with how our brains work, is that lots of things we may think are true are often wrong and only made up.

Wouldn't it be brain gain if we had better tools to tell which things are made up and which are not?

• *Limitation:* The human mind makes assumptions, often inaccurate, about the thoughts or intentions of others.

One highly positive feature of a healthy human mind is that it can read subtle clues, including facial expression, tone of voice, and body language, to ascertain the thoughts and intentions of others. Yet people cannot do this perfectly.

Mistaking someone else's intentions is a common occurrence and often leads to problems and embarrassment. This is even common among people who know each other quite well, including siblings and couples who have been together for many years. It is certainly commonplace in business and in all negotiations. The limitation on understanding the thoughts and intentions of others is exacerbated when people try, for one reason or another, to conceal their thoughts and intentions, as when they are negotiating or playing poker.

While this particular failing of our minds can at times provoke humor—as in, for example, Shakespeare's *Comedy of Errors*—in the extreme not understanding other's intentions and thoughts can lead to terrible problems, and even to war.

Wouldn't it be brain gain if we could overcome this limitation, even in part?

• *Limitation:* The human mind depends on educated guessing and verification (i.e., the traditional scientific method) to find new answers.

Because humans often cannot know or understand things just by looking at them, we needed to invent a good procedure for figuring

things out. That procedure, which was perfected only over recent centuries, is known as the scientific method. It consists of making educated
guesses (hypotheses) based on what is known and observed and then
doing experiments to see if results predicted by those guesses are true.

While the scientific method has proved enormously useful to
humanity, it is a particularly difficult, time-consuming, and inefficient way to find things out. It also doesn't lead necessarily to the
"correct" answer, because new data may appear later, and because
better-designed experiments or more sensitive equipment may detect
something different.

Wouldn't it be brain gain if there were other approaches that got
around these limitations?

- **Limitation:** The human mind cannot deal well with complexity
beyond a certain point.

Most real-life situations involve many interactions and competing forces. The human mind is actually good at handling much of this
complexity and weighing and evaluating many variables, particularly
with experience to draw on. Sometimes we call on "eggheads" and
"wonks" with advanced degrees to do this for us, but many people can
deal naturally with a great deal of complexity, even without any formal
training.[16]

Still, there are only so many variables the human mind can accurately keep track of. Many of the complex projects and undertakings
that humans are now capable of quickly exceed that limit. Unaided,
the human mind cannot track all the variables even in projects of
moderate size, and many of today's projects, whether they be space
exploration, scientific research, large engineering efforts, or worldwide
business endeavors, are, in their detail, far beyond the scope of any
unaided human mind or group of minds to deal with.

Wouldn't it be brain gain if this could be made more possible, and
even easy?

- **Limitation:** The human mind is constrained in its ability to predict
the future and construct what-if scenarios.

A great many useful things that humans do, from understanding
our climate to waging war, depend on our ability to think ahead and
predict what the consequences of various actions will be. The human
mind can do this, but only to a limited extent.

When projecting out into the future, at some point the mind can no longer keep track of all the possibilities; it must rely on shortcuts, hunches, and rules of thumb (technically known as heuristics). Such shortcuts are often considered wise, when they predict correctly, but very often they are inaccurate. No human can predict complex situations perfectly—many weather reports have us wearing snow boots for nothing. In order for human minds to simplify the process of making predictions so-called second-order and third-order effects (i.e., the effects of effects) are often misjudged or ignored.

Wouldn't it be brain gain if we could get better at predicting?

- *Limitation:* The human mind cannot see, hear, touch, feel, or smell beyond the range of our senses.

We know the human mind is terrific at integrating and interpreting the results of its built-in sensors for sight, hearing, smell, touch, taste, and detecting things like temperature, pain, and balance. That's how we get along in the world.

The range of a human's built-in sensors, however, is extremely limited. Human eyes can detect only a tiny portion of what we know is an extremely broad electromagnetic spectrum. Our ears and noses detect far less than those of many animals—dogs can have up to 300 million scent receptors, compared to a human's 5 million. We are just learning that human diseases and cancers can give off recognizable smells that dogs and other animals are able to detect. But even the best animals often detect far less than what is out there to be detected.

As we discover the full potential spectrum of the world in which we live, we increasingly come up against limitations in what we, as humans, can sense directly. Instruments such as radio telescopes, electron microscopes, seismometers, and so on, clearly do much to augment this.

But wouldn't it be brain gain if there were better ways to sense and integrate all the sensors' data into our brains?

- *Limitation:* The human mind finds it difficult to hold multiple perspectives simultaneously.

Most of us are familiar with the optical illusions in which one can see either the face or the vase, either the old hag or the young woman, but not both at once.

Our minds tend, particularly without help and training, to view things in a polarized way (as we say in the vernacular, as either black or white). Much of our education is learning to see and deal with the "grey areas" in between the extremes. There are always multiple perspectives of the same event, yet our minds, unaided, typically accept only one of them. The human mind is also subject to a number of other limiting biases, or "mental illusions," such the "priming" influence of things we see in advance of our decisions. Daniel Kahneman discusses several of these mind limitations and mental illusions in his book *Thinking Fast and Slow*.[17]

Wouldn't it be brain gain if we could hold and deal with multiple perspectives more easily and overcome other biases in our thinking as well?

- *Limitation:* The human mind has difficulty separating emotional responses from rational conclusions.

Humans are always balancing the emotional and the rational. Kahneman theorizes that the human mind has, in fact, evolved two separate and distinct modes (or "systems" as he calls them) for thinking: a quick emotional mode (what Malcolm Gladwell refers to as "blink"[18]) and a slower more rational mode.[19] It takes effort to distinguish between the modes and to know which is operating. "Engage brain before opening mouth" is a humorous way to express this.

Wouldn't it be brain gain if we could more easily both detect which system we were using and, even better, combine them to best effect in most situations?

- *Limitation:* The human mind gets bored.

Humans are not particularly fond of doing the same thing over and over, time after time (except, interestingly, when the reward is random, variable, and has a large potential upside, as with slot machines).

When required to perform repetition, the mind typically creates what neuroscientists call "patterns" or "zombies"—brain structures that allow us to go through the needed pattern over and over while removing it from our conscious thought. This is what happens when you knit while talking or find yourself suddenly arriving home when you had planned to stop at the cleaners: Your zombie took over. While zombies have certain advantages, they remove critical thought. We speak, for example, of "mindless" repetition.

Wouldn't it be brain gain if we could find ways to do repetitious tasks and still keep them under our conscious control when useful, and even enjoy them?

• **Limitation:** The human mind forgets.

Humans are horrendous at remembering. "Even as I read," says Pierre Bayard, author of *How to Talk about Books You Haven't Read*, "I start to forget what I have read, and this process is inevitable."[20] "I am a man of no retentiveness," said Montaigne.[21] "To think," says writer Jorge Luis Borges, "is to forget."[22] We forget far more than we remember, far more, generally, than we want to. Some, like Borges, argue it would harm us if we did remember everything, clogging up our mind with useless data. Our minds have evolved some ways of selecting what is important to remember, often by tying this to an emotional connection. But this is an imperfect system, sometimes leading to trauma from unwanted memories.

Wouldn't it be brain gain if we could store everything and recall whatever we want exactly when we want or need it?

The above is just a sample of the human mind's limitations, weaknesses, and failings. More examples can be found in Malcolm Gladwell's *Blink* (2005), Daniel Kahneman's *Thinking Fast and Slow* (2011), Nassim Taleb's *The Black Swan* (2011), and many other volumes.[23] Even though philosophers and psychologists have been thinking about these issues for quite a while, we are still learning more about our mind's limits. Some of these limits may have been, at one time, useful adaptations, such as the ability to clear our minds by forgetting. They have only become limitations as our culture has changed—which, of course, it has, dramatically.

This is why the kind of technology-enhanced evolution that I describe in this book is so important. In many cases, it is the limitations of the human brain that are now preventing twenty-first-century humans from reaching the heights to which we are potentially capable.

In the past these failings were more easily compensated for (and less widely acknowledged). Our unaided minds, in most cases, were sufficient to solve the problems presented to us. Today that is no longer the case. Today our minds, to be their most effective, require the addition of technology. As writer David Brin puts it, "Technology is the most recently evolved part of the brain."[24]

TECHNOLOGY'S WEAKNESSES (AND STRENGTHS)

Technology, of course, and particularly the digital technology we use today, has its own set of inherent weaknesses and issues. Technology has traditionally been thought of as "dumb," although the reality is that this is changing: "Smarter Than You Think" was the title of a 2010–2011series of articles about technology in the *New York Times*.[25] Writes Richard Dawkins: "There is a popular cliché . . . which says that you cannot get out of computers any more than you have put in . . . , that computers can only do exactly what you tell them to, and that therefore computers are never creative. This cliché is true only in a crashingly trivial sense i.e., in the same sense in which Shakespeare never wrote anything except what his first schoolteacher taught him to write—words."[26]

Still, machines do not think in the same sense that humans do. They cannot holistically grasp an entire context. They lack human judgment. They require programming and typically stay within its bounds. They have a reputation of being easily misled and for making what for humans would be stupid mistakes, which often amuse us. Machines have a great deal of trouble with many types of reasoning and with complex types of pattern recognition (such as recognizing human faces) that are trivial to the human mind.

On the plus side, machines are tireless workers. When programmed correctly, they will do the same task or analysis over and over indefinitely, totally accurately, with infinite amounts of data. They can instantly recall information from anywhere and combine and pool their resources, processing power, and memories. They can wait and watch eternally for a single event. They can, of course, do calculations—trillions and even quadrillions of calculations— incredibly quickly.

People's thinking about what machines and technology can do is often wildly outdated. Machines can now self-correct. They can learn from their mistakes. They can adapt to changing circumstances, weigh competing variables, reason (to a certain extent), and utilize some of the kinds of "fuzzy" logic that humans do. Machines can sense the world and act on what they sense, customizing their responses to each situation.[27] Machines like IBM's Watson (the computer that won on *Jeopardy*) can read and understand huge numbers of documents, recognize puns and plays on words, arrive at answers in multiple ways, and answer complex questions, with confidence, in time to beat a human contestant to the buzzer. Machines can also detect hidden patterns in very large data sets that unaided humans cannot find, or sense, at all.

The most interesting and important thing to realize about the strengths and weaknesses of human minds and the strengths and weaknesses of machines and technology *is that they are often complementary.* And that is the point of this book. It is because of the complementary nature of the two sides—innate human capacities, on the one hand, and technology-based extensions, on the other—and through their symbiotic combination that digital wisdom can and does emerge. The combination, says Ray Kurzweil (from whom we will hear much more at the end of this book), is "formidable."[28]

INCREASING OUR MIND'S POWER

Humans have always wanted and tried to increase their mind's power and have taken, in the past, two traditional paths for doing so.

One path has been to look inward and use more of the power we already have—or potentially have—in our own living cells. This is the approach of generations of meditators and monks, as well as of many analysts and "brain exercisers." That it is possible to achieve much via this path is shown, for example, in the many books on memory gains—Amazon has a list of 100 of these. Books also exist on increasing human capabilities to do art (e.g., *Drawing on the Right Side of Your Brain),* to do crossword puzzles, to meditate, to do Sudoku, to play video games, and, in fact, to increase our capacity for almost every mental activity. What these books demonstrate is that people can, in many cases, make their brains better (i.e., achieve brain gain) just by working those brains harder or in different ways. This is certainly a good thing, and it is a long-established path to mind enhancement. Humans have always known that working our brains produced gains—it's why we have school. And we have recently learned, from neuroscience, some of the ways that our brains respond *physically* to hard work, for example, by causing neurons to grow additional branches (dendrites) and connect them. Exercised parts of brains get denser and can grow larger. Today scientists can observe additional dendrites actually being grown by rats' brains in learning situations and identify useful chemicals being released as a result of efforts. So we know from this path that our brains—and, as a result, our minds—can be greatly improved through our own effort.

But we also know other things.

First, we know there are limits to these improvements. These limits almost certainly differ from individual to individual. People have different inherent capacities; we can't all become chess or memory champions—or pass the London cab driver test—no matter how hard we try.

But more importantly, we know that there is another road to brain gain, one that is often far more wide open, is accessible to many more people, and is more far-ranging in its effects and power. This road consists of *external* tools that we can use—some of which man has been using for millennia, and some of which are brand new—to overcome and push past many of the inherent limits in our brain.

Before the advent of language, for example, humans grunted and pointed, but then they learned to use external drawing tools as a way of enhancing their mind's ability to record and communicate their ideas—pictures and maps are powerful mind enhancement technologies and a source of brain gain.

Once speech (itself a huge mind-enhancing technology) developed, humans memorized and told stories—but later added the external tools of written records, stories, and eventually books—storytelling and books are among our most powerful enhancements and sources of human brain gain.

For a long time humans could only approximate measurement. Then they invented external technologies, such as rulers, geometry, and trigonometry, and, using these powerful tools, they calculated. All of those technologies provided brain gain.

THE EXTENDED MIND THEORY

Humans have always been dependent on external mind enhancements, and today we are even more so. Integrating these tools into our minds, however, is not dependence in a negative sense, but is closer to symbiosis. As philosophers Andy Clark and David Chalmers explain in a 1998 paper, "extended cognition is a core cognitive process, not an add-on extra." "The brain," they write, "develops in a way that complements the external structures and learns to play its role within a unified, densely coupled system."[29] According to Clark and Chalmers, the brain is continually actively integrating useful components it finds in the external world, such as our fingers for counting, pen and paper for writing, and more recently slide rules, calculators, and computers. They use terms like "active externalism" and "coupling" of internal and external mental parts.

According to their thinking, when today's young person says, "When I lose my cell phone I lose half my brain,"[30] he means it literally.

And he is right.

Many would express the same sentiment in regard to a computer or an iPad. Humans are already embracing a basic level of digital technology enhancement, and we will be offered—and most will accept—ever more sophisticated enhancements as that technology and other new technologies continue to develop.

ALL MOVING FORWARD

We are all moving, each at our own speed, toward digital technology enhancement of our minds. In terms of availability (although not distribution), we are already there; digital enhancement is or will soon be available for a large percentage of the cognitive tasks we do. Digital tools already extend and enhance our cognitive capabilities in a great many important areas (distribution of these tools, unfortunately, moves more slowly). Digital technology enhances our memory via data input/output tools and electronic storage. Digital data-gathering and decision-making tools enhance judgment by allowing us to gather more data than we could on our own. Digital enhancements enable us to perform more complex analyses of this data than we could unaided and increase our power to ask "what if?" and pursue all the implications of that question. Other cognition-enhancing digital tools facilitate communication and enhance understanding. Cognitive enhancement is a reality in almost every job and every profession, even in nontechnical fields such as law and the humanities. I will examine a large number of these cognitive enhancements in Chapter 3.

And as technologies that link directly into our nervous systems and brains become widely available, technology enhancement will become even more vital for everyone.[31] I sometimes joke to audiences that the piercings and studs that so many young people have inserted all over their heads and bodies are really places to attach new technology chips as they emerge. The nervous laughter I get shows that this is not out of the realm of their imaginations. People living in the very near future (i.e., ourselves and our children) will have instant access to ongoing worldwide discussions, everything ever written, all of recorded history, massive libraries of case studies and collected data, and highly realistic simulated experiences equivalent to years or even centuries of actual experience.

HUMAN GOALS

Human goals have of course expanded, but overall, they may not have not changed much over history. As listed and prioritized by psychologist Abraham Maslow in 1943, human goals are to survive, to obtain food and shelter, to make a living, to find happiness and self-esteem, and then, once those basic needs are taken care of, to "self-actualize," as Maslow puts it, by becoming wiser, more productive and creative members of society.[32] This last goal includes behaving morally, following personal ideas and goals, and working to improve and expand humankind.

But even as people get closer to achieving many of the more basic goals, they hit limits in their quest to achieve the higher levels. Because of limits in our brains and minds, we hit walls of misunderstanding. Our predictions about the future (and even our conclusions based on the past) are far too often wrong. The human brain—powerful as it is, and as far as it has brought us—is no longer adequate, on its own, to achieve our most lofty twenty-first-century goals. To do that we must enhance it, extend it, connect it, and maximize its powers.

One of our best thinkers—Albert Einstein—came to this conclusion, implicitly, when he said "a new type of thinking is essential if mankind is to survive and move to higher levels."[33]

New tools for thinking are required in the twenty-first century. Perhaps the most urgent of these tools is an "enhanced" mind. And the minds of those alive today have already begun to be enhanced—rapidly and radically.

OUTSOURCING: THE BRAIN AND MIND
EXTENDED, ENHANCED, AND AMPLIFIED

"It's all about outsourcing," says Ken Jennings, who lost to the computer Watson on the TV show *Jeopardy.*[34]

"In olden days," I recently heard a ten-year-old girl say, "you had to memorize phone numbers!"[35] Today, of course, we just outsource them to our phones.

More and more formerly internal cognitive functions are being outsourced to machines: How many of this book's readers would try to divide two multiple digit numbers in their head? We would almost all run for the nearest calculator or computer, which is, at least in many places, never far away and often on our person. While some people are appalled by this, it is really no different than consulting the watch we all strapped to our wrists (until it got incorporated into our phones). And watches replaced clocks, which replaced hourglasses, marked candles, and sundials.

BRAIN ENHANCEMENTS, PAST AND PRESENT

Outsourcing and enhancement of our minds is in no way a "new" phenomenon or issue suddenly confronting humans. Man has outsourced and enhanced parts of his brain and mind for millennia. Marking a trail outsourced memory. Writing outsourced both memory and retrieval as did drawings and photographs. So did calculations on paper—Nobel Prize winner Richard Feynman strongly maintained that his written notes were actually a *part of his thinking* that resided outside his head.[36]

Even other people are a form of outsourcing via conversation and communication: "What was that name, or number, again?" you might ask a friend. Much of our knowledge is outsourced to our family, sometimes with particular knowledge such as driving directions, stored in our partner's mind and not our own. We typically rely on the brains and minds of others for much knowledge and many specific tasks that our own brains cannot perform as well: memory, drawing, directions, art production. We hire assistants to remind us, and we offload many of our mental tasks to them. And the brain itself outsources some of its conscious functions to its unconscious, in the form of habits and zombies.

With the exception, perhaps, of school test proctors, almost no one is uncomfortable with much of this mental outsourcing—we don't usually hear complaints, for example, that our phone remembers our numbers for us. But some people still get upset when others outsource functions like calculating a tip or checking spelling. Somehow, they think, this makes us "lazy"—a complaint often heard from teachers. "There is a vast reservoir of bad will toward the idea of computers doing human-like tasks,"[37] says Ken Jennings. I believe this attitude holds us back.

What we need to move forward is not to stop the outsourcing, but, rather, to reflect on, revise, refine, and redefine what we mean by "thinking" when we are enhanced with modern technology as so many of us now are. Like the updated quiz shows that now permit us to "phone a friend," we can no longer think of our mind's activity as the work of only a single person in isolation. Certainly that's not the way most of the world functions these days; most of today's thinking—and work—is a symbiotic effort of people and machines. A person connected to the Internet might look up something he or she is thinking about, and be directed by the technology, to a great many additional thoughts and areas in an expanding virtuous cycle. Thinking and problem solving are increasingly done by people and machines—and often by large numbers of both of them, linked together.

Outsourcing doesn't just *replace* the capabilities that we have in our un-aided brains and minds—it improves, enhances, extends, and amplifies them, making us freer and more capable human beings. Outsourcing allows us to make more of the things we are good at and to add to our skill set many areas we're not. Shy or autistic people uncomfortable with in-person connections often connect using technology. People from around the world collaborate on-line around their shared interests. People who live alone find online gaming or dating partners. People who have difficulty with reading or math work cash registers by looking at pictures on the keys. (And if this last doesn't seem like a gain to you, think about if you had just moved to China and needed a job!)

Yet many people seem to reject cognitive outsourcing and fear its conse-quences. I think those people are wrong, and so should you.

"TRANSPARENT" COGNITIVE ENHANCEMENTS

Andy Clark, one of the creators of the extended mind theory (and a profes-sor of philosophy and chair in logic and metaphysics at the University of Edinburgh in Scotland), has written about "supersizing our minds" through cognitive enhancements.[38] To Clark, the enhancements are an actual part of our thinking, because "the cycle of activity that runs from brain through body and world and back again actually constitutes cognition."[39] Clark admits a possible distinction between "tools" and "parts of the mind," but says it is a "fuzzy" one. The difference, he thinks, turns principally on what he calls "transparency"—the more you don't have to "attend to" the technology to make it work, the more it can be considered part of your "core thinking pro-cess." In other words, the more automatic the technology gets, the more at-tached it becomes to our minds.[40]

"We haven't yet gotten used to inhabiting a world with tools so well-fitted to us that when they are with us they become transparent,"[41] says Clark. Clark offers as an example of a transparent tool a U.S. Navy flight suit for helicopter pilots that, in cases of instability, buzzes on the side that needs to be corrected. He claims the suit enables first-time helicopter pilots to cut the practice time needed to learn to hover from multiple hours to only 30 minutes.

Clark uses the term "cognitive prosthetics" for things we add on to extend our mind's capabilities, just as body prosthetics like artificial limbs extend our bodies'. Not only, he says, do the cognitive prosthetics extend the properties humans already have, but, like the physical prosthetics, they open up new ones. Clark offers text messaging as an example of a mental prosthesis that has extended our capabilities: "[Texting] didn't just fix or enhance [our former methods of communication]," he says, "it opened up a new channel." In fact, Clark sees the greatest potential of extending our minds as "opening up new worlds" to humans. I agree.

HUMAN PERFORMANCE ENHANCEMENT

The U.S. military has for some time been interested in mind enhancement as a way to enhance warfighters' capabilities. A 2007 report from the Institute for Defense Analyses (IDA) entitled "Overview of Developments in Human Performance Enhancement"[42] reports that "some leading militaries have adopted these technologies for military purposes." It goes on to say, "There is also evidence that potential adversaries are either conducting research on or wish to obtain HPE [human performance enhancement] capabilities for use against the United States and its allies," and that "significant research is already underway in many countries as part of their future soldier programs: many countries have programs underway that involve neurological and biological research that could be applied to internal HPE."

The report defines human performance enhancement (HPE) as involving "any measure that can enhance, modify, protect, or restore human activity." It examines a number of enhancement technologies, which include pharmaceutical/neutraceutical enhancements, molecular and genetic technologies, nanotechnologies, and cognitive/neurotechnologies. The authors remind us that there is a "dangerous duality" in these and other emerging technologies, in that the "opportunities for improvement" offered by HPE may be "either well or ill-intentioned." (I will return to these concerns later in the book.)

HPE technologies are often, for convenience, subdivided by researchers according to physical criteria, such as whether they are "skin-in" or "skin-out," "above the neck" or "below the neck." Some HPE technologies are already in use by the U.S. military, while others are still years away. Already in use today are pharmaceutical enhancements, including "using 'uppers/downers' and anti-sleep medication to extend continuous battlefield performance and alertness." This includes the widely used practice of giving pilots amphetamines to keep them alert on long flights.

There is also the use of nutrition to enhance performance. An emerging field that is under serious investigation by military researchers is nutritional genomics—how what we eat changes our genome. This is actually a subset of pharmacogenomics—how every compound that passes through our mouths changes our gene expression. For the military, the practical issues include both what to give to warfighters and how to keep steady-state levels of relevant compounds in the target organ—that is, the brain.

The study's conclusion is that "the convergence of nanoscience, biotechnology, information technology and cognitive/neuro science offers immense opportunities for the improvement of human abilities, social outcomes, and the nation's productivity, and has great potential for applications to enhancing the warfighter performance." But to underline the need for continued research, they also paint a darker potential scenario: "On the more extreme end of the genetic engineering spectrum, suppose genetic engineering becomes widespread and China's average IQ goes up by 30 points. Higher IQ causes qualitative differences in how people think. People with higher intelligence can think with concepts that are quite beyond the reach of lesser minds. But genetic engineering of the mind will not be done only for intelligence. It will be done for personality too. It seems very likely that there are personality types that are harder or easier to control. There may also be intelligence characteristics (e.g., inquisitiveness) that make one have a greater independence of mind, a lesser willingness to accept orders, a greater desire to feel unconstrained, and a lesser desire to bow to peer pressure. The biggest benefit and danger from human genetic engineering may come from the ability to do personality and intelligence selection. However, indications are that this is yet in the distant future of the technology (more than 20 years)."[43] Will this be brain gain? Will it happen to all of us? I discuss this in Chapter 8.

At the moment, one of the great *un*knowns is whether, or to what degree, technological brain enhancements can be passed on to offspring. The idea that humans can pass on such changes was proposed by Jean-Baptiste Lamarck roughly 200 years ago, but it was later rejected by many scientists.[44] It has recently been revived as we learn more about so-called "epigenetic" changes—changes to our genetic structures that are environmentally caused. This is an area where we should all stay tuned—big changes in our understanding are coming, with wide-ranging implications.

THE "LIBERATED" MIND: USEFUL PERSPECTIVE

In this book's introduction, I use the term "perspective." Perspective is very much what this book, and this subject, is about. The most interesting and useful perspective to take regarding technology, I believe, is the following:

We are all, as part of twenty-first-century human society, going through a period of intense transformation. Whether we like it or not, twenty-first-century humans are living through huge changes in how we behave and relate as people, as well as big changes in what we, as humans, consider important. Technology is a key part and driver of that change. It is important that we focus not just on the negatives, but rather on the positive changes that technology is producing in our lives. In particular, we need to look for, understand, and keep our focus on how technology is enhancing and liberating our minds to do new things.

For many in the world the changes now taking place are wrenching and difficult. In some places the changes are just beginning. But they are coming to everyone. And that is why there are new kinds of battles going on. As Thomas L. Friedman of the *New York Times* describes in his books *The World Is Flat* and *Hot Flat and Crowded,* the world is becoming equalized (or "flattened") because of technology.[45] Everything from school, to trade, to knowledge, to thinking is now more global. Places that used to be considered "backward" or "out of the way" by some now have the same power to influence the world as the so-called "big guys." The group that attacked America on 9/11 and the self-immolator in Tunisia who set off the Arab Spring are examples of this. As a result, we can no longer live in our own cocoons, however comfortable or physically isolated they may be, but must now, because of technology, continually interact with the entire world.

On top of which the unsettling combination of variability, uncertainty, chaos, and ambiguity is increasing in the world and in our lives.

And it's all happening faster and faster. These days, almost no matter where in the world one is, new technology is coming at humans and entering their lives, leaving them feeling, often, like they are on an out-of-control roller coaster. Word processing. Spreadsheets. Email. Instant messaging. Cell phones (even in remote villages in India and Africa). The Internet. Worldwide databases. Computers in our pockets. Instant connection to every person. Online shopping and banking. Social networking. Facebook. Twitter. Blackberries. Smart phones. Tablets. Personalized recommendations. Automated personal assistants. Electronic book readers. Personalized ads.

Something new, literally, every day.

And the technology arrives not just frontally, but it also inserts itself in our lives stealthily, without our often being fully—or even partially—aware. Many people find themselves caught up in a world of changing jobs, changing habits, changing attitudes, changing children—changing *everything*, it seems!

SHUT IT OFF? A DIFFERENT TAKE

In the midst of all this change, people look for means of control, and use of technology appears to some as one thing they have control over—control that they feel the need to assert. Many people whose lives have been made more stressful, complicated, or hectic because of today's rapidly advancing technology are starting to say "hold on."

This response does make sense. At some point *any* smart person would sit back and ask him or herself: Is this good? Is our quickly advancing technology helping or hurting us as individuals? As humans? Or are we being led downhill, toward dystopia, and perhaps even toward domination by our machines?

But we oughtn't overemphasize this problem. There are some real dangers, and I discuss them later. But I suggest we benefit more from considering technology not as a set of concerns and dangers, as many of these people do, but rather as the enormous boon to our lives that it is (a boon that comes, of course, with issues and trade-offs). Even though we should watch out for and guard against some things, modern technology is by far "net-positive" for all humans and for humankind. Those alive today and their descendants are fortunate to live, and think, in a much more powerful and positive world.

In many cases, the truth is that we can do little or nothing to change technology's course. As Kevin Kelly points out in his book *What Technology Wants*, technology emerges, often in multiple places, when conditions are ready and when the supporting technologies are in place.[46] "We have no choice but to embrace it," says Kelly, "because we are already symbiotic with it: Technology underpins civilization."[47]

But humans love to worry—and these days good money can be made from doing so publicly. Articles appear frequently presenting yet another aspect of technology to worry about (the latest article I saw was about the huge amounts of data collected on its customers by Target stores[48]). Speakers focus on specific threats: If you are worried about computers taking over, hire Ken Jennings (the guy defeated by Watson on *Jeopardy*). Concerned about your kids getting dumber? Hire Mark Bauerlein *(The Dumbest Generation)*. Concerned about what is happening to adults? Hire Nicholas Carr *(The Shallows)*. Concerned about overuse of technology? William Powers *(Hamlet's Blackberry)* and Sherry Turkle *(Alone Together)* will be happy to fuel your fires. They are all excellent speakers, and all draw applause. Each will be glad to tell audiences about the worrisome things that technology is doing to "our" minds (they almost always use the collective "we"). But few offer any solutions beyond "turn it off." The wisest admit "I don't really have the answer."[49] I differ from all those individuals and find little wisdom in their warnings and negative approach.

I do not see people getting dumber (including young people), I see them changing. I do not see public writing as getting shallower—I see more need to pick and choose what one reads and watches, and to look in new places.

I think what technology is doing to human minds is what we have the *least* to worry about. Instead, what technology is doing to people's minds is what we should all be celebrating.

It is, by any definition, brain gain.

TWO

THE QUEST FOR DIGITAL WISDOM

The Emerging Homo Sapiens Digital

B rain gain, certainly. But wisdom? That is a more complex question. In mid-2008, a small article—actually a letter—appeared in *Nature,* the leading life-sciences journal. The letter's authors were seven scientists—neuroscientists and ethicists—all well known, all highly regarded, all at the top of their profession.

The letter's purpose was to make a recommendation. The authors began by discussing a practice that had been going on for years, on college campuses and elsewhere, of people routinely taking drugs like Ritalin and Adderall to "increase executive functions" and "improve their abilities to focus their attention, manipulate information in working memory and flexibly control their responses." Because these drugs are widely prescribed as treatments for ADD and ADHD, they are often easily obtainable by students and by people in general.

But no one, up to the time of this letter, was advocating giving such medications to *everyone.*

The article's authors, however, were writing to support the practice of not just allowing but actually *encouraging* (their term) the "responsible use of cognitive enhancement tools—including the pharmacological," by "healthy" people (i.e., those not diagnosed with ADD or ADHD). Their reasoning, and their radical claim, was that these drugs "will be increasingly useful for improved quality of life and extended work productivity, as well as to stave off normal and pathological age-related cognitive declines."

The letter's title: "Toward responsible use of cognitive-enhancing drugs by the healthy."[1]

None of the letter's writers recommends just "putting these substances in the water supply"[2] (as the letter's lead author, Professor Hank Greely of Stanford Law School, put it to me), and all support further study. But all of these noted scientists recognize and agree that there is cognitive enhancement—i.e., mind or brain gain—from the use of these technologies. And Greely, the legal ethicist in the group, does not see pharmacological mind enhancement as morally wrong in principal.

Do *you* think what these ethicists and scientists are saying is wise?
Or not wise?

That is what this book is about: considering all the kinds of new technologies—a few pharmacological but most not—that are already enhancing and impacting our minds today, and considering the wisest uses of all these new technological capabilities. This is what I call the "quest for digital wisdom."[3]

It is critical for us to think about these questions now, before events overtake us. For example, in 2011, just three years after the publication of the letter in *Nature,* the *New York Times* reported on its front page that the United States was experiencing shortages in Ritalin and Adderall. These drugs and their generic equivalents, they explained, are in short supply and often difficult to obtain. "Shortages, particularly of cheaper generics, have become so endemic that some patients say they worry almost constantly about availability," wrote the *Times.* The main reason for the shortages, according to the paper, is "healthy" students. "Since the drugs have been shown to improve concentration, and not just in people with ADHD, they have become popular among students who are seeking a study aid," wrote the *Times* reporter. (Of course, not all of what students use these drugs for is studying. The *Times* also cites as reasons for the shortage the drug manufacturers' manipulating the supply, and "people, many of them college students, who use the medications to get high or to stay up all night."[4])

But with plenty of other alternatives available for getting high, why have so many non-ADD and non-ADHD students gravitated, in large numbers, toward these drugs? I agree with the scientists that it's because the students see them as technological mind enhancers—that is, as brain gain. Using these technologies, the students believe, makes them wiser, giving them a leg up.

We can, and should, debate the merits of achieving enhancement in this particular way. But given the huge changes in our technology, our environment, and our world in general, there is little question, and can be little debate, that we, as humans, are in desperate need of additional wisdom—wisdom that now comes from incorporating technology into our minds.

WHAT IS "WISDOM"?

I want to begin by asking two questions that may seem obvious but are probably not asked as much as they should be. First: "What is wisdom?" And second: "Why would we want it?" The answers to both of those questions will help us understand what digital wisdom is, and why we are—or should be—on a quest to find it.

Wisdom is a universal, but ill-defined, concept. It is often, although not always, associated with old age and experience, and yet we also talk about "the wisdom of babes"—we often see wisdom in our children.

Definitions of wisdom fill entire volumes. The Oxford English Dictionary suggests that wisdom's main component is judgment, referring to the "capacity of judging rightly in matters relating to life and conduct, soundness of judgment in the choice of means and ends."[5]

Philosopher Robert Nozick suggests that wisdom lies in knowing what is important.[6]

In his *Nicomachean Ethics,* Aristotle speaks of "practical wisdom," the ability to discern the best thing to do, in every situation we face, to achieve our worthiest goals.[7] In their book *Practical Wisdom,* professors Barry Schwartz and Kenneth Sharpe update Aristotle's concept for the current world, arguing that we need to integrate it further into our justice, educational, and medical systems.[8]

Many see wisdom mainly as the ability to solve problems—some think it is just a more complex kind of problem solving. Others talk about wisdom as finding the healthy thing to do.

Stanford law professor and ethicist Hank Greely sees wisdom as the ability to "usefully integrate our experiences to come to an understanding or plan of action."[9] Some include as part of wisdom how those plans and decisions are implemented as well.

An interesting definition of wisdom comes from Howard Gardner, who suggests that wisdom may be seen in the breadth of issues considered in arriving at a judgment or decision.[10]

And many definitions—although not all—attribute to wisdom a moral component, locating wisdom in the ability to discern the "right" thing to do. This is, of course, problematic since agreement on moral issues is frequently difficult to come by. What it implies, though, is that wisdom cannot be conclusively defined without a consideration of context.

Combining these sources, let me define wisdom as *the ability to find practical, creative, contextually appropriate, and emotionally satisfying solutions to complicated human problems.*

I believe wisdom involves considering the largest possible number of factors, analyzing them appropriately and well, and reaching and implementing useful and beneficial conclusions.

Digital wisdom, I believe, involves doing this for both the technologies we use and the ways in which we use them.

WISDOM AND TECHNOLOGY

Some might question why I put "digital" and "wisdom" in the same sentence, thinking "digital technology" is only—or mainly—for entertainment or pleasure. The truth is, though, that wisdom and *every* technology have always been closely linked.

Wise cave people, for example, used charcoal and paint to leave markings on trees or cave walls. Wise hunters used arrows and spears. In the Bible, David exhibits technology-based wisdom in slaying Goliath by knowing that a strongly propelled, well-aimed rock could be more powerful than large size and muscles. Leaders throughout history have understood that if they wanted to protect their people, or advance their cause, it was wise to develop advanced technology, which generally provided the best weapons. Even the fact that we often name our historical eras in terms of technologies (the Stone Age, the Bronze Age, etc.) may have some relationship to wisdom—some might say humans were wiser in each of the succeeding technology eras.[11]

And even that paradigm of wisdom, the biblical story of King Solomon and the baby, has a technology component. While Solomon knew that a real mother's instinct is to want her child to live, without a sharp sword (a highly advanced technology at the time) to potentially cut the baby into "equal" parts, his offer would not have been possible.

All technology requires wisdom in its use. Many, such as Neil Postman (*Amusing Ourselves to Death*), have warned us against the dangers of excesses of pleasure that can come from ill-considered uses of technology.[12] If one puts electrodes into the "pleasure centers" in animals' brains, lacking wisdom, they will use that technology to literally self-stimulate themselves to death.[13]

Technology-based wisdom is something we teach to all our children, starting at a very young age. The almost universally known children's story (at least in western culture) of the three little pigs teaches that those who are wise use better technology. (The wise pig employs the more advanced technology of baking clay bricks, rather than the earlier construction technologies of wood and straw.) Today, many teens learn about the relationship between technology and wisdom through computer games like Civilization and Rise of Nations, where, by investing in (or not investing in) various technologies, they lead a civilization, either successfully or unsuccessfully, through the various stages of history.

Each new technology humans invent presents us with a new need to think about wisdom, because almost all technology can be used in positive and negative ways. In the past, people needed to successively develop "stone wisdom," "bronze wisdom," and "steel wisdom." We are still struggling with "atomic wisdom" today. Digital wisdom involves integrating the technologies of *our* times into our thinking and decision making, doing it wisely, and sharing the results.

FIRE WISDOM

Although there may not as yet be a single paradigm for digital wisdom—that is, a story that everyone is raised on like the *Three Little Pigs*—it may be helpful for our understanding to review the trajectory of one of man's oldest technologies: fire (a technology that humans didn't invent, of course—it came from lightning—but one that we did tame for our uses).

There's no doubt that fire was frightening at first—after thousands of millennia, it still is. When it strikes, fire can destroy our most precious possessions: libraries, crops, fortifications, and even whole cities. But fire also brings humans great benefits. The ancient Greeks saw it as a "gift" from the gods (it was actually stolen from them, according to Greek mythology, and given to man by Prometheus). Over the course of history, humans have learned a great deal about fire's benefits and how to control it, in our hearths, homes, and factories. Over time, we have found, if you will, "fire wisdom."

While one could conceivably make the argument that because it is an "external" enhancement fire makes humans "lesser," my guess is you wouldn't believe it. Despite its many dangers, fire vastly improves us. How "human" would we be without this technology, without "home fires" to warm us and bring our families together? Without all of fire's industrial benefits? Without fire and its successors to cook with and to sit and read by?

Still, while we appreciate fire, we continue to teach our children to be very careful with it. "Don't play with fire" is a universal lesson and has even become a metaphor for safety. Most citizens are happy to pay their government to maintain highly trained fire fighters.

Despite its obvious danger, no one writes books about how "fire is destroying humanity." The story we tell, rather, is about how much this technology has improved our lives. We recognize the dangers of the technology and do our best to protect against them, but we accept that this powerful tool benefits us and strive to make better and better use of it. This is our fire wisdom.

Digital wisdom is similar. The difference is that humans are still at digital technology's very beginnings. And as with fire, the beginning is the scariest time. Just as with fire, the potential dangers of digital and other modern technologies, identity theft, cyber-attacks, worldwide electronic wipeout, for example, and even, at the extreme, nuclear annihilation, are real. Some dangers are still coming into focus.

But the benefits of these technologies are real, too. And just as with fire, the positives of digital and other modern technologies so far outweigh the negatives—and come in so many diverse ways—that we often ignore them. People often don't realize, for example, that their chief way to complain about technology is through the Internet and email!

This focus on the negatives, and taking for granted of the positives, is particularly true with respect to the ways digital technology is affecting the mind. Although it is not what we usually hear, the benefits of digital mind enhancement far outweigh the negatives, and many of our smartest people recognize this. I recently asked the former president of Harvard, treasury secretary, and presidential advisor, Larry H. Summers, what he thought were the biggest benefits of the new technologies for education. He responded immediately that mind enhancement (through pharmacological technologies like future successors to Ritalin and Adderall) was the most promising place to look.[14] Another smart observer is Hank Greely, the professor of law and bioethics at Stanford, who helped write the letter I mentioned earlier, and whose whole career has been spent studying the question of biological mind enhancements. Greely dismisses almost out of hand many of the objections to such enhancements, although with some caveats. He admits there are serious concerns around safety, fairness, and coercion to be worked out—in many cases—coercion of kids by parents pushing their kids toward enhancement. (I agree with Greeley that these are serious issues, and I discuss these and other legitimate concerns in some detail in Chapter 7.)

But even though Greely's personality, he says, leads him to an overall "middle position," he nevertheless views mind enhancement through pharmaceuticals as generally positive, and certainly not in any way "wrong." He points out in his writings and talks that mind enhancement is something people have always done and, in fact, strived toward; that it is something that brings many benefits, and that it is something we do today in many places. Today biologically based mind enhancement happens in our homes (vitamins), in our schools (Ritalin and Adderall), in our workplaces (caffeine), in our military (amphetamines for long flights), in our sports (energy drinks and steroids) and even in medicine (many doctors take drugs like modafinil to increase their alertness).[15]

Greely dismisses arguments about enhancements being bad just because they are physical (as in drugs) versus mental (as in teaching or coaching). All, he notes, affect our brain. He does not agree that mind enhancements obviate the need for effort—they just multiply, he says, that effort's effects. He does not accept what he calls the "integrity" arguments of "needing to play by the rules" and of not "cheating," because rules are arbitrary—we make them and change them.[16] And Greely doesn't agree at all with the "it's not right, it's not natural" arguments (what he calls the "yuck factor" arguments) against enhancements, even while noting that these arguments often have the most "political" resonance. "I frankly do not see much in [these arguments]," he writes, although, he adds, carefully, as the good professor and lawyer he is, "I am (somewhat) open to being convinced."[17]

We all should remain open to being convinced by new evidence. But it is important to recognize that the sorts of mind enhancements that I am talking about in this book are very large in both their number and scope, and that biological mind enhancement is only one of more than 50 kinds of enhancement I look at.

GAIN VERSUS WISDOM

There is, however, an important distinction to be made between brain gain and true digital wisdom. Gains due to technology can often be observed and recognized right away, such as when a technology extends our senses in some fashion. Technologies such as telescopes, thermometers, microscopes, hearing aids, as well as email, search engines, and other digital technologies, provide clear gains.

Wisdom, though, takes longer to recognize. It comes partially through our choice of technologies, but it also often comes in how those technologies are used by us. Even the most obviously beneficial technologies also have their downsides and can, if desired, be used in negative ways and for nefarious purposes. I have heard, for example, that more telescopes and binoculars are sold in New York City than anywhere else on earth. Do you imagine this is all for bird watching?

So just asking whether a technology—mind-enhancing or otherwise—is positive or negative, or good or bad, is generally an unhelpful question, since all technologies have the capacity to be both. We need to question whether the technology is being used wisely.

Yet the "good or bad" technology question gets asked a lot. Entire technologies get banned in schools or even countries, denying people obvious benefits (such as students' abilities to reach their parents in emergencies, or citizens' ability to find all the information on the Internet). Some U.S. schools have banned students' use of calculators, cell phones, YouTube, Facebook, and other digital technologies. China and other countries have banned access to parts of the Internet.

My approach is therefore *not* to provide an answer to the unhelpful question of whether each of the individual mind-enhancing technologies I discuss is "good" or "bad." It is rather to offer instead an alternate overall perspective that provides, I believe, a better lens for viewing technology and our future.

Practically, I also offer a more helpful set of questions to be asking. For any technology, or group of technologies, we encounter and want to evaluate, we should ask ourselves:

Is this use of technology wise?
Are there wiser uses of this technology?

The combined answer to these questions for all of our technologies is what constitutes our digital wisdom.

THE QUEST FOR DIGITAL WISDOM

The struggle to acquire digital wisdom—that is, to find the ways that digital technology can make us wiser and better as human beings—is an important piece of humankind's twenty-first-century development. Humans *need* digital wisdom, and I strongly believe we can develop it. I hope to show you why and how.

A key thing, in any evaluation, including of technology, is to overcome our personal instinctive affinity (or disaffinity) and look at both sides. This I will try to do. But that doesn't mean we can't, or shouldn't, make judgments. We must remember that as important as the risks of various technologies may be, they are *only a piece* of our assessment of the digital wisdom of using those technologies. As humans, we use many risky technologies on a daily basis— from pharmaceuticals, to nuclear power, to air travel, to explosives. We employ these technologies—despite obvious risks—because our assessment tells us that their use, in particular cases, is okay. A big part of digital wisdom is knowing when our decisions to use those technologies are right.

DIGITAL WISDOM

Digital wisdom is a dual concept, referring both to wisdom arising *from* the use of digital technology and to wisdom *in* the prudent use of such technology. Digital wisdom is similar to, but different from, Aristotle's concept of "practical wisdom"—what he calls *phronesis*.[18] It is similar in that, like practical wisdom, digital wisdom can only be assessed in terms of our aims and goals, which differ in individual situations. That a use of a technology might be wise (or digitally wise) in some situations, and unwise in others, is obvious from the way nuclear technology can be applied to generating energy or weapons. (And, as recent events in Japan have showed us, there is even need for digital wisdom in a peaceful context.) Digital wisdom is also similar to practical wisdom in that they are both "moral" skills rather than just technical or artistic skills; that is, they involve decisions about what is "right." Both involve good judgment.

But digital wisdom differs from practical wisdom in at least one very important respect. According to Barry Schwartz and Kenneth Sharpe, practical wisdom is learned primarily though trial and error. I believe we can be much more deliberate and proactive in creating and extending digital wisdom.

Schwartz and Sharpe point out that trying to induce wisdom though incentives, or rules, often produces unfavorable results, citing, for example, doctors who order fewer tests because that is what they are incentivized (i.e., rewarded) for doing, when the wise thing is for the doctors to order the *right* amount of tests, based not on the incentives but on their judgment. Wisdom, they say, lies in doing things *not* because we are incentivized to, but because we judge them to be the right things to do. "Incentives—even smart ones," they write, "may move the goal further away." A technology-related analogy would be when business or school system administrators keep their technology tightly "locked down" (that is, when they severely restrict what users can access) because they fear they will be blamed if something goes wrong. The goal of keeping their job leads them to make decisions that are personally protective but are digitally unwise for their organizations. (Doing this is known, in the vernacular, as "CYA."[19])

On the other hand, setting up hard and fast rules, such as "always do what the businessperson wants," is often, also, an invitation to disaster—Schwartz and Sharpe call such rules "pale substitutes for wisdom." "Rules without wisdom," they write, "are blind—and at best guarantee mediocrity, forcing wise practitioners to become outlaws, rule-breakers pursuing a kind of guerilla war to achieve excellence."[20] We can easily find examples in the technology world of this rule-based lack of digital wisdom, such as "blanket" bans on the use of pharmaceuticals, or smart phones, or any mind-enhancing technologies during exams.

Yet it is a measure of how far we have, in fact, advanced toward digital wisdom that many students are now allowed to use calculators on some exams and to use computers to take tests and write essays. The military also tends to be forward thinking on these matters, as do the many businesses that provide employees with personal technology tools. But we are still learning in these areas.

The valuable gains in wisdom that we get from technology do not come from enhanced convenience—although technology often does make things easier. Digital wisdom is rather about using technology—particularly the new digital technologies of our age—to improve our minds. Technology helps us most when it makes us *better thinkers* who make *wiser decisions and choices*.

Although there is certainly no guarantee about anything, I believe people are likely to become "wiser" human beings when they can do things like:

- concentrate harder,
- combine the intellects of hundreds of experts from around the globe to work on a single problem,

- apply the power of all the world's computers to their own individual issues and questions,
- communicate across the globe without barriers,
- take into account every relevant fact and precedent before making a decision,
- recall all of their past experiences,
- tap into the power of their unconscious mind,
- not just find information, but automatically rearrange, combine, and analyze it,
- understand what is going wrong in their own body and how to fix it,
- prevent crimes, wars, and other negative events from happening,
- see old and/or familiar things in totally new ways, and
- debate issues and ideas more fully.

This is, of course, a partial list of what technology can enable. We will see that these capabilities, and many others, are currently possible and are available to many people today. Many more technologies that go even further toward making us digitally wise are very close and will become available in only a few years. This is why I speak of *Homo Sapiens Digital*—the Digitally Wise Person. I believe that our species, *homo sapiens,* is, because of technology, getting wiser.

Not that every *homo sapiens* is there. But that is what we all should be striving to become: digitally wise people. We are not born with digital wisdom, but we can acquire it. Hence the book's subtitle: *The Quest for Digital Wisdom.*

The concept of the "quest" (i.e., a difficult journey to achieve a worthwhile goal), goes way back into ancient history, but it has taken on new meaning and relevance for many of today's young people through the medium of video games. In a great many of those games, the hero must complete increasingly difficult, risky, and dangerous quests in order to gain desired rewards. So, many of today's kids are used to "questing." (There is even a game-based school in New York City called Quest to Learn.)

I believe a quest for digital wisdom is one that twenty-first-century humans desperately need to undertake. I have certainly felt myself on such a quest. As digital technology enters more and more phases of my life, from communication, to education, to medicine, to entertainment, I have often felt myself struggling to find the right thing to do and the wisest path to take. Do I buy my six-year-old son an iPad? Do I push for more computers in his classroom? Do I demand that my family's medical records be digitized? Do I share my personal information on Facebook? Do I support stronger privacy legislation? These are questions to which there are no easy answers, but that we must all address in our search for digital wisdom.

THE VALUE OF THE PAST (IN A TECHNOLOGY-DRIVEN WORLD)

I believe strongly in extracting all the wisdom we possibly can from the past, using it in our own lives, and passing it to our children. But whatever else you take away from this book, there is one thing I hope you will learn and remember:

> The changes coming because of technology are far greater than you—or anyone—can imagine. And because of the changing context, the wisdom of the past, in a great many cases, will no longer apply.

This is true for a number of very important human areas. An enormous number of our fundamental assumptions are currently undergoing reexamination and change. They certainly include, at a minimum, privacy, physical and intellectual property, what is important, what is valuable, and even what constitutes and characterizes good and deep relationships.

Much of what has traditionally been considered totally private information is now going online, where it can be found more and more easily. Do we value privacy or transparency? And if both, how do we prioritize them?

New kinds of value are emerging from unexpected directions, such as from the ephemeral online relationships created by links and sign-ups to virtual communities. To whom does this value belong?

Relationships can be carried on via more and more channels and in more and more ways. Which are wise, and when? Minds can be accessed and influenced as never before. Who should have responsibility? Virtual goods are being created and sold. Who owns them? Many new behaviors are possible. Which are acceptable and under what conditions?

Because so many of these beliefs are central to our lives—who we are, who we are with and how we interact with them, how we earn our living, what we own—we have to find "new" wisdom in these areas. A large component of digital wisdom is figuring out which of our beliefs need to change and which we should keep.

How do we judge what is digitally wise and what is not? The answer is not yet crystal clear and perhaps will never be. But there are already some guidelines emerging.

For one thing, "top-down" authority is no longer the best way to make decisions. Because of technology, the voices of those at the bottom have been liberated and empowered, and wise decision makers need to listen to their opinions and take them into account. This is true in politics (the blogosphere), in business (where anyone can send an email to anyone, and doing so is often encouraged), in the military (where individual solders have started their own blogs to complain about conditions or equipment, and officers have created their own web sites to assist everyone at their rank), and in a great many other fields. "Bottom-up" has now entered our decision-making vocabulary. So one criterion for a digitally wise decision is whether it has taken into account the opinions of all the stakeholders from bottom to top.

Another clear direction is that people are becoming more fully informed, as information becomes more available. It used to be that one side—say the government—could easily withhold things that could be valuable to the other side's argument—something that we don't permit in our legal system, for example. Today we have WikiLeaks and digital hacking. The issues of what information should be kept secret is a tricky one, particularly in cases of national security, but the digitally wise direction is, I believe, moving toward openness. For example, information on the H5N1 bird flu virus was made public so that scientists could share access, even though there were concerns that terrorists might misuse the information.[21]

A third guideline is to learn to talk about these changes in neutral language that allows dispassionate discussion. If teachers shout "plagiarism" or "theft" or if people scream "less human" every time students do something new and different with technology, it will certainly not help. Our behaviors and expectations in many of these areas ought to be reframed not as absolute rules but rather as societal expectations, some of which may be changing.

We also see people's expectations changing regarding online availability and speed of response. We will need to decide, despite our resistance, when it is in our best interests to adapt.

Not all the wisdom of the past, of course, is or will become outdated or useless, and not everything will change. But much will become meaningfully different—and already is. I believe those who are quickest to understand this, to think about its implications and adapt, will be those who thrive in the twenty-first century. Those who hang on the longest to outmoded ideas and beliefs will almost certainly suffer.

Today we see this nowhere more than in our schools, many of which cling to pre-digital ideas, rules, and behaviors. That is why I devote an entire chapter (Chapter 6) to incorporating digital wisdom into the education system.

Despite the many Cassandras and other naysayers predicting our doom, what is happening to our minds because of technology is not, in the main, bad. As we will see in the many examples in the next chapter, the great majority of what technology is doing to us in this area is, rather, very *good*—good for each us and good for humanity. It is crucial to always keep this thought in mind as you listen to the critics.

A FEW EXAMPLES

One good example of our new digital wisdom is the late Steve Jobs's remaking of the music industry. (He did not do this totally on his own, of course, but many of the key ideas and insights were his or championed by him.)

In the early 2000s, new Internet sites, enabled by new digital technologies such as file-sharing protocols and fast download technologies such as BitTorrent, allowed music—mainly popular songs—to be shared and downloaded for free. Young people in particular started rushing in droves to use these technologies, and music became, for these people, essentially free. On the other side were the record companies (sometimes joined by the artists), who thought music should continue to cost as much as it had up until then—in order to support, in many cases, their high salaries and lavish lifestyles, and the investors in their companies. The record companies' most powerful weapon was lawsuits. They began to sue people, often poor, extracting some harsh judgments. A huge battle loomed.

With his unusual digital wisdom, Jobs saw a solution. He did not choose between those who wanted all music to cost a lot and those who wanted all music to be free. Rather he used technology to create a virtual store (iTunes) where people could purchase individual songs at the compromise price of just 99 cents each. While neither side was completely satisfied, both sides saw his solution as fair and wise. Although some music sharing still goes on (and some high-priced albums are still sold), the battle essentially ended.

What makes Jobs's solution digitally wise is that it was made possible only because of digital technology—the newly created abilities of technology to set up secure accounts, complete sales, and have customers download the music online. What is also worth remarking on is just how quickly technology can respond to a need or demand and create a solution.

Steve Jobs was also digitally wise in many of his other decisions. His purchase of Pixar (and early investment in digital filmmaking), his creation of the preferred music playing device (iPod), his remaking of the phone into an app-playing computer (the iPhone), and the integration of magazines and movies into a device you could hold in your lap (the iPad) all paid off big for Apple. Perhaps Jobs's most digitally wise decision of all was to link all those devices directly to his iTunes store.

Other examples of digital wisdom abound—I will discuss 50 of them in the next chapter. They include using technology to overcome our brain's deficiencies to improve our communication, to augment our physical well-being, to improve our relations with other people, to make our world a better place, to deepen our analyses, to derive new and useful insights, to increase our executive thinking (i.e., decision-making) ability, to increase our creativity, and to do new, wiser things and achieve better outcomes in almost all fields of human endeavor—including artistic fields—as a result of the emerging symbiosis of human mind and technology.

MIND, BRAIN, BELIEF, AND "BEING HUMAN": DANGEROUS MYTHS, FEARS, FALLACIES, AND BELIEFS THAT KEEP US FROM REACHING DIGITAL WISDOM

There are, however, a number of myths, fears, fallacies and beliefs that keep us from reaching digital wisdom. I now discuss several of them.

The Fallacy of "Human" as Being Special and Always Better

"Preserving our humanity" is a phrase, and a goal, that comes up frequently in discussions about digital technology. But what "our humanity" means, exactly, is often left to the imagination. This is because people hold very different opinions and beliefs about what makes us human, just as they do about our minds, our brains, and our technology.

There are some who believe that humans are not just a species, but are differentiated from the rest of the universe by something special, something not "natural" (in the sense of having evolved in nature). For some this difference is a God-given "soul" or "essence." For others, who may refer to themselves as "humanists," it is a belief that human beings possess some special kind of spark that technology can never replicate. Jaron Lanier calls this the "specialness of personhood."[22] "Being a person is not pat formula," he writes, "but a quest, a mystery, a leap of faith." Lanier differentiates his own "new digital humanism" from "computationalism," and "cybernetic totalism," preferring the former because he believes it is "a more colorful, heroic and seductive" approach to technology (which I'm sure it is). But Lanier also sees which view of people one adopts as being situational and practical: "There are some situations in which it is beneficial to think of people as 'special' and others where it isn't," he writes in *You Are Not a Gadget.*

To me, seeing people as special in this sense is a dangerous way to look at things.

I have no trouble with the idea that humans have something that other creatures don't, such as our abilities to talk, and to make tools—look at the great music and works of art we, alone on earth, have created. And we have not yet found any beings or intelligences outside our planet that are even there— let alone that surpass us.

But to assume this will always be true—that nothing on earth or in the universe will ever surpass humans, because it is the way of nature, or God, or anything else, is to diminish rather than extol humans. Humankind's greatest capacity is that we are capable of continually surpassing ourselves. Right now we have a symbiosis between man and machine that is more productive than either alone. Unless you are a clothing-less monk on a hilltop, it is hard to make a believable argument that the unaided human is better. But why get upset either way? Things evolve—almost nothing stays on top forever. If, as some speculate, technology surpasses the human brain and takes off on its own trajectory—see Chapter 8—so be it. Digital wisdom will only come if we accept things as they are, not as how we might wish they were. (This doesn't mean, though, that we can't try to influence things.)

The Fallacy of "Genuine"

"People are afraid," my editor told me, "that technology will cause them to miss out on the 'genuine' experience." Closely linked, perhaps, to the "man is special" fallacy above is the belief that certain things are more "genuine" than others. In particular, many believe that face-to-face interactions are more genuine than virtual (i.e., technology-mediated) ones.

I believe the problems with this thinking should be obvious to anyone who has ever watched any sport on TV and then later attended a live game. Unless you are fortunate enough to have obtained the very best seats, as close as possible to the action, what you see on the television is often far better and more of a "genuine" game experience: often these days you can even watch the game unfold from a participant's point of view. Some, of course, prefer to experience the smells and sounds and "feel" of being in an arena, which you do not get on television. But we should differentiate between the "being-a-spectator-in-a-crowd experience" (which you can, at least for now, only get in person) and the "watching-the-game" experience. For the latter, in-person is not the more "genuine" experience unless you are close. It has little to do with the genuine game if you are 100 rows back, where the players are specks (as I have been, for example, watching tennis matches. I once scored the last available seats to a Pete-Sampras–Andre Agassi match at the National Tennis Center at Flushing Meadows Park in New York City, where I spent the entire match freezing and wishing I was home watching a "genuine" tennis experience on TV). Similarly, I'd consider an encounter with a famous person online in which I actually got to ask that person a question a far more "genuine" encounter than just being in the same room listening to that expert from the back row of a lecture hall.[23]

To think that *any* technology-mediated experience, whether it be visual (e.g., video), audio (e.g., music), or an online conversation (e.g., text, audio, or on Skype), is *always* less genuine is a fallacy. Perhaps more importantly, avoiding such technology as "not genuine" means missing out on much of what life affords us today. We can now virtually attend a huge variety of concerts, plays, and operas around the world—even of performers who are no longer with us.

Another element of this particular fallacy is conflating "genuine" with "better." Is a poorly recorded live performance of a song, say, more "genuine" than a beautifully and highly produced studio version? Some might argue this. But is it better? Absolutely not! I have both the studio and live versions of Garth Brooks's "The River" on my iPhone, and I only ever want to hear the—far better—studio version.

The truth is that technology does not make us miss important or genuine experiences—it actually does the opposite. Technology *opens up* a great many kinds of interactions and experiences that are either impossible, or that most of us would never have, in person. So to equate non-technology-based with genuine is something that, I believe, is digitally unwise.

The Fallacy of Longer Always Being Better

Although many people praise and prefer long books like *War and Peace, The Brothers Karamazov,* or *Les Misérables,* and often seek out longer articles or musical works, it is important to understand that longer—by itself—does not equal better. It is, in fact, dangerous to confuse and conflate the two. A novel, although it may be easier for a publisher to publish and distribute, is no better because of its length than a novella or a short story. Any book with 500 pages, whether fiction or nonfiction, is no better—just because of its length—than a book of 50 pages, or even an article of 10. A long newspaper article is no better than one that is shorter and better written. A three-minute NPR report isn't necessarily better than a 30-second network news piece, even though the longer works, in each case, may contain more details.

It is not clear to me where the bias that many have in favor of length originates. Possibly it comes from a time when information was harder to come by, when details were less easily available, and when people had more time to spend. Putting a great many details into a work made sense under those conditions. But today, those conditions have turned around 180 degrees. Information is far too easy to come by (think about the Internet), there is far too much detail available (think about high-definition TV that suddenly shows heretofore concealed facial flaws of many actors and reporters), and time is at an all-time premium (think about your life).

Today it is even more important than ever for people to be able to value things not by length but by the quality of their content. In our era of too much to do, the more high-quality content that can be put into shorter forms, with details available as backup, the better it is.

There has always been a countervailing trend favoring conciseness over excess length. We have aphorisms, morals, quotations, commandments, and haikus that express deep thoughts in short, memorable, ways. Nobody calls these brain loss. These need to be reinforced and used more widely. Despite protestations of many to the contrary, technology is a great boon to us in this respect, because it allows us to more easily highlight what is important and to easily relegate the rest to backup. But digital wisdom is required to do this in a way that enhances, rather than diminishes, our understanding.

The Fallacy of Privacy Always Being Better

Privacy is something that many people value and wish to preserve. But it is a fallacy to think that privacy is always better—this is just not so. When you call 911, it is better that the operator can see your address. When the police have probable cause to think someone dangerous may be hiding in your house, it is better that the house can be searched. When one individual can blow up a plane, it is better that all passengers be scanned. From the perspective of population protection and epidemiological control, if you have a communicable disease, it is better that the world know about it than not know.

But if the information that you reveal about your disease is used to deny you insurance, or a job, that's a bad thing. There are valid concerns about "undue" invasions of privacy, that is, intrusions where there is no countervailing argument of good. Yet what is "undue" is generally based more on social norms and contracts than anything else, and those change with time and technology. The U.S. Bill of Rights specifies certain aspects of privacy that we have all agreed, by consensus, to guarantee in this country, such as the privacy of beliefs (1st Amendment), privacy of the home against demands that it be used to house soldiers (3rd Amendment), privacy of the person and possessions as against unreasonable searches (4th Amendment), and the 5th Amendment's privilege against self-incrimination, which provides protection for the privacy of personal information.

But there is no *requirement* that you keep your information private. If you don't feel you are incriminating or endangering yourself, personal information can be freely shared by individuals, companies, and even our government. (Remember the Freedom of Information Act?)

There are areas of legitimate privacy concern—information about minors, for example—and some things that people prefer—and in some cases have the legal right—to keep to themselves. It is digitally wise to be concerned about what happens to the information that we do share (e.g., health information with our insurance provider, or financial transactions we enter into with banks and credit card lenders), and about its being reshared (whether sold or unsold) without our knowledge.

But as a social norm and a legal matter, rather than a natural right, the concept of what information should or shouldn't be private is subject to change. And with the advent of digital technology, norms about privacy are shifting rapidly. To cite only one obvious example, Facebook and other social networking sites and activities have led to a generation that is (rightly or wrongly, for better or for worse) much less concerned about sharing and privacy, in many of its forms.

I believe our children will grow up in a world with very different ideas about what should and shouldn't be private. To a great extent, this is because once something has been put online digitally, it is very difficult—and often impossible—to remove it, or even to hide it from anyone determined to find it. We are all struggling with this—it is reported that there are 200,000–250,000 attacks *per hour* on the combined U.S. defense sites.[24]

Less (or no) privacy in the realm of information will clearly mean changes in people's lives and expectations. But will they all be bad? Here I think too many observers jump to unwarranted conclusions. Different does not necessarily mean worse.

Does it matter if our pictures, our incomes, and our digital details are easily available? Of course it will matter to some—today many lives, businesses, and governments are built on lies and illusions—but overall, and in the long run, I'm not sure it does matter. It will certainly require some serious readjustments in how we do certain things. We will still need to prevent things such as theft or discrimination, and we will have to find, in many cases, new ways of doing this. Today there are people—including all politicians and celebrities— who already live in a world of far less privacy. They survive, for the most part, quite well. Some of them may yearn to go back to a more "private" life, but they have made trade-offs they thought were beneficial. As will our children. If they accept less privacy in some areas than we had, so be it. Will they come to regret that we didn't protect them? I doubt it.

Science fiction writer David Brin has an interesting perspective on privacy, particularly privacy from the surveillance that is becoming more and more prevalent. The only thing privacy laws accomplish, he quotes Robert Heinlein as saying, is to make the bugs (i.e., the cameras and the microphones) smaller. "In a decade," says Brin, "you'll never know the cameras are there. Those with access to them will have devastating advantages."[25] A better solution than laws, Brin thinks, is to make everything transparent, that is, to give everyone access to everything. That way nobody gets any advantage. "The only alternative is to give the birdlike power of sight to everybody. Make the inevitable cameras accessible so anyone can check traffic at First and Main, look for a lost kid, or supervise Officer McGillicudy walking his beat. Only this way will the powerful have just as much—or little—privacy as the rest of us,"[26] says Brin.

Is it better to keep things private, or to make everything public and prevent and punish information misuse? Determining how much privacy is the right amount for each person and group in the digital age is a matter of digital wisdom.

The Fallacy of Depth and of Its Always Being Better

The term "depth" is often used when describing relationships, and for writing as well. That "technology is preventing us from having 'deep' relationships with people—or books—as we did in the past" is an oft-heard contemporary complaint.

Like wisdom, "depth" is a concept that is hard to pin down. It is a metaphor, often referring to the amount and/or the quality of the "content" in something. But it is impossible to measure depth, in this sense, with any degree of precision.

People sometimes try to get around this difficulty by using the "I know it when I see it" argument. "We all know what depth is, though it's hard to pin down precisely in words," writes William Powers in *Hamlet's Blackberry*.[27] Even though Powers goes on to say "it's the quality of awareness, feeling or understanding that comes when we truly engage with some aspect of our life experience," that still begs the meaning of "engage."

Unfortunately, the "I know it when I see it" argument provides no more clarity for depth than it did when Justice Potter used it for pornography. If we are going to use the word "depth" at all—and especially if we are going to use it as a yardstick for what is good—we need a better definition.

Some maintain, for example, that there is, *prima facie,* more depth in things that do not contain digital technology—writings, for example, or face-to-face relationships—than in things that do. I see this view as a dangerous fallacy. There are things online that are clearly of more depth than most face-to-face conversations (I'd cite David Brooks's *New York Times* blog as an example). People maintain intimate long-distance relationships using technology. Although it may not be the norm for some, one can have a deep relationship, a deep moment, or even a deep reading experience online as well as in person, and many of these have much *more* depth than in-person, non-technology-facilitated moments. (And by the way, let's note that this question is only asked in relation to newer technologies: no one disputes the potential for depth in the technology of writing letters.) Sometimes people will share much more about themselves in an email, for example, than when face to face. And if you haven't noticed, the bulk of face-to-face conversations in the world are about nothing more than the weather!

Digital wisdom requires that each interaction be judged on its own merits and not be stigmatized as less deep because it uses a technological medium.

The Fallacy of Slower Being Better

There is also a feeling, expressed by many, that it is somehow better to go or think or do things more slowly (and, they might add, deliberately). But it is a fallacy to think that slower is *always* better, and that the speeds enabled by technology cannot add value to what humans do. When a person goes into shock, or when a missile is on the way, there is only so much time one can spend thinking and deciding.

Certainly there are cases for humans where "slow thinking," as Daniel Kahneman calls it, is beneficial. But even he posits that humans have two separate thinking circuits and that each has its own strengths and weaknesses. Teachers everywhere have always praised and encouraged slow, deliberate thinking.[28] Others, such as Malcolm Gladwell in *Blink,* have praised fast, intuitive thinking as often good and useful. (Note that Kahneman and Gladwell speak behaviorally, not anatomically—we cannot currently observe these two types of thinking in brain circuits.)

But while there may be discussions about the varying speeds at which humans think, there is no question of the speed at which machines work—they are designed to go ever faster. Is that ever an advantage? Of course. There are clearly situations in which the time to reflect and weigh options is quite limited, say before another player's buzzer sounds or before a bullet arrives. Slowly weighing all the factors (and perhaps "sleeping on it," which has also been shown to aid decision making) is not, in many situations, a possibility. The ability of machines to think fast then becomes a powerful asset. So much so that in many cases we program machines to make decisions on their own, such as when to close floodgates or shut down nuclear reactors. Interestingly, Kahneman even defines expertise as the shifting of decision making from slow thinking to fast thinking based on accumulated experience. And no individual can store more accumulated experience than a computer.

Slower thinking is also supposed to allow us to more easily separate out emotional components, which play a big part in the fast, or "blink," type thinking from our decisions. In this way we can sometimes avoid or overcome the many biases that cloud our thinking.[29] Machines do not have these biases and are also particularly good at not getting emotional, even when under pressure. So the interaction of human and machine is almost certainly likely to produce a more emotionally unbiased decision at faster speeds.

Digital wisdom requires not just looking at the speed at which decisions are made, or even just at the human system that makes them, but at the wise interaction of minds and machines in the process.

The Fallacy of "One Thing at a Time" Being Better

Although my mother is long gone, I can still hear her voice in my head shouting, "Marc, concentrate on one thing at a time." It was common wisdom in her generation that doing this was always better. Some things clearly are better. It is certainly better (at least in the sense of statistically safer) not to talk on a cell phone while driving.

But there is no reason to believe that this is true in every situation, and, in fact, it is—just as clearly—not. It is certainly not how most people, particularly successful people, operate most of the time. There are tasks that demand our highly focused concentration, and many others that do not. Even when we try to focus on a single task, other thoughts, whether they be conscious ideas, emotions such as anxiety, or physical needs such as hunger or going to the bathroom, typically intervene. Often those "extraneous" thoughts are useful: Suddenly something important that you'd forgotten pops into your head, and you can go off on a tangent and take care of it.

Research has uncovered situations in which people get no more out of giving something their full attention than they do out of giving it their partial attention. In studies done for the television show *Sesame Street*, researchers found that young children who watched a program in a room full of toys (and were distracted by those toys a great deal of the time) got the same information out of the program as similar kids without toys.[30] Linda Stone, now a researcher at Microsoft, coined the term "continuous partial attention" to describe—negatively, I believe—what many of today's people do. I do not, however, think this is anything new, and it isn't necessarily negative. In fact, it is terribly misleading to say that concentration on only one thing is always important.

One reason, as noted, is that many things do not require our full attention. But additionally, researchers are now finding that people *can* multitask successfully when doing two or more highly demanding tasks.

A recent article in the journal *Scientific American* labeled these people "exceptional multi-taskers."[31] It is not clear, as yet, what causes this, and whether it can be transferred to others. Certainly most people are capable in certain situations—often with training and practice—of concentrating intently and blocking out distractions. Our bodies have evolved mechanisms, such as the rapid production of adrenaline, to help us completely focus on the task at hand in emergencies. But most people, most of the time, do not have a single focus—and there is nothing wrong with that.

The much more important issue—on which far less focus is placed, unfortunately—is understanding in which situations concentration and focus are important, necessary, or even crucial, and in which they are not. Because the appropriate mix varies considerably by individual, digital wisdom requires adding this type of understanding to both our self-knowledge and, additionally, to our school curriculum.

Digital wisdom also requires knowing in what situations we need to interact frequently with our technology and when we can let it operate independently. For example, I can give my computer certain tasks, like searching or calculating, hit "enter," and let it go off on its own. But if I don't watch from time to time, it may get stuck (e.g., on a dialog box) and just sit there awaiting my response. Other technologies, like some cooking technologies, need to be closely and continuously monitored—miss the precise moment to intervene and something spins out of control.

Andy Clark adopts this as his criterion for considering whether a technology is a cognitive enhancement—the less we have to pay conscious attention to it, he believes, the more it becomes part of what he calls our "core consciousness." Today there are, typically, many technology enhancements working with our minds at once, and there is no need for us to pay attention closely to all of them. In fact, in many cases, we can set the technologies to signal (or warn) us when an event occurs that we need to pay attention to, as pilots—and cooks—often do.

To sum up, digital wisdom includes knowing, as individuals, when it is okay to multitask and when it isn't.

The Fallacy of "Brain Science" Providing All, or Even Enough, Answers

As I discussed earlier, neuroscience, and our understanding of how the physical brain works, is making great strides. I am optimistic that someday we will understand almost everything about how the brain functions. But that day is not today, nor will it likely be in my lifetime (and probably not in the lifetime of my son, although that is more open to question). Today we are still at the stage of uncovering particular mechanisms, and finding, as one neuroscientist says, the scientific rules by which our brain operates.[32] We are just at the beginning of learning many of those rules, are still totally ignorant about others, and are even earlier in the process of finding new actionable steps we can take based on the knowledge we have. (This has happened in a few places. The neuroscience-based company Scientific Learning, for example, has helped many kids read based on a neurological understanding of their issues. But our current process of treating depression, for example, is still a crude hit-or-miss, trial-and-error affair.[33])

Big problems occur when people apply the label "brain-based" where they really shouldn't—that is, when they extend the link between what we actually know and the actions we should take further out than our knowledge justifies, as John Bruer warned in his 1997 article, "Education and the Brain: A Bridge Too Far."[34] Because having the term "brain-based" in the title appears to sell books, too many recent volumes titled brain-based this or that (particularly brain-based learning) are either just reformulations of old ideas in new "brain-based" language or, in far too many cases, based on false understanding of the neuroscience research. (This last notion is something that a conversation with almost any reputable neuroscientist will confirm.[35])

The key point is that while it is important to keep abreast of developments in neuroscience, it is even more important not to over-rely on them. Many conclusions presented by writers, reporters, and even some less-responsible scientists are based on single experiments and exceeded the bounds that the experimental data truly allow. Most scientific papers contain a section at the end labeled "discussion," where the authors speculate on some of the implications of their work. When examining research, the information from these sections—while useful for understanding the scientists' thinking—is dangerous to take as fact or truth, as some appear to do.

It takes a great many experiments and verification before the findings from individual research studies become generally accepted science. Digital wisdom involves understanding scientific methodology and processes well enough to know what information to rely on and what to be critical of and skeptical about, and where to keep an open mind. Nowhere is this digital wisdom needed more than in interpreting neuroscience.

The Fallacy of Relying on "Tried and True" Solutions in New Contexts

Some people object to technology—and to technological mind enhancement—on the grounds that our old "tried and true" approaches and solutions work just fine. Why use calculators for subtraction and multiplication, for example, when we have "always" done these things in our heads?

I include this as a fallacy, because the people who champion the tried and true typically ignore two important factors. The first is our changing context. The second is the mental cost of doing it the old way, which includes the cost of checking and rechecking for human error.

To rely on humans to do certain things is to invite error. Have you ever found a repeated word in a printed book? I have, in my own work, despite several readers and proofreaders. Despite all that we have learned about checking and rechecking our work, and "putting more eyes" on it, we still often wind up with mistakes. But there are many things that we can rely on machines to do *completely without error,* once the inputs are right, and digital wisdom demands that we identify these places and delegate them to machines. Spell-checkers can flag every repeated word in a huge manuscript, something that human proofreaders often miss. Of course we can't rely on spell-check alone, because some things, like spelling and grammar, are more contextual and still rely on people. But it is a much better use of human time to decide about the situations that are equivocal than it is to actually look for them. (A computer, for example, can find, in the Gettysburg address, the repeated word "that that nation shall live." A human needs to decide—at least for the moment—that it belongs there.)

Complex calculations are similar, and we typically get math completely backward in this respect.[36] Human time is best spent getting the inputs and methodology right in mathematical situations and in verifying that the answers make sense. Manipulation and calculation are tasks best done by machines. Doing calculations in your head is certainly still a valid way to solve problems (assuming you are accurate in your mental math and it provides the right answer). But does it really make sense to spend large amounts of time learning and practicing mental (and even paper) calculations—particularly of complex math—in a twenty-first-century context, when almost everybody has access to a machine that does it for them? Shouldn't this, rather, be something that is more like looking at your watch to tell time? Today, chips with four-function calculators cost a tiny fraction of a cent each and can easily be built into everything. Is it worth spending years teaching kids types of calculation (beyond, that is, the most simple examples) that they will never do? Or is this a waste of our limited twenty-first-century educational time, particularly given that we often have only limited success? I go into this idea more deeply in Chapter 6.

It is not that tried and true methods like memorizing the multiplication tables are not useful—they can be. It is rather that the trade-off of the time and effort needed to memorize versus the time and effort it takes to calculate the answer may no longer be worth it in today's context. I am sure that at one time many memorized the multiplication tables up to 20 x 20. But today, who would know the answer to 19x17 by heart? We would almost all see memorizing that as a poor use of our time. Our context has changed.

Similarly, note-taking is a tried and true way to remember what a professor or speaker said. But does it really make sense when your pen can also function as a recording device?

Flying by the seat of your pants (i.e., without instruments) is generally considered a useful skill for pilots to have. But does it make sense to teach this to pilots who will likely, in the future, only fly planes that cannot stay in the air without computer control?

I know many would answer "yes, it does" to the above questions, and in some situations they may be right. My goal here is not to judge the specifics but to emphasize that digital wisdom means that we should continually be asking these questions and reassessing our decisions.

As we enhance our minds with technology, a big part of digital wisdom is learning how and when to abandon old beliefs, habits, and skills, or to put them into backup for retrieval when needed. The "backup and retrieval" is part of technology's job, but the determination of what skills humans need to actively retain is a decision for humans.

The Fallacy of "Reflection" Being Slow

People often cite "reflection" as a skill that humans can do and machines cannot. Although this may once have been the case, it is no longer entirely true. Many of today's computers, like IBM's Watson, are capable of reviewing their own actions and making corrections in future attempts. Reflection—and continuous improvement based on reflection—is enormously important for making progress, and reflection is an ideal place for human and machine to work together symbiotically. Andy Clark believes it may even be possible, eventually, to develop a technology-based "prosthetic" to help with reflection.

The problem, I believe, comes in thinking that such reflection needs to take a great deal of time. Educators have often made reflection into a long, drawn-out process of "thinking hard" and articulating one's ideas, out loud or on paper. But although this may be one way to produce reflection, it is certainly not the only way, and it is not clear at all to me that this is the normal way human reflection actually happens.

My experience in watching people reflect is that our reflections often happen very quickly. We instantaneously put together information into patterns and observations. For example, a video game player who just lost a life might quickly flash through all the things to do differently in the next life.

Lengthy reflection may be, in some cases, nothing but a series of these almost instantaneous events. It may even be analogous to the way IBM's Watson parallel processes by putting the same data into a series of different analysis packages or algorithms, going through hundreds of them at once and comparing the answers.

This may be why reflection is best done not in a single session, but over time, with insights coming "in flashes" whenever they do. Or, as Kahneman suggests for thinking, there might be more than one type of refection that needs to be combined for the best results.

The digital wisdom, I believe, is not that we need more time for slow reflection, as many suggest, but rather we need *more cycles* of reflection, at whatever speed, by both humans and machines. Reflection now certainly consists of a new and better symbiosis of a variety of types of human and computer "thinking."

The Fallacy of "Expertise" Meaning "Knowledge and Analysis of Data" and of Expertise Coming Only from Professionals

One of the things that technology has already changed greatly is the meaning of "expertise." An "expert" used to be someone who possessed a great deal of knowledge—much of which was gained through experience—and who was able to do analyses in order to answer new problems.

In today's digital age, much of the knowledge that experts formerly uniquely possessed in their heads and books (and far more) can be found online by machines. And much of the analysis that experts would previously have done can be outsourced to machines, which can do the same analyses, and more, in a fraction of the time. An example is the web-based Wolfram Alpha analysis engine and database (wolframalpha.com), developed by mathematician Stephen Wolfram. Its goal is to "analyze any data in the same way that an expert would"—but in only seconds.[37]

In terms of expertise, digital wisdom calls for a new division of tasks between human and machine and a new definition of what it means to be a human expert. Human expertise will clearly consist more of understanding context and what to look for than of knowing specific information or being able to do specific types of analysis. And human experts will always turn to, and always rely on, machines as helpers (as we saw earlier with the APACHE example) in order to make the wisest decisions.

Another important and positive trend in the digital world is that expertise is expanding from only a concentrated group of professionals, where it has formerly resided, to many amateur experts out on the margins. In many fields, technology tools are allowing interested and knowledgeable individuals, who make their primary living in other jobs, to make important contributions. One example is astronomy, where amateurs scanning and analyzing available pictures and data with new tools have already made important new discoveries.[38] Another is protein folding, a skill requiring human manipulation of large molecules on a computer screen (important for pharmaceutical development) where amateur users of the publically available Fold-it program have produced new and important solutions.[39] A third field, surprisingly, is neuroscience, where new understanding of the brain's electrical micro-fields, combined with inexpensive new tools to measure them, is now opening up brain research, as one neuroscientist put it, "to guys [and, hopefully, girls] in garages."[40] Digital wisdom requires that we encourage these directions.

The Fallacy of Short Attention Spans

Do young people have short attention spans? Do people today have shorter attention spans than in the past? It certainly seems so to many people, particularly parents and teachers, and many people say this about themselves. It might even be true in some cases, but to generalize it to all today's people, or even to all today's young people, is a fallacy.

One could probably be forgiven for such thinking, as this is almost all one hears on the subject. But the truth is that people's attention spans depend—and have always depended—very much on what they are doing and how they feel about it. As a college professor once put it to me, "Yes today's kids have short attention spans—for the old ways of doing things."[41]

Many of the individuals who think that today's people have short (or shorter) attention spans can generally concentrate for long periods when there is something they really want to do, such as a hobby, a sport, or, in some instances, their work. Most healthy young people can as well. Many young people accused of having short attention spans spend long periods playing video games, listening to music, or watching movies in a focused way.

One reason we may feel that concentration spans are shorter is that we now so often multitask. But the reason we do this may not be because we *can't* concentrate, but rather because we choose (often wisely) not to. In the world of today, it is often highly inefficient to focus only on one thing. Movies (and lectures), for example, typically have slow parts (during which it may make sense to text friends). Kahneman posits that our system for focused thinking is, by nature, "lazy," and that without strong motivation, it often slows or shuts down. Intense concentration on something we are not passionate about may therefore *require* breaks. We also tend to forget, I believe, the extent to which we were all distracted in our youth. We idealize our own ability (or former ability) to concentrate.

Concentration is a complex area, where discussions generally contain more heat than light. Digital wisdom demands we get more understanding here. This understanding includes, I believe, each of us knowing our own varying attention spans as a function of the different things we do and the different contexts in which we do them.

The Fallacy of "Limited Capacity" and the Need for In-Person/Online Trade-offs

How much capacity does a human mind have? We don't really know.

We do know pretty definitively that most of us have a very small "buffer" for storing facts that we don't intend to remember, such as telephone numbers.

(Research suggests we can generally retain seven digits, plus or minus two.) But what about the human capacity for carrying on multiple simultaneous projects? Or for reading and putting together ideas from multiple books? Some call this "working memory" and equate its size with a person's intelligence. Many business and other consultants thrive on working on multiple projects simultaneously. (At the Boston Consulting Group, where I spent six years, this was required—not just because more work got done, but because *better* work got done through the cross-fertilization of ideas.) Bill Clinton has said he typically has seven or so books he is reading and thinking about, among his many other endeavors.[42]

So while capacity may vary from person to person, we have little idea of its upper limits.

The fallacy, though, is in thinking that humans lack the capacity to do multiple things in their heads, and that to do one thing (or do it well), we have to do less of others. A particularly egregious example of this fallacy, I believe, is the idea advanced by some that we can't have strong in-person relationships and strong online ones simultaneously—that this is a necessary trade-off. Some even cite studies to back this up, but I have looked at these and they do not, in my opinion, justify jumping to this conclusion (although like all hypotheses, this one could be further tested.[43])

It is, of course, true that we get better at things we do frequently (especially with good feedback) and that skills we use less frequently can get rusty and disappear. Some brain research even shows new dendrites and synapses being created as animals learn better skills and dendrites being pruned as some tasks are abandoned. There may, in fact, be trade-offs among tasks competing for the same resources. But exactly what trades off against what is largely unknown.

Here the digital wisdom consists, I think, of not jumping to premature conclusions about limitations of *either* people or machines. And we should certainly not do this about their combination, because the human-machine combination is something whose power we have hardly begun to tap.

The Fallacy of the "Cultural Now"

We all have a tendency to believe that what goes on in our own lives and times has a great deal of importance. And much of it does, at least for us. But the bulk of what happens in our lives, in our times, and in the culture we create

and experience is, with any distance and perspective at all, much less important than we think.

Purveyors of popular culture try hard to make people think that anything
recent or new is more important than it actually is, and their efforts are often
abetted by technology. But technology is also increasingly, freeing us from "the
recent's" grip. Technology now allows us to interact with practically any music,
any book, or any movie, no matter when it was created or where it physically
is. There is a reason that so many narrowly specialized TV and radio stations
exist, and that people gravitate toward personalized services like Pandora,
YouTube, and Pinterest—we are all, in the details of our personal preferences,
different and individual.

A recent article, titled "In Praise of Not Knowing," suggested that life was
more fun when information was harder to find and knowledge more "secret."[44]
I couldn't disagree more with this point of view. To me, the ability for each
person to more easily know, find, and experience a wider variety of things is
a clear example of brain gain. Digital wisdom lies in finding among all that's
available the things that are meaningful to you.

Another way that technology now allows us to happily escape the "tyranny of the now" is by allowing us to circumvent simultaneous scheduling,
that is, situations where seeing or doing one thing precludes our doing another
thing of equal interest. In the past, TV stations tried to schedule all their most
interesting programs in the same time period—head to head. You could watch
Carson or Letterman, but not both. I still attend many "multi-track" conferences where I must choose between two simultaneous sessions both of which
I want to attend. But in more and more places and ways, technology is over-
coming these limitations with time-shifting (i.e., recording for consumption
when desired), allowing us to experience one of the events later. Marketers are
realizing that it is digitally wiser to put things online for people to watch when
they prefer than it is to prevent people from seeing them.

Technology allows all human events—lectures, TV coverage, concerts,
plays, and many other things—to be recorded and stored for future reference. This will continue to radically change how people behave—think of how
much iPods, movie downloads, and digital recorders have already changed
people's listening and viewing habits. We are just beginning to feel the impact
of these kinds of changes, which also have huge implication for education (see
Chapter 6). Digital wisdom, I believe, includes making our cultural (and other

experiential) choices not in terms of immediacy, or what is the latest, or what is available, or even what the most people prefer, but in terms of quality and personal connection.

The Fallacy of "Wisdom" as Coming Only from Humans

Despite the "wise old owl" of folklore, up until recently wisdom was regarded as a purely human attribute. But that is changing. However we regard wisdom, technology now must be considered a component of the wisdom equation.

Among the earliest to foresee this were science fiction writers. Isaac Asimov, for example, gave much thought to the future human-machine relationship. In 1950, in his story collection *iRobot,* Asimov proposed three "Laws of Robotics": (1) A robot may not injure a human being or, through inaction, allow a human being to come to harm; (2) A robot must obey the orders given to it by human beings, except where such orders would conflict with the First Law[45]; and (3) A robot must protect its own existence as long as such protection does not conflict with the First or Second Laws. (Asimov later added a fourth [or "zeroth"]: A robot may not harm humanity or, by inaction, allow humanity to come to harm.[46]) It remains to be seen whether Asimov's laws will actually apply to all human-robotic interactions, but the idea of technology and machines working together symbiotically is now firmly with us. A science fiction concept I have always found intriguing is George Lucas's creation (in the Star Wars films) of two separate categories of robots: working robots (such as R2D2) who speak only their own machine language, and communications robots (such as C3PO) whose function is to translate between those machines and humans.

DIGITAL WISDOM: THE WISE SYMBIOSIS OF MIND AND TECHNOLOGY

Who in the twenty-first century wants or needs a weatherman without radar? A scholar without the Internet? A doctor without diagnostic technologies? A lawyer without automated research capabilities? An auto mechanic without a computer? (A Dalai Lama without Twitter might still be desired by some, but even that is no longer possible.) Today wisdom—as I hope you are now at least starting to believe—is a joint property of humans and technology working together. Anyone who continues to think of wisdom as the sole province of human minds is missing, I believe, humanity's greatest opportunity—perhaps ever—to get wiser.

It is already very clear that, because the human brain is highly plastic and continually adapts to the input it receives, the brains of those who interact frequently with technology will be restructured by that interaction. With the possibility of inherited, epigenetic changes, the brains of wisdom seekers of the future are likely to differ, in both organization and in structure, from our brains today, in ways we cannot now completely understand or foresee. Neuroscientist Dr. Michael Merzenich observes that "We can say unequivocally that the brain that is massively exposed to all our modern stimuli is going to be substantially different."[47] Bearing in mind that different does not necessarily mean worse—or better—we can ask, "What might this mean in terms of people's achieving wisdom, and digital wisdom in particular?"

My belief is this: While future wisdom seekers will likely still be able to achieve *today's* level of wisdom without the cognitive enhancements offered by our increasingly sophisticated digital technology, that level of wisdom will not be sufficient, either in quality or in nature, to navigate the complex, technologically advanced world of our future (and even of our very near future). For that we require the cognitive enhancements and extensions of technology, and the digital wisdom to use them well.

Are *you* already becoming a wiser person because of technology? Has *your* brain been extended? Almost certainly. But the extent of our digital wisdom also depends, to a great extent, as I said at the beginning of this book, on our *attitude,* on how we choose to see technology and the world, and on the enhancements we decide to accept and let in.

Most people dislike and resist change—even a detour on our route home from work can cause a great stir. Ask people to change their behavior in almost any way, and they will almost certainly say no, or at least resist.

But there is one type of change that people have much less resistance to. It is a type of change that humans do all the time and, for the most part, do very well.

It's called adapting. As humans, we have evolved to be excellent at scoping out our environment and adapting our behavior to maximize our benefits in that environment. We do this every time we move, for example, or change jobs.

Our new, rapidly expanding technology means a changing environment, and our success as humans means adapting, as quickly and completely as possible, to that environment. Whether we are comfortable with or discomfited by this new technology, all of us, if we are going to succeed, need to learn to use it wisely.

We all need digital wisdom.

Now, let us look at some examples.

THREE

50 CANDIDATES FOR DIGITAL WISDOM

Are We Wiser if . . . ?

S o, how goes humankind's quest for digital wisdom? Are we there yet? How close are we? And how much brain gain has there been so far?

My sense is quite a bit. Although the digital age is still extremely young (less than a blink in human time, a not-even-findable speck in geological time), I believe that we are already coming closer and closer to digital wisdom, and that, in some cases, we have already found at least some of it. I have been searching for examples of digital wisdom for the past year, and I have found a great many technologies, and technology uses, that I believe to be digitally wise. I have found many people who are exhibiting what I think is digital wisdom.

Of course, most uses of technology (and most people who use it) are not digitally wise. Almost all fall into the category of what I call "digital cleverness" of varying degrees (both positive and negative). A large number also fall into the unfortunate category of "digital stupidity." I discuss these two categories, and concepts, in the next chapter.

But a great many technologies, uses, and users are digitally wise, or at least approaching digital wisdom. They are the harbingers of this much-needed human attribute.

In this chapter, I present a great many examples of what I see as brain gain and digital wisdom for your consideration. And because digital wisdom is not a well-defined attribute but, rather—as we have discussed—a quest, I will encourage you to reflect on each case. So each example is preceded by the question, "Are we wiser if . . . ?"

You decide. And you can cast your vote on the book's web site.

It is also important to note that even if a particular action or development is, in my—or your—opinion, "digitally wise," that certainly doesn't mean we can't, or won't, get *digitally wiser* in that practice or area. In fact, chances are good that we will. I hope that once people know what digital wisdom is, they will continually strive for and toward it.

CATEGORIES OF DIGITAL WISDOM

Because there are so many examples of digital wisdom, I have arranged them into categories—I hope this method provides some understanding of the breadth of areas in which digital wisdom can manifest itself. These categories are, clearly, not the only ones that human mind-technology enhancements can be grouped into. So I challenge you to think about others and, if you like, to share them with other readers on the book's web site.

My categories of "Brain Gain" and "Digital Wisdom" are the following:

Brain Gain and Digital Wisdom from combining mind and technology:
1. to overcome our brain's deficiencies
2. to improve our communication
3. to augment our physical well-being
4. to improve our relations with other people
5. to make our world a better place
6. to deepen our analyses
7. to derive new and useful insights
8. to increase our "executive thinking" (i.e., decision-making) ability
9. to increase our creativity
10. to involve our whole planet
11. to do new, wiser things

While these categories do not cover everything and, in fact, overlap considerably in some places, they form a useful set of starting points for us to begin to examine where brain gain and digital wisdom are emerging.

For each of these categories, I have selected a few salient examples of what I think is digital wisdom. I strongly encourage you to think of your own examples as well.

BRAIN GAIN AND DIGITAL WISDOM FROM COMBINING MIND AND TECHNOLOGY TO OVERCOME OUR BRAIN'S DEFICIENCIES

Combining our brains and minds with technology allows us to overcome specific brain deficiencies. For example:

Are we wiser if we record everything our senses experience?

One of the biggest limitations to our brain is our inability to remember everything we see, experience, read, and, in general, take in.

We know that there is much stored in our brains that we are not consciously aware of, either in full or in part. This is apparent from the fact that prompting (and, in some cases, hypnosis) can often help us recall things. However, it is unlikely that every detail our senses have ever come across—say the weather every day of our lives, the details of every room we have been in, or every conversation we have ever had—is somehow stored in our brain, even though there are occasionally people who can recall much more of this. Much of what remains in our heads does so because it is associated with strong emotions we experienced relative to it, or because it was oft-repeated. But irrelevant details are lost to us. Could it be helpful, and wise, to be able to recall everything? Some see this as a potential burden, but others think it could be very useful.

Recording and storage technology has now reached the point where we can record pretty much all the details of our lives. People are already doing this. Mathematician and inventor Stephen Wolfram, for example, has recorded every keystroke he has ever typed.[1] But it goes much further. We can now, if we choose, record video of everything we look at, audio of everything we hear, and details of temperature and other things we experience.

Although touch, smell, and taste data are not yet recordable in useful form, the digital storage space is available to do so. Ongoing research will no doubt make it possible at some time to record and recall the taste of every food we have eaten at every meal of our lives.

In their book *Total Recall: How the E-Memory Revolution Will Change Everything* (later renamed *Your Life Uploaded: The Digital Way to Better*

Memory, Health and Productivity), Gordon Bell (a longtime, distinguished computer engineer and current research fellow at Microsoft) and his colleague Jim Gemmell discuss the idea of what it means and what it would take to record and store everything a human experiences.[2] Doing this, they argue, is not only well within the capabilities of today's technology, but will get easier and easier to do as storage capacity increases. Bell is already doing it, calling it "lifeblogging."

An important issue is, of course, useful retrieval. How do we search this vast archive to retrieve the particular information we need? If all the words we have ever heard and read are stored, how do we retrieve just the salient ideas or quotes? "The hard part," Bell writes, "is no longer deciding what to hold on to, but how to efficiently organize it, sort it, access it, and find pattern and meanings in it."

But suppose we could do this (and Bell and Gemmell claim that technologies are on the way)? Is this brain gain?

I would argue yes. In fact, in allowing access to all these data, and sorting and mining it well, we may, in fact, re-create, with technology, the famous madeleine of Proust that unleashed so many of his associations and memories. Bell describes how, when asked to speak at an event honoring a friend, he was able to go back to his lifeblog to recall significant encounters with that person that he had completely forgotten.

Bell hypothesizes that we will "uncover patterns in our lives that we could never have gleaned with our unaided brain," and that we will "generate a virtual [me] long after we are dead" to "reach out and touch lives in the future." We may, however, merely create only a new cave, without a map. Just because things get recorded doesn't mean they will ever get retrieved or used.

Do *all* our interior thoughts, memories, and ideas that we can't yet record remain encoded somewhere in our physical brain, able to be unleashed and released by these prompts? In some cases, such as the one Bell cites about his forgotten friend, it appears that the answer to this is "yes"—storing what our senses experience allows us to retrieve our interior experiences. But this may not be true for all situations. My father being an inveterate movie maker (just as many of today's parents are inveterate videographers of their children), I have many of my early life experiences, such as birthday parties, available on film. The images are nice to see, but they don't unlock my inner experience of being there, which may be forever lost.

So is this kind of life recording digitally wise? I think it is likely to be digitally wise only if we find a way to decide whether the benefits it brings, and the places where it does spark our memories, are worth the effort involved to record, find, and retrieve them. What, for example, about traumatic memories? Are these wise to have access to for use in therapy, or should we, as our conscious mind sometimes does, delete them for self-protection? Someday, perhaps soon, we might be putting cameras on all our soldiers. Will that increase or decrease their trauma? What about privacy? These are some of the important and difficult places where digital wisdom is required.

Are we wiser if we combine our minds with technology to pay closer attention?

Although some recent evidence suggests that we can pay attention to more than one thing at the same time,[3] humans do not, and cannot, pay attention to everything at once. In today's digital age, there are so many new things competing for our attention that many now refer to "attention" as a twenty-first-century human's scarcest and most precious resource.

There are several technology-based ways to increase attention. One is biofeedback, which lets us monitor the kinds of waves our brain is producing (e.g., alpha or theta) and shift the mix in ways that calm us down and increase our ability to concentrate. This technology has even made its way into tapes teachers can use in school[4] and games people can play at home, such as *The Search for the Wild Divine*.[5]

Pharmaceuticals are a well-known example of technologies that enable us to pay closer attention. As we saw in Chapter 1, drugs are currently available that can help any healthy human direct and maintain attention to necessary tasks. Amphetamines have long been given to warfighters in situations where their attention needs to be maintained, such as long flights. In fact, according to a military-sponsored report, "stimulants have been used by the world's militaries throughout history. For example, the Chinese sentries along the Great Wall took herbal treatments in the form of ma huang. Incan warriors chewed coca leaves in the Andean passes in order to remain alert. More recently, the British reportedly used pharmaceutical enhancers during Falklands conflict. Similarly, the U.S. Air Force used stimulants during its air strikes of Libya years later. The French too reported using them during the first Gulf War. The Belgian and Dutch militaries also have some experience with using stimulants to extend periods of cognitive alertness."[6]

Amphetamines have also long been used by students—particularly college students—to stay alert to study. I remember being first offered such drugs by a college roommate in 1963. Adderall, which is an amphetamine, is used widely by college students today.

And there are even better cognition-enhancing drugs now available. A new class of pharmaceuticals is now available called eugeroics (from the Greek "good arousal"). One of these, modafinil (brand name Provigil), has become widely available and, according to reports, is being considered for use by the U.S. military.

Modofinil, originally developed to treat narcolepsy, "is not a traditional stimulant such as amphetamines,"[7] says a government-sponsored report. "Instead of bombarding parts of the brain with arousal signals (by producing neurotransmitters), it promotes alertness through certain pathways by possibly increasing serotonin." "I think it [Modafinil] is a subtle enough drug that it doesn't just activate everything,"[8] says Dr. Thomas Scammel, an associate professor of neurology at Harvard Medical School.

Ampakines is another class of cognition-enhancing pharmaceuticals currently under development. They "subtly ramp up brain activity by enhancing the action of its main excitatory neurotransmitter, glutamate."[9] It is not yet clear, however, whether they provide significant enough advantages to replace drugs currently in use.

Do all these ways to help us focus our attention lead to brain gain? The U.S. military, the scientists who recommend giving the drugs to healthy people, and even the former president of Harvard say yes—and I concur.

But is this use of drugs to increase healthy people's ability to concentrate on tasks digitally wise?

Many think so. However, there are issues and trade-offs, and the digital wisdom comes often in how we make them. Some of the current drugs come with side effects that are unwanted and possibly, in some cases, unsafe (although some of the future drugs promise to mitigate or eliminate these risks). Yet all drugs—from aspirin to alcohol—have multiple effects on us, some of which we have yet to discover. Alcohol has many potential negative effects, particularly when consumed in large quantities, but it is prized in many human societies, including ours, for its relaxation abilities. (Other societies ban it.) Aspirin, that wonderful extract from the willow tree, relieves pain—but it also thins the blood, which, while good for certain people, in other situations can be dangerous.

So it is for cognition-enhancing drugs. There are positives and negatives, but digital wisdom seems to be moving in the direction of accepting them as mind-enhancers. Moreover, pharmaceutical-creating technology has reached the point where scientists can aim to deliberately create new drugs that retain the effects we want and lose the unwanted side effects, as they did with Modafinil.

If the people who take these drugs have a clear advantage in their ability to perform necessary tasks, like flying planes and studying, and the side effects are tolerable or minimal, isn't it digitally *un*wise not to give them to everyone?

Still, many questions remain about how to do it and, if we do it, how to afford it. Will cognition-enhancing drugs become a new kind of technology-based divide between haves and have-nots? Digital wisdom tells us to avoid this.

Are we wiser if we combine our minds with technology to do more than one thing at the same time?

Some studies have shown that, at the neurological level, the brain does not truly parallel process to multitask, but quickly switches serially between tasks. But at the behavioral level, people certainly *do* do things in parallel. We drive cars, listen to the radio, and often talk on the phone at the same time, without consciously interrupting one task to do the other.

Is this brain gain? At some level it clearly is, but it is not a new phenomenon. Women have always had to be terrific multitaskers, whether at home or when combining home and work. I have heard women tout their superior ability to multitask—only partially facetiously—as evidence of their superiority over men. In a widely circulated YouTube video, students add up all the hours they need to complete a day's work and conclude, since the total is well over 24, that they have to multitask to get everything accomplished. Clearly, people who are capable of doing multiple things at the same time get more done. And recent studies have shown that some people multitask even complex tasks capably and easily.[10] What is new, in our time, is the ability to increase our multitasking with technology.

But is doing this digitally wise?

Whether multitasking is a wise thing is a different matter—it certainly is not in all cases, as the statistics on texting and driving clearly show, and that is why many states are creating laws banning it. Even though many of the tasks we do simultaneously may be assigned to what neuroscientists call "zombies" (i.e., automatic, below-conscious processors) in our brain, whenever we do multiple things our full attention (or enough attention) may not be given to any of these tasks. There are certainly limits to the wisdom of multitasking.

But is it possible to use technology to do more multiple things in parallel, safely and efficiently? Many think the answer is yes, and the digital wisdom lies in finding out more about who can and can't do this, along with when and where.

Moreover, it is also possible, with technology, to be in more than one *place* at the same time. This is one of the great opportunities the virtual world offers us—we cannot only be in more than one place, but, we can conduct parallel lives. Even my six-year-old can be in two places at once, holding a conversation with me (in person or via Face Time—videoconferencing—on his iTouch) while he is simultaneously in the world of Club Penguin, chatting with friends in his igloo. The virtual worlds for teens and adults are becoming ever more realistic at an incredibly rapid pace. If you haven't looked lately, the people (i.e., the avatars) you see in these worlds are now far more lifelike than even a few years ago, and you interact with them by talking, just like you would with someone standing in front of you. Some of the virtual places are fantasy worlds, but others, such as the virtual worlds promoted by IBM, are work spaces (they use the term "BEST" spaces for these, standing for business, economic, social, and technical spaces).[11] Today you can be simultaneously working in your own office, attending a business meeting in virtual space, and roaming the virtual forests of Azeroth.[12]

Is this brain gain? I would say so. It was impossible for people, and brains, to do this in the past. But is it digitally wise to be in two (or more) places at once? That clearly depends on one's choice of places (and times and tasks). Certainly there are issues about how "present" we are, or have to be, in each world.

As technology offers humans more and more ways to do more than one thing and be in more than one place at the same time, digital wisdom is needed to determine how best to do this.

Yet another important type of brain gain that results from combining mind and technology to overcome our brain's deficiencies is therapeutic enhancement for people with mental disabilities and difficulties. This includes such fields as depression management and memory restoration,[13] sensory prostheses and restoration, and digitally engineered personalities and drugs that help us to overcome our fears.[14] Therapeutic enhancement is a large and important category that I have deliberately left out of this book, choosing instead to focus on brain gain for healthy people.

BRAIN GAIN AND DIGITAL WISDOM FROM COMBINING MIND AND TECHNOLOGY TO IMPROVE OUR COMMUNICATION

Are we wiser if we combine our minds with technology to eliminate illiteracy (i.e., the handicap of not knowing how to read and write) from the world?
With the technologies of text-to-speech and speech-to-text largely perfected and already in wide use around the world, I believe that what stands between universal literacy (i.e., everyone in the world having the ability to read and write) is no longer the difficult, intensive, and time-consuming work of education. It is, rather, just a matter of our spending money on the right technology. Doing so would certainly produce brain gain.

Lest this seem an outrageous claim, let me explain.

Almost all of us, long before we have any formal schooling, can speak and understand verbal language, often quite well and at a very sophisticated level. Yet reading, as useful as it is, is an extremely complex skill that, for most people, takes enormous effort to both teach and learn.

So, if technology enabled anyone to easily turn any printed text (and in some cases handwritten text) into verbal language that they can readily understand, it would qualify, I believe, as brain gain. And we can do this today.

People can, today, using tiny machines, scan any text, word by word, line by line, sentence by sentence, or paragraph by paragraph, and have it read aloud to them. The technology is extremely accurate and can be incorporated into technologies like cell phones and pens. Devices such as the Wizcom Reading Pen, already on the market, will read to you whatever text you pass them over.[15]

Would it be digitally wise to incorporate this capability into the kinds of devices that most of the world already possesses, such as cell and mobile phones or even eyeglasses? I believe so.

I am not suggesting that people do not need to know how to read. I am suggesting that technology now *enables* non-readers to understand written text, and that this is brain gain.

Is it digitally wise?

Many people's jobs and professions today clearly depend on not just reading, but reading quickly. They depend as well on the human mind's ability to know when to skim, when to read carefully, and when to process, in a variety of ways, written information. Even with head phones, it might not be digitally wise, or even practical, for professionals and others who can easily learn to read to use this technology. (Although for these people another form of brain gain—machines reading and understanding text on their own—may help.)

But in the twenty-first century, a distressing percentage of the world's population, not just in the so-called third world, but even in the United States and other developed countries, either struggles to get by without being able to read or does almost no reading, even after having spent all of that school time to learn how. I have heard it suggested that many Americans never read a book after high school.[16] More and more people around the world—and most Americans—increasingly get their news from television, their stories from movies, their skills from short videos on websites such as YouTube, and their work instruction and training via multimedia. Giving both non-readers and reluctant readers easier ways to access printed materials that they now shy away from (but need to use in many instances)—rather than continuing to force them through reading classes, often unsuccessfully—would constitute, I believe, digital wisdom.

Doing so would not, of course, eliminate the need for teaching understanding. But in many cases, it might actually make understanding easier.

Writing is similar. While a great many people depend on—and even earn their living from—their ability to write (as I do), the vast majority of the world's people rarely, if ever, write and often try hard to avoid doing so—even when they know how.

In fact, I am not "writing" this book at all, in the physical sense. I am dictating it into my computer via a speech-to-text program, Dragon Speech. I don't even have to be able to read the words to make corrections; I can have the program read my words back to me and correct them orally (although I don't, personally, choose to do this).

Much of this reading technology was developed for blind people, who often use it quite fluently. Computer voices that once were flat and devoid of meaning and emotion can now be programmed to project both.

Interestingly, it is another, newer technology that has led to this ability (and that has also improved speech recognition to the point that you no longer have to "train" it to your voice). That technology is the recording by Nuance (the maker of Dragon), Google, and others of billions of utterances that people make online—on help-desk calls and other speech interactions over technology. This huge volume of real speech allows computers to recognize not just words but also phrases, along with the intonations that generally accompany them. The huge computing power required to do this can often reside not on your local device, but on large banks of remote servers (often referred to as "the cloud").

For the illiterate—and for all of us who use this technology to do something we clearly couldn't before, such as write with our voice—this is brain gain.

Is it digitally wise to use technology in these ways? I believe it certainly is, at least in many cases.

The increased productivity that dictating provides has long been a source of brain gain for corporate executives, initially with secretaries who took shorthand and then with dictation machines and digital voice recorders. A version of Dragon Speech even comes with a high-quality recorder that you can walk around with and talk into, and later plug into your computer for transcription. This is such an obvious feature for a smart phone to add that there may already be, by the time this book is published, "an app for that." Personally, using voice-to-text technology allows me to go much faster with my writing. It also allows me to be more active and write in many more physical positions, including while walking around and while lying down (as I am currently doing).

There are, nonetheless, some downsides—even aside from the screams of those who hate the thought of people not learning to actually "read" in the traditional way ("What will happen to society?!"). Recognition of children's voices is still not very good, because there as yet is no comparable database of young people's voices. Anything requiring listening is limited by either external noise and distraction or the need to cut one's self off with earphones. But this last is something the younger generation is already quite used to and, in many cases, prefers.

The biggest reason that using these technologies widely provides not just brain gain but also digital wisdom is that there is still a huge percentage of the world's population that is totally, or functionally, illiterate. Even in a developed country like the United States, some estimate that there may be as many as 40 million functionally illiterate people.[17] Wouldn't it be wise—digitally wise—to invest in providing all of these people around the world with the capabilities to "read" and "write" in this way? My hope is that doing this is such a no-brainer that it will happen as part of the normal, competitive process of upgrading smart phones. But that may be wishful thinking on my part.

Are we wiser if we combine our minds with technology to eliminate language barriers?

The inability to speak a common language has long created a wall between people. It is why we speak, metaphorically, of a language "barrier."

One way technology is providing brain gain in this area is by moving the world toward a common language. A great many observers feel that this is now happening, and that that common language is English. English is now spoken and understood, to some extent, by up to 27 percent of the world, by some estimates.[18] It is spoken more widely outside of countries that speak it natively (i.e., as a first language) than inside those countries. In fact, depending on how you measure, the world's largest English-speaking country may be India, rather than the United States. The desire to teach and learn English in other countries, including those with large populations, such as China, is very strong.

Because of this strong demand, and because technology in this area complements a human teacher in many positive ways, the technologies used for teaching languages—English in particular—have been given much attention. And they have made great advances. Computer programs can now remember everything a student says, correct mistakes, present material in a constant graded and logical order, and, most importantly, customize the content, vocabulary, and learning activities for each student. A wide variety of computer programs exist to help people of varying nationalities acquire English skills. One group in India has even found that merely (and inexpensively) subtitling English-language television programs—in English—helps considerably both with understanding and reading English. (This also works for local languages.) Hundreds of apps, many free, can help build a learner's English skills.

The same tools and technologies also make it easier to learn a language other than English. Programs like Pimsleur and Rosetta Stone have made the difficult process of language learning more appealing, as have the many language-learning apps. (I am studying Japanese and have about 20 apps on my iPhone, including phrase books, writing guides, quizzes, and one that even helps me practice talking on the telephone!)

At the same time, the technology of the Internet has opened up to language learners—many for the first time—the possibility to have real, meaningful communications with peers who natively speak the language they are learning. If you go to YouTube, you will find hundreds (if not thousands) of videos made by language learners, mostly on their cell phones, or using their computers, that they have "broadcasted" to the world for feedback. That feedback is sometimes in the form of written comments, but it often comes in the form of video as well.

Is the ability of technology to enhance our ability to communicate in more than one language—including one that much of the world speaks—brain gain? I think so.

Is it digitally wise to encourage this? I believe it is.

An additional, complementary way in which technology is helping eliminate language barriers is though instant translation. Long a dream, this, too, is now with us thanks to technology.

For most of history, translation was a human effort requiring great skill: Although language-to-language dictionaries have long existed, they do not, alone, do the job of translating one language into another—there are too many phrases, constructions, idioms, nuances, and differences among languages that, in the past, only human translators could understand and bridge (to varying extents, of course). Early machine-based translation attempts led to many laughable results, such as the famous case of the English proverb "out of sight, out of mind" coming out in Russian as "invisible lunatic."

It turns out, however, that once machines have enough human-created translations to analyze, the task of translating "basic" meaning is something they can handle reasonably well. They do this not by "learning" language in the traditional sense that people have always done, but by comparing, statistically, huge numbers of examples to find the best contextual fit. Google Translate, for example, works by looking at an enormous database of documents produced in multiple languages by human translators for the United Nations and various countries. Using this service, interviews that I give that are published in languages like Turkish and Hungarian (languages that, unfortunately, I do not speak) are now accessible to me for review.

Language translation is, I believe, a clear case of brain gain and, to the extent it is helpful in bridging language barriers, of digital wisdom as well. But digital wisdom also suggests not trusting the machines completely for any documents or understandings that are—or could be—particularly sensitive.

Are we wiser if we become more concise in our communications?
As most of us know and feel, one of our greatest scarcities in our current age, along with attention, is time. With the explosion of information to deal with, *and* the number of people with whom we can be in contact, *and* the shortening of the time frames in which people are looking for answers, time is, for more and more people, at a premium.

One possible solution for doing more in less time is to be more concise. As people in higher positions have always known, the "executive summary," a short resume of the major points in a longer report or document (which contains supporting details there for backup and reference), is often fully sufficient for their needs. In fact, it is generally the preferred method of information delivery to more and more readers in general.

Interestingly, one of the things that technology has brought us, at the same time as the explosion of information, is conciseness. Twitter, for example, whose messages are limited to only 140 characters (a limit imposed by technical constraints on the size of easily sent SMS messages), has become far more successful than many (including me) ever believed it would. One reason, I think, is because the ability to be concise—something we get better at the more we are constrained and practice—is a form of brain gain. Communicating meaningful amounts of information in short bursts is both valuable and difficult, and Twitter is helping many to get better at it. I believe this increased ability, contrary to what many might say, is brain gain.

But is shortening our communications digitally wise?

Although many hold the opinion that the longer a written work (or other communication) is, the better, richer, and deeper it is, I beg to differ, and I would point out that this is only occasionally (and in fact rarely) the case. Most media of communication—books, articles, papers, manuals, and so on—are, in fact, far too long. Their length and desire for "completeness" and "depth" often stand in the way of their precision, ease of use, and usefulness.

I recently asked English professor Mark Bauerlein, author of *The Dumbest Generation* (whose main complaint is that our students no longer read enough), whether he thought that most books—both fiction and nonfiction— could benefit from some trimming. He totally agreed and was able, when I asked, to suggest only a handful of novels that he, personally, would not cut. (My own re-reading of some of these works suggests that they, too, might benefit from some further editing.)

Often a few pithy quotations from an author can be as useful, or more useful, than a whole book: There is a good reason why quotation sites are so popular online. The newspaper *USA Today*, decried at first by many as too short, has flourished—as have 30-second news segments.

In my view, the reason for this move to shorter forms has little to do with "lack of depth" or "dumbing down," as some would have it, and more to do with our need in this technological age to take in more, to process more, and to do it more quickly. Of course depth and detail can be important in many situations. But what technology allows us to do is to put the depth of detail into easily accessed storage. It does this via hyperlinks, via images, and via the way we organize information online. A whole field of web site design has arisen to make this happen. Technology allows us to put most of our enormous amount of information into backup and to, increasingly, easily retrieve it as needed.

This is brain gain.

In fact, an oft-heard criticism of many web sites is that they have *too much* text. Today's online readers and browsers expect headlines and pictures that they can explore in detail as they wish.

So where is the digital wisdom?

I believe that the digital wisdom comes from not focusing on the length of the communication. It is in accepting that that length—except, at times, for artistic purposes—is best as short as possible. We become digitally wiser by focusing, rather, on content and conciseness. In writing, digital wisdom lies in distilling things down to the shortest possible length. To paraphrase Einstein: "Things should be as short as possible, but no shorter."[19] We see this even in fiction and other artistic writing: Novels in Japan have begun appearing in short bursts for reading on cell phones. This is not to say that we won't ever have another 5,000-page, Harry Potter–type series. But those same types of escapes are coming, increasingly, in other, shorter, media.

Additionally, shared context also helps the shortening process. One of the shortest conversations in history occurred when Oscar Wilde telegraphed his publisher the following question, inquiring about his latest book's sales: "?" The publisher wired back "!"[20]

Technology also enables us to experience both audio and video faster, that is, at double (or more) their original speed, without changing the pitch of the voices: It just appears as if the people are talking more quickly. Although Microsoft has long buried controls to do this deep in the interface of its media player, and variable speed tape voice players have long existed for language learning, none of these techniques has as yet taken off widely. But I predict that they will. If key video sites, such as YouTube, Ted Talks, Big Think, and the many how-to video sites, gave the automatic option to play their videos more quickly, I believe this feature would get wide use.

At the same time, the ability to slow down audio and video is useful in cases such as understanding foreign languages and hard-to-comprehend accents. It is also useful in the remedial reading program FastForward, which slows down sounds for kids who have difficulty hearing and saying them, and then gradually speeds them up.

Is the ability to do such speeding up or slowing down of recorded communication brain gain? Yes. Our brains can use these technical enhancements both to take in far more information in the same amount of time and to get more understanding.

Is it digitally wise?

Focusing on content rather than length is wise, I believe, both digitally and in general. Assigning students work measured in pages, as many teachers do, is, I think, a digitally unwise way to do it. But technology's ability to sometimes make things more concise does not add to our wisdom on its own—the digital wisdom lies in when and how we use these tools. To take in more information with understanding is digitally wise. To merely read, or watch, faster is clearly not.

Are we wiser if we stay more current?

In former times, when communication technologies were much slower, people typically didn't know what happened in far-away places until long after events actually took place. The news of wars being started, lost, or won often didn't arrive for weeks or even months. This has always been a frustration, particularly to decision makers and those with loved ones across the world. Few like being the last to know something, and it often works to our detriment. So people have always searched for ways, and created new technologies, to speed up the flow of information.

Today's digital technology allows us to keep current with what is happening everywhere on the globe, often in real time. Think of President Obama watching the raid on Osama bin Laden's compound as it happened.

This is brain gain.

Keeping truly current in terms of events, politics, and even friends has become a modern goal for many of us. Search engine providers, such as Google and Microsoft (with its search engine Bing), work continuously to tweak their search algorithms and content to offer more up-to-date results. The engines have been enhanced to include social media such as Facebook and Twitter. Many people now use these media obsessively to keep up with what is going on with people and events that they care about.

Companies use "push" technologies to send us information (hopefully at our request) directly as it becomes available. I get updates of breaking news on my iPhone from *The New York Times* and CNN. No major event would happen in the world without me, and most of the world, knowing about it in seconds. As a New Yorker watching the events of September 11, 2001, unfold live, the first call of concern I received was from Tokyo, where my friends were watching the towers burn in real time.

BRAIN GAIN AND DIGITAL WISDOM FROM COMBINING MIND AND TECHNOLOGY TO AUGMENT OUR PHYSICAL WELL-BEING

Are we wiser if we know when our bodies are malfunctioning and how to fix them?

We can go for years, even lifetimes, without knowing there is something wrong inside us. Slow-growing cancers and incipient diseases often give no signs of their existence that we, as humans, can recognize. In what is being referred to as the "digital revolution in medicine," technology is changing this to a remarkable degree. We can now increasingly quantify what happens in our bodies and use this to work, in concert with the healthcare system, to increase our physical well-being substantially.

Monitoring techniques exist for more and more bodily functions. These start with tracking our food intake (calories and nutrients), our sleep (not just amount, but quality), and our daily exercise, minute to minute. We can also, with increasing ease, track more and more of our bodies' key biochemical markers. We can track cumulative exposure to harmful effects like radiation. We can even track our brain waves. The devices to do these things are being miniaturized to the point where we can wear them constantly (some are already embedded under people's skin) and can have the data sent continuously to our own databases and our physicians'.

Larry Smarr, a scientist at the University of California, San Diego, monitors 60 of his biochemical markers in addition to his weight, sleep, and exercise. He claims that this intense monitoring helped him discover an incurable chronic disease he didn't know he had and predict a painful attack that his doctors had pooh-poohed as unlikely. "I've come to understand," he writes, "that I can't count on intuiting or 'feeling' the quantitative state of my body's key markers."[21] In other words, you have to measure.

Fortunately, digital technology allows and enables all of this. Healthy people can now wear Band-Aid–sized devices that monitor our heart and other functions.[22] We can, if we care to, observe these functions on our smart phones in real time.

More importantly, the technology can immediately detect abnormalities and alert us and our healthcare providers. Other technologies allow even less invasive monitoring. Pulse and other functions can be detected from subtle changes in skin color. Databases can evaluate and alert us to potentially dangerous drug interactions. Often the technologies can take corrective action on their own, as implanted insulin pumps already do for diabetics.

These technologies are quickly proliferating, shrinking in size and cost, and becoming available to more and more of us at a rapid rate.

The ability to measure more and more previously unknown details and trends in our body, and to compare our results across our human population to detect abnormality and disease—something we could not even conceive of doing in earlier times—is clearly brain gain.

Is it digitally wise?

I believe so. Many think it will improve our healthcare system dramatically by altering in our favor the balance of power between the informed patient and the healthcare system.[23] Both brain gain and digital wisdom come from using modern social networks to share among people with similar health situations. "Medicine is breaking out of its cocoon," says Eric Topol, professor of genomics at the Scripps Research Institute and author of *The Creative Destruction of Medicine*. "[Previously, the term] digital applied only to rectal exams," he quips. "Now it applies to almost everything."[24]

Interestingly, issues similar to those that many are having with the transition from paper books to digital books, and from old technologies to digital technologies, are currently being experienced by doctors with regard to new digital versions of old tools such as sphygmomanometers and stethoscopes. There now exist digital replacements, for example, for everything the stethoscope does, many of them already in wide use. But "I'm so comfortable with it—I don't want to change" is often heard from doctors asked about moving to the newer equipment. "What if the new one breaks down?" many ask. So they continue to do twenty-first-century medicine using an almost–200-year-old device. Is this digital wisdom?

Are we wiser if we combine our minds with technology to increase our lifespan?

Over the course of history, the human lifespan has continually increased, from a score or fewer years in the early days of humankind to more than four score years in many places today (sadly there is still far too much variation here). Just over the course of the twentieth century, technology—particularly technologies allowing us to analyze our own nutrition and improve it—has extended the human lifespan, in some places, by as much as a decade.

But today's digital technology puts us on the verge of extending human life by much, much more.

Using digital microanalysis tools, scientists are beginning to determine the causes of aging in animals and humans, and in some cases, they are beginning to reverse them. For example, they have discovered that DNA parts called telomeres continually shrink during each cell division. When they get too short, telomeres prevent cells from dividing—something that is essential for maintaining a healthy organism. This has already led to treatments that repair and enlarge those telomeres, allowing the cell division processes to go on and, in some cases, reversing the effects of aging.

A number of scientists are working on the aging issue. They include people like Aubrey de Grey, chief science officer of the Strategies for Engineered Negligible Senescence (SENS) Foundation. He is author of *The Mitochondrial Free Radical Theory of Aging* (1999), co-author of *Ending Aging* (2007), and editor in chief of the academic journal *Rejuvenation Research*. He also co-founded the Methuselah Foundation. Dr. de Grey's research focuses on whether regenerative medicine can "thwart" the aging process. He has already identified seven types of molecular and cellular damage caused by essential metabolic processes (he calls these "The Seven Deadly Things") and proposed a panel of tissue-repair strategies or therapies (he calls these "Strategies for Engineered Negligible Senescence" [SENS]) intended to rejuvenate the human body and allow an indefinite lifespan.[25]

Stephen Coles, an M.D., Ph.D. with more than 150 published papers to his credit, is a co-founder and director of the Los Angeles Gerontology Research Group (GRG) and director of the Supercentenarian Research Foundation (SRF).[26]

Gregory Benford, a professor emeritus of physics at University of California, Irvine (and a science fiction author), started a company called Genescient, "a new generation biotechnology company that combines evolutionary genomics with massive selective screening to analyze and exploit the genetics of model animal and human whole genomes.[27] This enables Genescient to develop novel therapeutics that target the chronic diseases of aging."

These researchers and many others are hard at work to use technology to expand and extend our lifetimes by several more decades, and potentially indefinitely. Some of the technologies that allow them to do this are those that enable us to see where our body is breaking down and intervene to fix it, much as we would do to maintain a car indefinitely.

Is this brain gain? It is—literally—if our brains live longer.

Is it digitally wise?

Living much longer, or even indefinitely, is attractive for many individuals, particularly those who feel they have much to do or accomplish. But it also brings up many issues. These issues include overpopulation, difficulties in younger people moving ahead, financial support, and many others. The digitally wise thing to do is to consider all of these issues carefully, even as we try to extend, if we wish, our own individual lives. (Ray Kurzweil, who we will hear more about in Chapter 8, currently takes more than 250 supplements daily for this purpose.[28])

Are we wiser if we combine our minds with technology to modify our own behavior?

And what about modifying our own behavior? Can technology help us with that? In many cases, it can.

In the early twentieth century, B. F. Skinner demonstrated that it is possible to modify both animal and human behavior via a process of reinforcement and feedback over a long period of time. More recently, companies like Scientific Learning have applied these and other techniques to particular learning problems.

In fact, an entire category of feedback-based behavior change has emerged. You may have driven past electronic signs that flash at you, in large digits, exactly how fast you are going. It has been found that just giving people this information gets them to self-modify their behavior. This process is known as a "feedback loop."[29] The old knowledge that feedback works has suddenly become far more relevant and useful thanks to technology: the development of small, cheap, and accurate sensors. "The plunging price of sensors has begun to foster a feedback-loop revolution," writes Thomas Goetz in *Wired*.[30] Sensor-based feedback loops are now used for promoting positive behavior change in energy consumption, weight loss, and health care, even helping with the not-so-trivial problem of getting patients to take their medicine. The feedback-based Glow Cap medicine bottle reminds patients to take their medicine through light cues, musical cues, and even, when needed, text messages and phone calls. It has increased compliance by "an astonishing" 40 percent.[31]

Another very promising use of the combination of the feedback principle and digital technology goes by the name of cognitive bias modification (CBM). This computer-based approach "appears to be effective after only a few 15-minute sessions, and involves neither drugs nor the discussion of feelings. It does not even need a therapist. All it requires is sitting in front of a computer and using a program that subtly alters harmful thought patterns."[32] CBM is being used successfully by researchers around the world for treating disorders such as anxiety and addictions, and it is being tested for alcohol abuse and post-traumatic-stress disorder.

CBM is based on the idea that many psychological problems are caused by unconscious biases in our thinking. The technique has people repeat a procedure around 1,000 times over two hours, in 15-minute sessions, using smart phones. The goal is to overcome people's automatic, unconscious, unhealthy, and unwanted attentional bias to threats (such as alcohol). "A common way of debiasing attention is to show someone two words or pictures—one neutral and the other threatening—on a computer screen. In the case of social anxiety these might be a neutral face and a disgusted face. Presented with this choice, an anxious person instinctively focuses on the disgusted visage. The program, however, prods him to complete tasks involving the neutral picture, such as identifying letters that appear in its place on the screen. Repeating the procedure around a thousand times, over a total of two hours, changes the user's tendency to focus on the anxious face. That change is then carried into the wider world." It's "like administering a cognitive vaccine," says Emily Holmes of Oxford University.[33]

Is this ability to shift our brain's activity to overcome deficiencies and biases in a relatively short amount of time brain gain? Almost certainly.

But is it digitally wise? According to Dr. Michael Merzenich, his FastForward program has helped tens of thousands of kids overcome reading problems. CBM has helped many people as well.

But we do need careful testing. Colin MacLeod of the University of Western Australia, one of the pioneers of the CBM technique, "thinks CBM is not quite ready for general use. He would like to see it go through some large, long-term, randomised clinical trials of the sort that would be needed if it were a drug, rather than a behavioural therapy."[34]

BRAIN GAIN AND DIGITAL WISDOM FROM COMBINING MIND AND TECHNOLOGY TO IMPROVE OUR RELATIONS WITH OTHER PEOPLE

Are we wiser if we combine our minds with technology
to know what others are thinking?

One of the greatest barriers in life is our inability to know precisely what someone else is thinking, whether it be someone close to us, a negotiation partner, or anyone else. But digital technology is now beginning to break even this barrier down.

Although we are just at the beginning, scientists can now detect brain signals and interpret them in ways that help them understand what someone is thinking about. In a widely reported experiment conducted by researcher Jack Gallant of the University of California, Berkeley, and published in the September 2011 issue of *Current Biology*, researchers watched a set of known films in an fMRI scanner and recorded the brain signals in their visual cortexes, frame by frame. They then watched two hours' worth of other, random YouTube movie clips and recorded those signals as well. Next they used a powerful computer to search through the brain signals recorded from the random YouTube clips that matched the signals from the first movie and had the computer create a composite of the pictures that those signals represented. The resulting composite, as you can see for yourself online at gallantlab.org, was strikingly similar, in its general outlines and movements, to a scene from the first film.[35]

Additionally, Tom Mitchell and his colleagues at Carnegie-Mellon University have been able to accurately predict words people are thinking about by observing their fMRI patterns. Their next step will be to extend this to whole thoughts.[36]

Christopher James of the University of Southampton has succeeded in sending brain waves over the Internet to another location, allowing a distant observer to read and interpret them.[37]

Bin He and his colleagues at the University of Minnesota have succeeded in getting volunteers to fly virtual helicopters on computer screens just by thinking about it.[38] This, for obvious reasons, has long been a goal of military researchers.

Going even further—though still a long way from being tested in humans—scientists have found that cognitive function can be improved with a device that plays back into rats' brains a previously recorded memory trace or firing pattern of neurons.[39]

This is brain gain. When we can visualize what someone else is seeing from their brain signals, figure out from their brain signals what words people are thinking about, send those signals to another person, and reproduce something in the other person's brain by playing back the right brain signals, we are, essentially, reading minds.

Is it digitally wise to do this?

It will certainly change a lot. Although we do not as yet have true telepathy (as in a conscious thought forming in one person's brain and the same thought appearing in another's), these experiments push human brains well down the road to getting there. Digital wisdom would dictate that we no longer treat this as far-off science fiction but start to explore its implications in our schools, workplaces, and lives.

Are we wiser if we combine our minds with technology to know how others feel?

Our feelings are some of our most private possessions—it is both difficult to share them directly with others and difficult to know if we are perceiving others' feelings accurately. In a 2004 experiment, Professor Kevin Warwick of the University of Reading wired his own and his wife's nervous systems directly to their computers via jacks inserted into nerves in their arms and sent their nerve signals to each other over the Internet. Warwick claims that he was able to discern his wife's feelings over the Internet at a distance.[40]

Is it brain gain if we can perceive, accurately, the feelings of others from far away, and even from across the world? Almost surely.

Where, however, in the digital wisdom in doing so? These new capabilities raise many ethical and practical questions. Should family members track each other's feelings? Where does privacy end? How accurate can we be, and what are the dangers of relying on this kind of technology and getting it wrong? Warwick's controversial work "directly tests the boundaries of what is known about the human ability to integrate with computerized systems."[41]

Are we wiser if we combine our minds with technology to be more cooperative and trusting?

Researchers at the University of California, Santa Barbara, are using technology to figure out how to both understand the evolutionary bases of cooperation and get people to cooperate better. In their studies, reported in the *Proceedings of the National Academy of Sciences,* they modeled computer agents to represent humans, who gained or lost "fitness points" by cooperating or competing, and then passed on those traits to more than 10,000 generations (representing, essentially, the full span of human history). What their modeling showed is that the cost of early selfishness is greater than the cost of trust—while selfishness may pay off in the short term, cooperation, generosity, and trust is by far the best long-term strategy for humans.[42]

Can technology even help understand guilt? Economists and neuroscientists at the University of Arizona have teamed up to use technology to research cooperation by examining human feelings of guilt in an fMRI machine. "The thrust of the study," said researcher Luke Chang, "is trying to understand why people cooperate." "One idea is that most people cooperate because it feels good to do it. And there is some brain imaging data that shows activity in reward-related regions of the brain when people are cooperating. But there is a whole other world of motivation to do good because you don't want to feel bad. That is the idea behind guilt aversion,"[43] said Chang.

Is this brain gain?

"Civilized society is based on cooperation and trust, from behaviors as simple and informal as opening a door for someone carrying heavy packages or tipping a restaurant server to complex legal agreements between corporations or countries. Understanding the neural structures behind these behaviors promises to offer new insights into complex behaviors of trust and reciprocity,"[44] according to *ScienceDaily*.

Is this digital wisdom?

The *Economist* reports that such studies "Show the value of applying common sense to psychological analysis—but then of backing up that common sense with some solid mathematical modeling."[45] The knowledge gained from such technology is likely to be incorporated, in the future, into software that provides particular rewards for longer-term cooperation and stronger penalties for selfishness.

Another clear piece of digital wisdom is using technology to increase our sample sizes in research and experiments from only a few graduate students to large, worldwide samples, and populations representative of all humankind. Doing this—via both modeling and the web—should give us far more accurate answers and information in many economic and social areas.

Are we wiser if we combine our minds with technology to share more?
One of the things that Internet technology has made possible is much broader sharing—in a great many new places and in ways that were never possible

before. Even very early in the Internet's history, people began getting answers much more quickly and accurately by posting questions on Internet bulletin boards than by just contacting people they knew. (Watching my programmers do this, over and over, and come up with better answers than I could was one of the seminal experiences that got me started on this book's whole line of thinking.)

A new culture of sharing has arisen, particularly among young people, that is far different from the "knowledge is power" and "keep it close to the vest" attitudes of my own generation. This propensity, and even need, to share widely, frequently, and often quite openly can be seen, of course, in the rapid rise and spread of social networking sites like Facebook (which, as this is being written, has engaged almost a billion people—more than 12 percent of the people on the globe), YouTube, Delicious, Tumblr, and a whole host of other sharing sites oriented toward various media and special interest groups. Information that used to be regarded as private or proprietary (and still is, by many) is now available to all. Encyclopedias in the past used to be closed and proprietary; today Wikipedia makes this knowledge available to all for free—it is a worldwide sharing of human knowledge. Huge amounts of data collected by governments and organizations that used to be extremely difficult to access are now available on the web for free and can often be incorporated into sites or apps with simple code. Many of today's elementary school kids could easily figure out how to add a stock ticker or a news feed to any web site or app.

Is this brain gain?

Certainly it is in the sense that humans know as a species, and as individuals can easily find out, so many more things than before. The many gains produced by these sharing technologies—finding old friends, looking up a zip code—are now often taken for granted. So many people have gotten so accustomed to this that it is safe to say, I believe, that sharing of more and more information by more and more people is the direction of the future.

But is this digital wisdom?

Sharing does have enormous benefits. An important one is that the group that shares the most, learns the fastest. Sharing online has opened up entirely new ways of learning from each other. It has democratized the process of learning, with openly accessible materials available from our best universities (e.g., Stanford's open-enrollment courses, MIT's Open Courseware[46]), from the enormous number of how-to videos that individuals have produced on their own motivated purely by the desire to share and from worldwide sharing projects such as Wikipedia.

But of course this cuts both ways—unbridled sharing also has many downsides. The impulse on the part of many users to share everything and anything they know and do, whether teenagers sharing naked pictures or Julien Assange sharing state secrets on WikiLeaks, has raised many concerns, particularly among people raised to maintain their privacy and share as little as possible. Digital wisdom is needed to balance these concerns and, at the same time, stay sensitive to the changing mores and preferences in the younger generations, as I have already discussed in Chapter 2.

Are we wiser if we combine our minds with technology to detect when people are lying?

When I first began this project, I thought that digital technology for detecting lying and falsehood would most definitely represent a big source of existing brain gain. But I was wrong. Our lie-detecting technology is far less advanced than I had assumed.

Unfortunately, many of the technologies that have been invented to detect lies—such as the classic lie detector or polygraph, which measures breathing and galvanic skin response—do not produce reliable data at all. This is why there has always been great controversy over the use of lie detectors in court. The military and intelligence world, which is, as you can imagine, very interested in detecting lying, has looked at these technologies carefully. As one person who has studied lie detection extensively for them puts it, "The entire body of work on the polygraph is 80 years of bad science led by the inventor of the idea who also was the author of the Wonder Woman comics."[48] Other past technologies for lie detection have failed similarly.

The problem is that there is no reliable connection, or cause and effect, between lying and the "affect" changes we have measured. In fact, we do not yet know whether lying produces a reliably detectable signal in the brain and body, or whether, as many suspect, lying produces a wide variety of effects depending on a number of elements, such as the context in which the lie is made, the "severity" of the lie, and prior training to prevent detection. It also makes a difference, apparently, how someone feels about the lie—if one is telling a falsehood for what one deeply believes to be a noble purpose—to protect one's clan, for example—it might not even be perceived by the brain as a "lie."

Still, it would be of great benefit to some (and cause great problems for others) if we could detect when people were lying, so researchers continue to look for reliable ways of detecting falsehood. One line of promising research is being conducted by psychologist Mark Frank, professor of communication in the School of Informatics at the University at Buffalo. By applying computer technology to the emotion-driven nature of nonverbal communication, Frank has, according to the university, devised methods to recognize and accurately read the conscious and unconscious behavioral cues that suggest deceit.

Frank's work is based on that of his mentor, Paul Ekman, who found that a wide range of facial expressions—that is, furrows, smirks, frowns, smiles, and wrinkles—are related to specific emotions and are identical from culture to culture. These combinations, he believes, offer surprisingly accurate windows to the emotions.

Frank has identified and isolated specific and sometimes involuntary movements of the 44 human facial muscles linked to fear, distrust, distress, and other emotions related to deception. "These micro-movements, when provoked by underlying emotions, are almost impossible for us to control," says Frank. He has developed computer programs that make it possible to automatically identify every facial expression, including those tied to deceit, shown by subjects in taped interviews. "I want to make it clear that one micro-expression or collection of them is not proof of anything," Frank says. "They have meaning only in the context of other behavioral cues, and even then are not an indictment of an individual, just very good clues." But Frank's work is already being tested or used by several agencies and police departments, and many who are looking for better solutions to detecting falsehood think he is on a useful track.[49]

Another recent approach to using computers to spot deception is that of Julia Hirschberg of Columbia University. She and her team are programming computers to parse people's speech for previously identified patterns in order to gauge whether a speaker is being honest. Some researchers have found that emotional "speech hallmarks"—for example, loudness, changes in pitch, pauses between words, "ums" and "ahs," nervous laughs, and dozens of other tiny signs—can indicate emotions like deception, anger, friendliness, and even flirtation.

"The scientific goal is to understand how our emotions are reflected in our speech," says Dan Jurafsky, a professor at Stanford whose research focuses on the understanding of language by both machines and humans. "The engineering goal is to build better systems that understand these emotions."[50]

The newest computer programs are already doing better than people at some kinds of emotional identification. "Algorithms [developed by Dr. Hirschberg and colleagues] have been able to spot a liar 70 percent of the time in test situations, while people confronted with the same evidence had only 57 percent accuracy," Dr. Hirschberg said. Other researchers are taking different approaches to the same problem, such as analysis of word choice.[51]

Is the ability for machines to detect and analyze emotion in facial expressions and spoken language—even if technology can *never* detect lies 100 percent reliably—brain gain? To the extent that it is more accurate than unaided people, I believe it is.

But is it digitally wise?

Using these kinds of tools could be considered wise, for example, for people who have trouble recognizing emotions on their own, such as those along the autistic spectrum. The downside, though, is false positives—that is, the machine's identifying an emotion that isn't there. Another potentially wise use might be to apply linguistic analysis to stock picking, by analyzing for veracity the comments of executives speaking about their companies, as one researcher has already tried to do.[52] But the digitally wisest thing to do here is probably to wait for further developments.

One particular emotion that it might be particularly wise to be able to detect—humor—has turned out, according to researchers, to be one of the hardest things for computers to understand. The digital wisdom here, I believe, is to keep trying.

BRAIN GAIN AND DIGITAL WISDOM FROM COMBINING MIND AND TECHNOLOGY TO MAKE OUR WORLD A BETTER PLACE

Are we wiser if we combine our minds with technology to stay safer?
Technology and questions of safety have always been deeply intertwined. But those questions often revolve around whether technologies are safe to use, rather than whether technology keeps us safer. Yet the latter is almost certainly more important.

As I discussed earlier, every technology has its risks. I focus on these risks and how to think about and mitigate them in Chapter 7.

But it is also important to focus on the great many ways that technology does keep us safer, from traffic lights, to airbags, to redundant systems, to testing of food and equipment. New advances are being made in all of these fields every day (although they are not always immediately, or universally, adopted). Our military is continually using technology to counter the effects of other technologies (i.e., weapons) and keep soldiers, and civilians, safer: New types of threat detection and armor are continually being developed and employed.[53]

In the area of digital technology, there is a never-ending battle between people who would use the Internet and other digital technologies to do harm, and the technological advances the rest of us use to defend against them. Both sides, in a sense, produce brain gain. Although their creativity is often put to work in less than socially positive ways, hackers are among the most creative people in this regard. (They have greatly extended, for example, our capabilities to find and do many things online.) Those creating defenses against hacking also create brain gain by showing us ways to be safer.

Where is the digital wisdom? Some of it lies in taking advantage of the best and latest defenses available to us, by installing and using the latest software for backups, firewalls, malware protection, and other threats, and keeping them up to date. Some digital wisdom lies in how we deal with the hackers: Is it wiser to punish them severely, or to turn their talents for good? (Many school administrators whose systems have been hacked by students have faced this dilemma.) Digital wisdom also lies, in the realm of safety, in remaining skeptical of blanket safety claims regarding new technologies whose effects are still unknown. Today, for example, some people feel certain that cell phones don't harm us, and others are certain they do. The World Health Organization takes what I believe is a digitally wise position, recently reporting that the jury is still out on long-term cancer risks. "The biggest problem we have is that we know most environmental factors take several decades of exposure before we really see the consequences,"[54] said Dr. Keith Black, chairman of neurology at Cedars-Sinai Medical Center in Los Angeles. Given that, it is also digitally wise, I believe, to use earphones or speakerphone features as much as possible, and to avoid holding phones for long periods next to our brains.

Are we wiser if we combine our minds with technology to know and share where (on the planet) we are?

A technology that has made great strides in recent times is geolocation. With the many Landsat (stationery-orbit global positioning) satellites and other communications satellites now in place, and with our ever-growing number of cell towers, a device that you can hold in your hand or attach to, or even embed in, your body can tell you, with excellent accuracy, exactly where you are on the globe. (For security reasons, the military, which can determine this with the most extreme precision, has actually limited civilian accuracy to within a few meters.) A third positioning dimension, altitude, has been added as well: There are now sensors, soon to be in our phones, that can tell us, for example, what floor of a building we are on. When we are going somewhere, we can now know precisely how far along we are and when we will arrive.

Programmers have been incorporating the sophisticated geolocation capabilities now available on most smart phones into more and more apps. People using these technologies can now share their current location with others, find friends nearby, participate in location-based games, and, using an app such as Foursquare, which lets you "check in," track the number of times they have been to various places.

Accurate geolocation opens up a variety of new possibilities. Because most digital photographs are tagged with geolocation (also called global positioning satellite [GPS]) data, they can be automatically positioned on an online map. Google Maps now shows you amateurs' pictures from almost anywhere on the globe that you click on. Are you interested in the Gobi desert (or is your child perhaps)? Just click on the map to see pictures. Textual information can also be associated with coordinates, so that an app can show you historical and personal notes left by visitors at any particular location. A whole new activity called "geocaching" has arisen, where people hide things for other people to find. Many parents do this with their children for both recreation and learning.

Is having geolocation ability brain gain? Almost certainly. A sense of direction and location has always been considered an important function of our brain, so the ability to enhance this sense—considerably—has to be counted as brain gain.

But where is the digital wisdom? The digital wisdom of geolocation technology lies entirely in how it is used. Clearly it is wise for the military to know precise locations—that is how it targets its smart weapons, finds downed pilots, and so forth. Being able to track shipments and truck fleets is also useful.

But the ability we now have to put chips into *people*—or into the devices they always carry around, which amounts to almost the same thing—requires more digital wisdom. It is a good idea to be able to locate lost children and pets. However, it is now easy for marketers, using geolocation, to identify where and who a customer is and to offer each customer a customized message or discount on the fly. This use of geolocation is far more controversial and raises important privacy concerns.

One marketing site, noting that "Sharing location is a high-trust activity," suggests that the wise thing to do is to build brand trust to overcome customers' privacy concerns. "In fact," they say, "brand trust is the only way geolocation technologies will move into the mainstream." They cite as examples of such brand trust Nike's letting people track their runs on their site and Yelp's letting people build personal reputations through reviewing restaurants they've eaten at. (They also cite Taplister, which lets people find out what beer is available near them, although I personally would not include the ability to find beer more easily as digital wisdom.[55])

The beer example, along with, for example, the iPhone's incorporation of geolocation into the digital assistant Siri to find things such as nearby restaurants, might be considered merely clever (though useful) rather than wise (see Chapter 4). But the ability to find the location of the nearest hospital or gas station in an emergency could be critical, as could be the ability to find accident victims by the geolocation signals of their phones or cars. Technology-based systems like GM's OnStar not only help rescuers quickly locate accident victims but immediately alert a central station of the location of accidents when they happen. Digital wisdom lies, I believe, in having and using these capabilities whenever possible.

Are we wiser if we combine our minds with technology to predict and deal with natural disasters?

Natural disasters such as floods, tsunamis, earthquakes, and others still cause enormous problems and take thousands of lives. Sadly, we do not yet have the technology to prevent these events. But we do have more and more technology that can help predict such disasters and help us deal with them after they occur.

Sensors in the earth can now measure the depth of offshore earthquakes and, combining their readings in milliseconds via the Internet, predict the likelihood and location of tsunamis with enough warning time to allow most people to get out of the way. Today, such systems are finally starting to be put into place where they are needed. Flood and earthquake prediction technologies are similarly improving, and, although they are not yet perfect, they will keep getting better. Technology allows us to model the flow of water more precisely to show where risk of flood is the highest, and where and how we should build breakwaters, dams, and levees.

More and more technologies are appearing that help us deal with natural disasters after they happen. Robots can now find people buried in earthquakes in places where rescuers cannot go. In addition, communication systems, some of which failed tragically on 9/11, for example, are being improved and upgraded.

Is this brain gain? I believe our increased ability to predict disasters in time to save lives is a form of brain gain. Yet although we have made great strides in this area, it remains a place where much more work, technology, and brain gain is needed. The recent tsunami and resulting nuclear disaster in Japan is a good reminder of how much we still have to learn and do.

Is this digitally wise? Much of the digital wisdom in this area comes not from the technology itself but from the willingness, on the part of leaders, to put the new technologies and warning systems into place—not doing so is almost certainly digitally unwise. Digital wisdom also comes from learning from our mistakes, such as failures at nuclear plants, levees, seawalls, and other structures, and continually improving these technologies. A third area where we could become digitally wiser is in testing technologies in stressful situations similar to those of disasters, to be sure they will work when needed.

Are we wiser if we combine our minds with technology to see what is happening in all places?

Not so very long ago, most people didn't even know what was happening in the next town, or on the next block, or even around the corner. Today we have cameras and other sensors in so many places that we are approaching the point where almost everything is being, or can be, recorded. You can watch your baby in her room on your iPhone when you are at work. You can watch the New England leaves change to their fall colors on web cams broadcasting on the Internet and determine when is the best time to go watch in person (or you can just watch them online). Satellites with cameras powerful enough to read the numbers on license plates are observing the whole earth in great detail from their orbits and can be repositioned at will for even greater coverage. And for the times and places where the satellites cannot see, we now have drones that can be positioned to circle or hover permanently. At a more local level, there are now traffic cameras in more and more places.

Add to this recording capability the vast number of individuals who now have video cameras in their pockets—either as separate devices or, increasingly, in their phones. Most of these videocams can be easily connected to the Internet, either to broadcast live or upload videos to YouTube, news portals, or other sites. News media are actively soliciting and using these amateur videos. It was such a video, of a frustrated individual lighting himself on fire, that set off the whole Arab Spring movement and led to worldwide political changes.

Over the past decade, the U.S. military and security apparatus, largely in an attempt to hunt down Osama bin Laden and his confederates in al-Qaeda, has poured huge amounts of money into the development of technologies enabling us to locate a proverbial needle in a haystack, by analyzing literally trillions of data points from human reports, cell phone conversations, and many other sources. As a result, our technological capabilities to do this are further advanced than they were a decade ago.

Is this brain gain? Unless you believe that ignorance is bliss, it surely is. Our brain's ability to see and know what is going on in all corners of the globe is now extended far beyond what it could do in even the recent past.

Is this digitally wise? Clearly, it cuts both ways.

Seeing what is going on can be a positive force. The whole world observed in real time the protests in Tahrir Square in Egypt and the Occupy Wall Street protests in the United States—in ways they couldn't do, for example, in Tiananmen Square in 1989. Technology has allowed our government to see what is going on in many dangerous places in the world and to catch dangerous people.

And this new power to observe what is going on is no longer reserved for governments. Workers in Bahrain were able to go onto Google Earth and see the size of the land and palaces the rulers lived on, versus the tiny part of the country they were all crammed into. "A big issue," writes Tom Friedman of *The New York Times,* "particularly among Shiite men who want to get married and build homes, is the unequal distribution of land."[56] Friedman reports that on November 27, 2006, on the eve of parliamentary elections in Bahrain, the *Washington Post* ran this report from there: "Mahmood, who lives in a house with his parents, four siblings and their children, said he became even more frustrated when he looked up Bahrain on Google Earth and saw vast tracts of empty land, while tens of thousands of mainly poor Shiites were squashed together in small, dense areas. 'We are 17 people crowded in one small house, like many people in the southern district,' he said. 'And you see on Google how many palaces there are and how the al-Khalifas [the Sunni ruling family] have the rest of the country to themselves.' Bahraini activists have encouraged people to take a look at the country on Google Earth, and they have set up a special user group whose members have access to more than 40 images of royal palaces."[57]

On the flip side, however, these new technological capabilities also greatly invade what many people have traditionally regarded as private space, and they open the door to what many consider to be dangerous and unacceptable levels of government control of citizens' lives.

The digital wisdom lies, I believe, in finding the proper balance between these extremes, which may be different in every situation. It is highly unlikely that the ability to see more and more will go away—there are too many benefits. Rather, it is likely to go much further as it becomes increasingly easier and cheaper to do. In some places, digital wisdom (at least from one point of view) may consist of figuring out ways to get around these technologies, as Iran is doing by building bunkers deep underground. Banning or controlling parts of the Internet, as China and other countries are currently doing, may have temporary success but will get increasing hard as people discover technological workarounds. In situations like these, as I discuss in Chapter 5, digital wisdom lies in making the best trade-offs for all concerned.

Are we wiser if we combine our minds with technology to get closer to nature?

A big complaint and criticism often heard about technology is that it removes us from nature, and therefore from the world of which we are a "natural" part. In the past, wisdom has often been associated with getting back to nature, for example, by the ancient Greek philosopher Diogenes, by St. Francis, and by more modern writers such as Walt Whitman and Henry David Thoreau.

But it is not always the case that technology separates us from the natural world. Technology can also do just the opposite, that is, bring us closer to nature. This is an area where new thinking, and new digital wisdom, is required.

Technology brings us closer to nature in a variety of ways. For many, getting closer to nature involves learning about it—learning the names of trees, or rock formations, or the names and habits of animals and birds. This used to require a great deal of out-of-nature study, searching in many books. Today's digital technology has made this something we can do while actually immersed in nature, and has made doing so, literally in many instances, child's play. Apps, for example, allow you (or rather your phone) to "listen" to a bird call and then tell you what bird it is. You can use your phone to snap a picture of a leaf and immediately identify and learn all about the tree it is from. You can point your phone at the stars, and it will tell you precisely which stars (or other heavenly bodies) you are looking at.[58]

When you are hiking, you can find out if the weather is going to change and get dangerous—something that can often happen quickly. Using technology's ability to leave virtual notes attached to geographical coordinates, you can read or hear what others have experienced in the place you are in and pass along your own observations.

And if getting closer to nature though camping in the woods is your goal, technology can help there, too. Writer Bruce Feiler, in a 2011 *New York Times* article entitled "Our Plugged-in Summer," describes all the ways that technology enhanced, unexpectedly, his family's back-to-nature camping vacation. These included using the tree and bird apps noted above, using an iPad for better storytelling around the campfire, consulting videos for learning how to make a perfect cross hatch pattern on grilled fish (and how to make a traditional lanyard), finding solutions on the Internet for nature-related problems (such as eliminating slugs), using trivia games for family fun and distraction, using apps for information finding ("who was the Benedict in eggs benedict?"), and using technology for emergency care (bug bite first aid and finding a hospital), as well as using technology to check in with other family members who were not able to be there and were missed.[59]

Is this brain gain? The many new ways that technology allows us to connect more deeply with nature, particularly through more knowledge, are all examples, I believe, of brain gain. We can now find out far more easily about aspects of nature and natural phenomena (e.g., meteor showers, comets, pretty leaves) that we want to connect with and discover the best times and conditions under which to connect. Consider, for example, all the ways you could use technology today to plan and enhance a vacation to our national parks.

Is this digital wisdom? As in most cases, there are different ways to think about this. Some would say, I am sure, that connecting with nature is best done (or only done) when we eliminate technology altogether. However, very few of these people would likely venture out into their preferred natural environment naked (i.e., without clothing technology) or leaving behind their Gore-Tex, bug spray, hunting or fishing equipment, and other modern technological aids. Camping in particular has now become, for most, a highly technology-enhanced experience—and as a result, in many cases, a brain-enhanced one.

Regarding his own camping trip, Feiler does acknowledge some downsides, such as the temptation to check his email, but concludes that there are "more benefits" to having technology along. "While the Internet is often accused of making us more shallow," he writes, "I found that time and again our devices helped deepen a moment, or extend it a bit longer." He also cites the positive benefits of connecting with his own family's past nature relationships through recorded stories, pictures, and videos, and the ability to connect with a larger societal past, such as when he found the Rip Van Winkle story online and read an edited version to his kids. (Others might prefer reading passages from *Walden*.)

The point Feiler makes, and that I would emphasize, is that it makes little sense to continually "moralize" (his word), as many do, about dropping technology and returning to a more "natural" state. We live in a new world and context, and digital wisdom comes from finding the right balance of "nature" and technology for every situation in which we find ourselves. This is, in fact, what our parents, grandparents, and all our ancestors did. I would bet that almost no pioneer or scientist ever set off to explore nature without bringing along as much current technology as they could possibly and comfortably carry.

Are we wiser if we combine our minds with technology to enhance the environment?

My guess is that most people, these days, would like not only to understand their environment better, but also to enhance it when possible, both for themselves and their posterity. Many technologies are now in place that allow us to do this, both locally and globally.

In fact, these days it is far harder—not to mention less effective—to attempt to enhance our environment *without* technology.

Modern farming could certainly not be done, on a worldwide scale, without technology. "We used to farm by the acre; now we farm by the square inch," a farmer once told me. What he meant was that we can now analyze the growing environment on a micro scale to see what works best. Crops that are genetically engineered to grow better and yield more now make up a large percentage of the world's food supply.

Today, whenever we contemplate undertaking large projects that will affect the environment, we have powerful technological tools to do impact analyses that we could never do before (leading, of course, to new battles as we can take more factors into account).

On an individual scale, we can also do much more because of technology. We can much more easily join organizations and contribute time and money to environmental causes via the Internet. We can monitor the effects of pollution on people's lungs via imaging technology. We can view and show our children the decline of our forests (and, conversely, the cleanup of some of our rivers) via Google Earth and other programs. We can participate in worldwide debates and discussions and more easily find evidence to support environmentalist points of view.

Is this brain gain? We certainly know, thanks to technology, much more about the environment than ever before, and we can do more about it. Although much remains controversial, knowing how not to starve, and how to protect our increasingly threatened environment, is, I believe, brain gain.

But where is the digital wisdom? It lies, I believe, both in taking advantage of technology to stay as informed as possible about environmental issues and in using technology to be an active participant in the many environmental debates that characterize our times. One kind of brain gain that comes from technology is empowerment to take action in support of what we believe in this and other areas. Digital wisdom lies in doing so. Writing in the *New York Times* about what they call the new "Anththropocene" age (i.e., the age shaped by humans), writer Emma Marris and a group of scientists suggest we can accept the reality of humanity's reshaping of the environment [via technology] "without giving up in despair."[60]

BRAIN GAIN AND DIGITAL WISDOM FROM COMBINING
MIND AND TECHNOLOGY TO DEEPEN OUR ANALYSES

Are we wiser if we combine our minds with technology to collect and analyze more data?

Digital technology now allows us to easily collect and store immense amounts of data, in quantities and over timeframes that were previously considered either impossible or not very useful. It also enables us to extract useful knowledge from this data in new ways. Many refer to this new opportunity (and issue) as the use of "big data."

Some of this big data—for example, all the phone calls people make, all their search requests, all their health records—is regularly generated from normal activities. Today, because of great advances in storage technology, this information can be kept, if desired, indefinitely. Although this creates trillions or even quadrillions of records (and someday more), we now have the technology to store and analyze these vast quantities of data, and to combine them in useful ways. By keeping the records forever, we allow researchers to study trends (so-called "longitudinal analyses") and to (hopefully) discover patterns that we couldn't see before.

By looking at the pattern of Google searches, for example, we can now see what whole areas of the world are interested in at any given moment. (The most frequent search topics in the United States can be viewed online at http://www.google.com/trends/.) Some people, like *Wired* magazine's editor Chris Anderson, claim that big data is creating a new and different kind of scientific method that involves finding things rather than hypothesizing and theorizing about them. Anderson wrote about this in 2008, calling his article, provocatively, "The End of Theory: The Data Deluge Makes the Scientific Method Obsolete."[61]

In addition to saving our old data longer, we are collecting vast quantities of new data. A sailing trip around the world in 2003 by scientist Craig Venter and his colleagues collected millions of new DNA and gene examples, extending our knowledge of the world's genome by more than 100 percent. We have now found more than 29 million genes, only 24,000 of which are in the human genome.[62] Remote sensors can now be placed almost everywhere, including inside our bodies. Nanotechnology, which reduces the size of these sensors to smaller than a speck of dust, is accelerating this process.

But having all this data means nothing if we cannot analyze it and derive useful information. More and more technologies are being developed—some still classified by our government—to analyze the mass quantities of often seemingly unrelated data, looking for correlations and patterns. Sequencing a human genome, for example, which used to take 13 years, can now be done in just a couple of hours.[63] Boding well for the future is that much of this technology is now becoming available for purposes other than just "hunting enemies." Among the fields likely to benefit first from these new technology-based analysis capabilities are health information and neuroscience.

One of the powerful new technology-based analysis tools that allows us to analyze and correlate large volumes of data—one that is currently available, free, to anyone with an Internet connection—is Wolfram Alpha, available online at wolframalpha.com. A brainchild of the scientist Stephen Wolfram, known for his powerful and enormously popular (among scientists, engineers, and technical types) mathematical analysis program Mathematica, Wolfram Alpha is both a data collection and curation project, and a powerful analysis engine.

Dr. Wolfram's goal in creating the Wolfram Alpha tool was to allow "almost anyone to analyze all human knowledge in the way experts now do." The data collection side consists of his people's obtaining access to and putting into analyzable form as many existing data sets as possible. It turns out there are enormous numbers of these data collections—from detailed population statistics to data on airplanes currently in the sky—collected by governments and organizations around the world. Just the site www.data.gov, for example, gives access to 390,255 raw and geospatial data sets. Access to a great percentage of the world's data is free or requires only a minimal cost.

The Wolfram Alpha analysis engine program (free on the Internet and part of the Siri virtual assistant on the iPhone) allows users to ask a detailed question involving data, just as they might question an "expert." For example, you can ask it, "How much arable land would be available to each person on earth if it were shared equally?" The program will interpret your request, divide the world's arable land by the world's population, and almost instantaneously produce the answer: 2.471 acres (approximately 1 hectare) per person [in 2009]. Or you might ask, "How many people have ever lived on earth?" (answer: 106.5 billion people).[64]

Wolfram Alpha answers such questions by putting together, on the fly, the necessary parts of its data sets to calculate results—results that may never have been calculated before. Request, for example, the "average world temperature," and the program will produce a graph, in seconds, of a number of different measures of world temperature, from 1900 until today. (Yes, all of these measures are rising.)

Is this brain gain? It is hard to see it as anything but.

Is this digital wisdom? At first blush, one might focus on just the digital wisdom that comes from using Wolfram Alpha to answer interesting questions that rarely, if ever, get asked, because in the past, these questions were unanswerable without expensive and time-consuming analyses by experts. But there are other issues involving the need for digital wisdom as well. Although Wolfram would like to answer *any* question, even he wonders how much personal information should be included in the program's analyses. "You would be amazed at the data I can find on you from just a simple analysis online," says Wolfram. He himself sees digital wisdom as steering "a middle course."[65]

Fortunately, because Wolfram curates the data himself (or rather his organization does), he can choose what to include. But some analysis engines are not as picky or concerned. Some, in fact, are designed to deliberately find and combine as much personal data as possible. Many of their advertisements show up almost daily in my email inbox.

We may be unaware that some of this data even exists. For example, I was recently surprised to learn that there is a publicly available database of the names of everyone in prison. I suppose I should have been cognizant of the fact that this information was collected, and likely made public, but I wasn't. As it turns out, much of the data recorded about what we do online—where we go, what we buy, or what we look at and don't buy—is bought and sold on a daily, or even real-time, basis.[66] A large part of digital wisdom is our being aware of this and, if we are opposed, knowing what we can do to keep our own data private. In the age of "big data," digital wisdom is a constant balancing act of what we get versus what we give up. It also includes, as I argued earlier, *not* thinking that privacy is always better. Contributing information to databases that are then used for public benefit is probably wise, although having all of it attached to your personal identifiers may not be.

Are we wiser if we combine our minds with technology to analyze new (and old) areas?

A variety of fields of human endeavor and study have not, in the past, been subjected to very much technology-based, or even quantitative, analysis. This is particularly true of those fields known collectively as the "humanities," including literature, history, philosophy, languages, philosophy, archeology, religion, and the arts. Most of the analyses of literature and art, for example, have, historically, been almost completely subjective, based on scholars' and experts' research and opinions. But technology is now allowing many of these fields that were previously considered matters of opinion to be analyzed more quantitatively and scientifically. In 2010 and 2011, the *New York Times* ran a six-part series entitled "Humanities 2.0" about this phenomenon. The writer, Patricia Cohen, cited numerous examples of technology being used for humanities research. They include digital mapping, both of historical places (an emerging field known as "spatial humanities") and of ideas, such as the mapping of exchanges of letters between intellectuals in different countries during the Enlightenment (part of an emerging field known as "culturomics").[67] Although fields like culturomics and spatial humanities are still in their infancy—and are regarded with skepticism by many older professors—they are firing up new generations of both teachers and students. Swarthmore, Haverford, and Bryn Mawr colleges, for example, recently jointly held a digital humanities conference for undergraduates. "We're really participating in something that's happening right now,"[68] commented a student. Much of this work is being supported in the United States by the National Endowment for the Humanities as well as by multination projects in Europe.

Is this brain gain? "People will use this data in ways we can't even imagine yet," says one scholar. "The digital humanities do fantastic things," said another. But is it digitally wise? The big caveat cited by many is that technology can't do or find everything; their biggest worry is that electronic tools have the potential to "reduce literature and history to a series of numbers, squeezing out important subjects that cannot be easily quantified." "So much of humanistic scholarship is about interpretation,"[69] says Princeton historian Anthony Grafton.

Another humanities field where technology is making important contributions is the history of art, which includes, among other things, the provenance and attribution of paintings and other art works. Today, technology has thoroughly invaded (and enhanced) this field. Conservators use technology to analyze pigments and detect forgeries made with materials that we know didn't exist at the time the works were supposedly created.[70] X-ray and other technologies are used by scientists and scholars to find earlier works of art hidden under existing ones.[71]

Even recognizing and analyzing an artist's style, long considered a purely "human" skill, can now be improved upon by computer analysis. New insights can be obtained as well. "Judging artistic styles, and the similarities between them, might be thought one bastion of human skill that machines could never storm," wrote the *Economist* in 2011. "Not so," they continue, "if Lior Shamir at Lawrence Technological University in Michigan is correct. A paper he has just published in *Leonardo* suggests that computers may have just as good an eye for style as humans do—and, in some cases, may see connections between artists that human critics have missed."[72] Shamir fed 513 works by well-known artists (57 for each) into his computer and had a program look, on its own, for features that most differentiated different artists. (This is a newer, and better, technique for doing computer analysis than just telling the computer what to look for in advance.) Shamir's aim was to "look for quantifiable ways of distinguishing between the work of different artists." Although he has not yet achieved that goal with perfect accuracy, he did discover some surprising new things, such as that the works of van Gogh and Jason Pollack, usually considered very different styles, have a lot of factors in common—more, by his analysis, than van Gogh shares with other so-called "impressionist" artists of his time such as Monet and Renoir.[73]

Is this brain gain? Yes, in that it provides a new way of looking at art and, as the *Economist* puts it, "a new line of analysis."

Technology is producing similar brain gains and new lines of analysis in the other humanities as well, including, for example, literature and historical writing. Literature researchers now use computer-based semantic analyses (i.e., word frequency counts, and links and relationships between documents) and computer-based stylistic analysis of commonly used language and turns of phrase to determine authorship and even when something was written. This has recently been done to analyze themes in Victorian literature.[74] Shakespeare has also been subjected to a lot of analysis in an effort to prove or disprove the authenticity of his works. For scholars of literature, at least, this is brain gain, although many scholars still reject it—one associate professor doing computer-based work reports that many of his senior colleagues regard his work as "whimsical, the result of playing with technological toys."[75]

Visual analysis technologies designed originally for other purposes have been repurposed for new uses in humanistic fields. One example is a technology called "Captcha"—you have probably, on the web, encountered these funny-spaced and strangely oriented letters and words that you must decipher in order to enter a site. Captcha was originally invented by Carnegie-Mellon researcher and Macarthur "genius grant" winner Luis van Ahn as a way to distinguish human web site visitors from machines (or "bots"), intending to insert spam or do other harm. Van Ahn has repurposed the technology, with a technology he calls "reCaptcha," to electronically decipher blotchy old newspapers and poorly printed documents, something that the human eye does fairly easily, but computers typically can't do well at all. The reCaptcha program creates captchas from elements that the computer has difficulty reading and reuses these captchas for the original purpose, that is, authentication by a human. The result is that hundreds of millions of humans are now, unknowingly, flagging undecipherable words in old texts for either more analysis or human assistance. The program has proved extremely successful, in some cases achieving an accuracy rate of more than 90 percent, comparable to that of professional human transcribers. ReCaptcha is being used to clean up the digitized versions of the older volumes in the *New York Times*'s archives and has become the principal method used by Google to authenticate texts in Google Books, Google's project to digitize and disseminate rare out-of-print texts on the Internet. The technology provides brain gain in terms of improving human-machine cooperation to do a tedious but important task much more quickly and accurately.[76]

This underscores two of the greatest contributions that technology has brought to the humanities: communal participation by scholars, and participation by amateurs. It is now possible, and becoming more frequent, for many scholars around the world to be working in collaboration on the same document at the same time. "This is fundamentally changing the way we do our work," said Martin K. Foys, who is using the technology to analyze the huge Bayeux tapestry.[77] In addition, tools have been developed that let amateurs do some of the work formerly reserved for scholars, which is helpful, because there is far too much for experts to accomplish on their own: The transcription of Thomas Jefferson's handwritten papers, for example, which was begun in 1943, is projected to take until 2025 to complete. Online tools such as those developed for the Bentham Project to transcribe all the notes of Enlightenment philosopher Jeremy Bentham allow ordinary people to help transcribe the large volume of pages that have been scanned. To date, hundreds have participated.[78]

And let us not forget the field of music, which has now been influenced almost everywhere by technology. Almost all aspects of music, from electronic instruments (and traditional instruments built with new, composite materials), to recordings, acoustics, and sound enhancement, to composition, to music distribution and consumption, are now affected by technology. Toyota's amazing robot Toyotashi, can actually play the trumpet, quite virtuostically, in fact.[79]

Scientific analytic technologies are now being used to build and evaluate new musical instruments. High-tech digital frequency analysis is used by many makers to provide a picture of the exact sounds and overtones a particular instrument produces. While this was done, primitively, in the past with analog oscilloscopes, newer digital techniques, combined with digital methods of data analysis and display, allow makers to reproduce almost exactly the sound of older prized instruments. The effects of this analysis were recently demonstrated in dramatic fashion in "double-blind" tests, which compared old and modern instruments in the violin family. (The tests were double-blind in that neither the player nor the listeners knew which instrument was which.) The results showed scientifically, for the first time, that some elements of "traditional" quality—such as a verified Stradivarius label on a violin—do not necessarily mean higher quality of sound, as many had previously assumed. It turned out that most listeners and players in the test frequently mistook old instruments for new and vice versa. The instrument that the (all very experienced) players "most wanted to take home" was a modern one, and the least preferred of all was a Stradivarius. In a fun test of digital brain gain, you can compare two of the violins online for yourself and try to pick which one is the Stradivarius.[80]

My view is that all of these digital analyses of new, previously unanalyzable (or unanalyzable in easily doable ways) information provide brain gain.

But do they lead to digital wisdom?

In some cases, undeniably yes. If we can definitively ascertain the creator of a particular work of art, or find a work that is hidden, in ways that experts previously were not able, or willing (so as not to destroy an existing work) to do, we have added to their wisdom. If we can use techniques to produce more beautiful-sounding instruments, saving players huge amounts of money, that is (leaving psychic and emotional attachment to famous old instruments aside) wisdom as well.

But just having more knowledge does not constitute wisdom. We need to be careful in many of these traditionally subjective areas not to let technology and technological knowledge get in the way of our non-technological understanding and appreciation of true works of art. In the play and film *Amadeus*, the emperor Joseph II tells Mozart that his music has "too many notes." We must avoid making judgments just because we are able to count. (When the emperor suggests removing a few notes, Mozart's answer is, "Which few did you have in mind?"[81])

As the sign hanging on Albert Einstein's office wall reminded him daily, "Not everything that counts can be counted, and not everything that can be counted counts." Substitute "analyzed" for "counted," and the statement still applies.

BRAIN GAIN AND DIGITAL WISDOM FROM COMBINING MIND AND TECHNOLOGY TO DERIVE NEW AND USEFUL INSIGHTS

Are we wiser if we combine our minds with technology to read everything written?

There once was a time—actually only a couple of hundred years ago—when a human being could read, in his or her lifetime, everything ever written on this planet (assuming he or she had access). That time is, of course, long gone (although it still is possible, as Stephen Wolfram pointed out to me, to read everything written *on a topic* if the topic is narrow enough, and even—and this is more brain gain—to have access to almost all of that writing via the Internet).[82] Still, since the invention of the printing press almost 600 years ago, there has been such an explosion of writing that we have reached the point where no individual could possibly read everything written in a single lifetime.

But computers *can* do this. Technologies are currently available that make it more and more possible for human minds and computers to take into account all human writing and knowledge.

One is the IBM Watson computer program that defeated two human champions on the TV program *Jeopardy* in 2011. According to Dave Farrucci, Watson's inventor (he is actually the leader of a large team that created Watson), Watson was able to find the answers it did, in part, because it was able, on its own, to "read" and "understand" hundreds of thousands of pages of text. There is no reason that a larger (in power, probably not size) version of such a computer could not ingest, in a similar way, everything ever written—in every language—and then use that material in the same general way as Watson did, to make connections and come to various conclusions.

This is, of course, not precisely what we mean by "reading" when a human does it. But since humans can't read everything (or even remember most of what they do read), a Watson (or a "Baby Watson," as another IBMer put it) might make a helpful assistant.

A second way technology can help us to "read everything" (or, more accurately, to at least take everything written into account) is for humans to finish the job of scanning all books and other materials ever written. Google, which has undertaken this project—and run into some controversy in the process—has so far scanned more than 11 percent of the entire corpus of published books.[83]

Yet a third way is to complete—or at least advance considerably—the so-called "semantic web." This version of the web will have an engine (or series of engines), available to everyone in the way search engines are now (and likely a part of what search engines evolve into), that will quickly find every topic, phrase, sentence, paragraph, or chapter *ever written* on a topic of our choosing, providing useful connections and correlations along the way. A very early example of this ability is already online at http://books.google.com/ngrams/. We are still a long ways off from completing it, but the idea is being championed by the inventor of the world wide web, Tim Berners-Lee. Based on his track record, I wouldn't call it impossible.

The Watson approach, though, is here today. Is it brain gain?

Being able to combine all writings into a single database clearly opens a new symbiosis between scholars and texts. It will allow people to search, for the first time ever without tedious years or decades of counting, for every printed use of particular words or phrases. Scholars have already moved ahead with this kind of technology, analyzing the Bible, the Federalist Papers, Victorian literature, and the Dead Sea Scrolls, among other texts.

Is this digital wisdom?

One might just as well ask, "Is scholarship wisdom?" or "Is the ability to connect complex ideas wisdom?" To the extent that one's answers are yes, this is digital wisdom as well. To the concerns of humanists that the essence of their art is "the search for meaning," practitioners of the digital humanities respond (and emphasize) that their analytic techniques "simply provide information." "Interpretation," they say, "remains essential."[84] But the fact is that in the modern age, even the humanities now require the digitally wise symbiosis of human and machine for finding wisdom.

Are we wiser if we combine our minds with technology to create new business models?

Technology is quickly transforming business in a great variety of ways. One of the most interesting to me is the creation of new technology-enabled business models. This is, for example, what Steve Jobs and the record companies famously did with music distribution. Jobs knew, as we all did, that new technology had enabled a way to easily download individual songs. But Jobs realized that, while initially these were downloaded and shared for free, a micropayment system could be added. He thought that if he made his system extremely convenient, and the songs were priced low enough, people would be likely to use such a system. (It also helped that the industry was adding threats and pressure of prosecution for stealing.) This led to a totally new way to distribute and buy music—iTunes—a model that now dominates the industry. "The Internet set out to destroy existing business models—Jobs just noticed their lack of relevance and came up with new ones,"[85] writes David Carr in the *New York Times*.

Other technology-enabled business models include:

- *Online auctions.* The ancient auction business model was given new life by Pierre Omidyar in 1985 with the founding of eBay. That company is now worth more than $45 billion.

- *Individually targeted advertising.* Once Google and Facebook began collecting and analyzing user data, they were able to target ads directly to specific consumers. Facebook is worth, as of its IPO, more than $105 billion. Google is worth almost $200 billion.

- *Micropayments by the "spending minority."* The game company Zynga soared from startup to IPO with more than a $9 billion valuation in only four years, with a business model that let most users play for free, but sold virtual goods to anyone who was willing to pay. These players, called "whales" (the term originally referred to the "big players" in gambling casinos), spend enough each, on a regular basis, to have made the company cash positive and profitable almost from the outset.

- *New ways of funding startups.* The web site Kickstarter.com bills itself as "a new way to fund and follow creativity." And it is. People looking for money post descriptions of their projects, to which individuals can contribute small amounts. Kickstarter, just two years old as this is written, has already passed the million-donor mark. Some businesses looking to raise only several thousand dollars suddenly found themselves with several hundred thousand.[86] At least two businesses have raised more than $1 million, and others have come close.[87] Their model is sometimes known as "crowdfunding."

- *Cloud-based music storage.* Google music lets you have all your music stored "in the cloud" (i.e., on their servers) so you can access it from any device. They claim this is a different and better business model than the model of downloading music and storing it on your own device. Says a spokesperson, "Other cloud music services think you have to pay to listen to music you already own. We don't." However, there are still issues of transferring your music that need to be worked out to make this business model grow.[88]

- *Bargains on perishable inventory.* Priceline's "name your own price" feature lets hotels accept or reject any offer a potential customer makes, on the theory that getting "some" revenue for something that is about to expire (i.e., that night's hotel room) is better than getting none. This business model provides both the customers and the hotels with new, technology-enabled advantages. Hotel Tonight, a free app on the iPhone and a feature on Priceline and Expedia, takes this even further, allowing travelers to show up in a city without a hotel reservation and get a very cheap one, at a decent place, starting at noon. Even the high-end Intercontinental hotel chain is trying this new business model for ensuring its rooms stay full. According to *Bloomberg Businessweek,* these new business models are "Threatening the decade old business model of online travel agencies."[89]

- *Micropublishing.* The company Hyperink employs software algorithms to predict narrow, in-demand e-book topics based on recent book sales figures and popular Internet searches, and then churns out thousands of narrowly focused online e-book titles a month on these topics. (An example: *How to Get into Amherst.*) Their costs are kept way down by using cheap freelancers found on Craigslist, mediabistro.com, and journalismjobs.com to do two-hour interviews and then quickly create the e-books.[90]
- *Device-based services.* Amazon's Kindle Fire tablet has no camera and no microphone, but it does have wi-fi. Amazon sees it not as a device, but as a new business model. "We don't think of the Kindle Fire as a tablet. We think of it as a service," says a spokesperson. It is designed to let Amazon customers sit back on the sofa and shop. "It allows us to offer premium products at non-premium prices." The device has already increased traffic, becoming a "huge tailwind for our [i.e., Amazon's] business."[91]

Professor Nancy F. Koehn of the Harvard Business School sees the Kindle Fire, which comes with an optimized shopping application preinstalled that funnels users into Amazon's meticulously constructed world of content, commerce, and cloud computing, as symbolic of Amazon's "remarkable ability to adapt and create new business models."[92] [The company], she adds, "is like a biological organism that through natural selection and adaptation just keeps learning and growing."[93] Of course new business models lead to new business wars: Apple has restricted Amazon from directing iPad users to its web site in order to avoid giving Apple its cut.

Other new business models that Amazon is exploring include "locking in" authors to online publishing contracts and same-day delivery.

Both Apple and Amazon (along with many other companies) have persuaded customers to entrust them with their credit cards, allowing them to shop in the least bothersome of fashions (e.g., with "1-click"—a registered "service mark" phrase of Amazon's).

- *Online grocery shopping.* Would you have predicted that grocery shopping online would become a successful business model? It wasn't at first, and many companies fizzled. But with the eventual success of Peapod, Freshpicks, FreshDirect, NetGrocer, and other companies, the big supermarkets (and even Amazon) have climbed on the get-your-food-using-technology bandwagon.

- *iTunes, app stores, and the Apple store.* Apple, like Amazon, is a company that delights in inventing new business models, often by starting with the customer and work backward. "Before the iPhone, cyberspace was something you went out to visit. Now cyberspace is something you carry in your pocket," says Paul Saffo, a noted futurist.[94] Saffo thinks the iTunes and app stores may be Jobs's most remarkable creations. While publishers have long struggled to create a mechanism that separates consumers from their cash, Apple has about 200 million credit cards on file in an online environment where people can buy with the push of a button. "Consumers are happy and Apple got fat," says Saffo.[95]

- *Reselling of unwanted digital files.* A frustration of many who buy electronic goods such as music is their inability to resell what they no longer want, as they can do with physical books and CDs. A startup called ReDigi has developed a system that it calls "a legal and secure way for people to get rid of unwanted music files and buy others at a discount." This new business model may lead to an entirely new secondhand digital marketplace for virtual goods, just as the Internet created an online market for new goods, and eBay created one for used goods. Once someone buys a copyrighted physical item like a CD or book, that buyer is free (according to the legal principle of "first-sale doctrine") to resell it. The law is unclear when it comes to digital goods, because, says the *New York Times,* transferring a digital file from one party to another usually involves making a copy of it, something generally not allowed under copyright law.[96] There is much uncertainty in this area, and we may see big changes—stay tuned.

- *New ways to find cheap labor and to sell one's services:* If you happen to have a few spare hours, or even a few spare minutes, you can now offer that time for sale through a web site. Conversely, if you need a simple task done, you can get people to bid to find who will do it for the lowest price. A new online business model helps many people find extra cash (or hire temporary workers) by making these matchups on a micro basis. Services such as Amazon's Mechanical Turk, Elance, oDesk, TaskRabbit, Slivers of Time, and MinuteBox (the last two in the United Kingdom), all online, hookup "doers" and "doees" in the tiniest of possible increments. (For example: "Go to the cleaners for me." "Work for one half hour." "Do one or two small tasks.") Mechanical Turk is particularly interesting in the context of this book, because it lets programmers coordinate the use of human intelligence to perform tasks that computers are as yet unable to do. Among the most oft-requested Mechanical Turk "Human Intelligence Tasks" (or HITs) are podcast transcribing, rating and image tagging, and writing or rewriting sentences, paragraphs, or whole articles. These have rewards ranging from one cent to about $10 per task.[97]

Are all these new business models brain gain? Maybe. Certainly some of them have created great financial value. One interesting thing to observe is that while humans have always invented new business models (such as paying with money rather than barter), in the past successful models generally lasted for a great amount of time. Now, with digital technology, new business models often last only for months before something better comes along. Perhaps the brain gain comes in the increasing ability of people to think about "business" and "business models" in new terms, as something they can create and change themselves.

Is creating these new business models digitally wise? I believe it is not only digitally wise, but imperative. Some businesses, already doing well, such as Twitter, and even Facebook, are still looking for their ideal business models. But it is important to get the models right. At one point Netflix managed to mess up an excellent business model of "mail plus online" delivery of films by trying to split it into two businesses without sufficiently consulting its customers. Many of those customers resisted mightily, using the power of technology to cancel their subscriptions online.[98] This shows us that while digital wisdom requires trying new business models, it also requires keeping in very close touch with customers about what models work for them.

Are we wiser if we combine our minds with technology to imitate nature?
Nature and evolution may work slowly, but they have had millions of years to do their work. Nature typically tries trillions of combinations before it finally

hits on, and preserves, what works well. As a result, nature has found many ingenious solutions to a variety of difficult problems—from spreading seeds widely, to staying put against tough forces, to locomotion, to construction, to camouflage, to survival, and many others. Plants have developed ingenious was to spread their seeds, such as by growing burrs that cling tenaciously to passersby. Spiders have developed the ability to produce threads of enormous strength. Marine creatures have developed superstrong glue to attach themselves to rocks and other objects. Many animals have developed ways to camouflage their appearance, and to deal with temperature and other environmental changes. A great many of nature's solutions surpass anything yet invented by humans.

Many scientists and inventors have now turned back to nature as a source of inspiration and solutions to problems. Human intelligence and technology have come together in a field known as "biomimicry" (or "biomimetics") to produce both brain gain and digital wisdom. New digital technologies provide ways to take advantage, in our human lives, of these solutions developed by nature.

One of the best-known examples of technology-based biomimicry is Velcro, invented in 1948 by the Swiss electrical engineer George de Mestral, who had trouble getting burrs off his clothes. He was able, using the microscopes of his time, to see the hooks and loops on the burrs, which he succeeded in imitating.[99] In 2011, scientists found an organism (a crustacean called *Crassicorophium bonellii*) that produces a remarkable fiber with both the adhesive characteristics of barnacle glue and the structural properties of spider silk. With modern technology, and nature as our guide, we can now create, on a nano scale, man-made materials with these and similar properties. "There is great interest, in biotechnological circles, in using [man-made] silk more extensively as an industrial material. Its lightness, flexibility and strength would make it widely deployable."[100] Add additional properties like a tolerance for salt water, and the possibilities become even greater.

Also based on natural models, glues are being developed that can be injected into broken bones to help them heal in only weeks.[101] Entire new bones can be created using additive technologies that build up nature-like internal structures. Scientists are now isolating the kinds of signaling proteins our bodies use to recruit different kinds of cells as those cells are required by the body, and artificially re-creating those proteins as needed. They are looking beneath the outside appearance of animals to see what they are capable of doing, and building robots with locomotion systems based on animals as diverse as shrews, octopuses, lizards, clams, and insects. "You do not need to look like an animal in order to behave like one"[102] says a researcher.

Biomimicry has even reached the human brain. Scientists are working to design computer processors and artificial intelligence algorithms that imitate the efficient way in which the brain does its processing. The human brain, for example, uses just 20 watts of power, while the Watson computer that won on *Jeopardy* consumes a whopping 85,000 watts. The scientists are not trying to "replicate" the brain. "That's impossible," says Dharmendra S. Modha, an IBM researcher. "We don't know how the brain works, really."[103] But researchers are trying to replicate what they believe are some of the ways the brain functions, and they are having some success. IBM has produced prototypes of what it calls "neurosynaptic microprocessors" or "neuromorphic chips," according to John E. Kelly of IBM, that do their work with a design drastically different from today's computers.[104] The creators base the chips on their observation that neurons—what they call the human brain's processors—are, in computing terms, massively distributed; there are billions in the human brain. They further observe that each neuron's processes are wrapped in its synapses (what they see as its data memory devices). This suggests to them that the brain's patterns of communication are extremely efficient and diverse. Their hope is that their attempts at biomimicry of the brain will lead to better processors, even though our knowledge of the brain is currently so limited that there may be things—electrical micro fields, for example—that the current generation of "neuromorphic" processers are not even taking into account.

Are these new generations of biomimetics brain gain? Probably, since our minds are gaining the ability to "copy" some of nature's most successful solutions, compressing millions of years of engineering into only a couple. Computers are rapidly improving at the sort of tasks that humans find effortless and that computers struggle with, such as the pattern recognition of seeing and identifying someone, walking down a crowded sidewalk without running into people, and learning from experience. This will hopefully lead to advances like "robots that can navigate a battlefield environment and be trained . . . and computerized healthcare monitors that watch over people in nursing homes and send alerts to human workers and for residence behavior suggests illness."[105]

Is there digital wisdom in biomimicry? Digital wisdom involves, I believe, adapting nature to us in ways that enhance, rather than destroy, our inherently human capabilities. As author and naturalist Diane Ackerman writes, "We may fantasize about possessing superhuman powers, but we are able to compensate. It's just that [we're now adapting] nature to us, instead of the other way round."[106]

BRAIN GAIN AND DIGITAL WISDOM FROM COMBINING MIND AND TECHNOLOGY TO INCREASE OUR "EXECUTIVE THINKING" (I.E., DECISION-MAKING) ABILITY

Are we wiser if we combine our minds with technology
to make faster decisions?

Speed cuts both ways—it can be both our friend or our enemy. While in the past there was often time for long reflection before making decisions (and in some cases there still is), both because of the electronic pace of our communications and, concurrently, the expectations that that engenders, a great many more of our decisions have become time-sensitive.

People who grew up in slower times often rebel against, or are uncomfortable with, the need and expectation for faster decisions and replies. ("My colleagues expect an email to be answered within hours," said Sherry Turkle, a professor and researcher at MIT and author of *Alone Together,* at a recent conference.[107]) But we have entered a new context and culture, and, just as when a person moves from Mexico to New York, time expectations are different. Because it expresses this truth so concisely, one of the great song titles of all time, in my opinion, is Jimmy Buffet's "Changes in Latitudes, Changes in Attitudes."[108] We perhaps need another Buffet song about the changing cultural expectations of the digital age.

We certainly need digital wisdom to make the best decisions in every speed-filled, high-pressured, twenty-first-century situation.

Daniel Kahneman, as I have discussed, posits two separate thinking systems, one faster and one slower. As both he and Malcolm Gladwell point out, fast thinking has its uses. Part of our brain is very adept at pulling together subtle cues from the environment and, often without conscious thought, reaching conclusions. Many of our "snap" judgments of people turn out to be correct. As we gain expertise, Kahneman believes, our thinking moves increasingly to our quicker more intuitive form of thinking (what he calls "System 1"), allowing us to make faster decisions.[109] Kahneman strongly recommends we use our slower, more deliberative way of thinking (what he calls "System 2") as a supplement to, and a check on, the fast part as often as possible.[110]

The problem, of course, is that a great many decisions in today's world are time-sensitive—often extremely so, exacerbated by the speed of our electronic communications. If we are to apply both types of thinking to our problems, digital wisdom requires speeding up our currently "slow-thinking" System 2, via a better symbiosis with technology. One way to do this, for example, is to use technology to set up, in advance, automated triggers for trading, or warfare, or other things that often happen too quickly for any deliberation at all. Particular types of events can automatically set off alarms and even shut systems down. We already do this for certain types of financial trading and in nuclear power plants. However, triggering school computers to set off a loud alarm siren whenever a student (or teacher) tries to do a "forbidden" search (as was done in the Chicago public school system) may not be digitally wise at all.

The U.S. military is very keen on augmenting, with technology, every commander's and warfighter's decision-making capability on the battlefield. One way they achieve this is by using technology to increase every warfighter's "situational awareness." Displays of information, with multiple screens, enhanced visualization techniques, and information overlays are employed where possible to allow decision makers to scan a great deal of information at once. Things that humans are particularly sensitive to, such as movement and color, are used as the most salient visual cues. New channels of information are added, in some cases, to indicate extreme urgency, such as when a recorded voice warns a pilot to "pull-up! pull-up!"

Is all this brain gain?

I believe that our use of technology to enhance and speed up our slower, more deliberative thought processes is an important form of brain gain.

Is doing so digitally wise?

I think this is something we need to keep a close watch on. We do not as yet have a definitive answer, and I suspect that answer will vary greatly by situation and individual. It would be quite helpful if, as part of our quest for digital wisdom, researchers studied this aspect of brain gain far more carefully in the future.

Are we wiser if we combine our minds with technology
to take more prudent risks?

Analyzing risk is something that humans have always attempted but have not always been good at: Icarus is an instructive example. Much ancient wisdom regarding risk was that it was, well, risky, and therefore best kept to a minimum. Taking risks could incur the wrath of the gods, as happened when Prometheus gave man fire. "Risk-taker" is still, in many circles, a pejorative term.

At the same time the concept of risk and reward being a tradeoff (colloquially expressed as "no pain, no gain") has also long been with us—taking "calculated" risks is often how generals won battles, particularly against overwhelming odds.

Assessing risk has always been a difficult job—something that wise individuals did from long experience. But the digital age has brought several new tools and capabilities to this area.

One is our growing—but far from perfect—ability to quantify risk, to give it a number. Assessing risk accurately is important: Take too little and you may leave things on the table; take too much and things can fall apart. Over time humans created tools for assessing risk, such as considering a person's income and debts before granting him or her a loan.

Computers and statistics enable far greater sophistication in using such tools. One approach is more advanced calculation. Rather than just calculate each individual borrower's assets, for example, one can compute, based on past data, the statistical probability of large groups repaying, compare the revenue gains and probable losses, and therefore compute how far on the "risk curve" it is profitable to lend. Combining the data from many institutions, agencies now assign individuals a "credit score," that is, a number that attempts to quantify, in relative terms, the risk of lending to them.

Another new capability is to "model" risk, and to use those models to manage it, moment to moment. With the advent of digital technology, risk management has become a highly technological venture. Companies have "chief risk officers" who rely, along with their associates, on complex computer models. Investment banks (and investors) often compete on the basis of their risk-modeling capabilities. Governments and militaries are constantly using models to assess and quantify their risks as well. The results of these are, typically, combined with human judgment to make decisions. (And as Nassim Taleb points out in *The Black Swan*, digital wisdom requires that the decision makers remain open to events that lie outside technology's statistical parameters.[111])

An additional new capability that technology has given humans to help them deal better with risk is simulation. Computer simulations create artificial but realistic risky situations, present them to people for decision making, and provide feedback in what is known as a learning loop. This way of learning about risk, that is, taking large numbers of risks in simulated environments and getting feedback, has become, to a large extent, the basis of contemporary computer and video games. Most of today's video games are based around large numbers of risk-return decisions of varying sophistication. Underneath their fancy graphics, the games are really just large computer models that provide rewards and penalties based on the risks players choose to take or not take, and on the judgments players make.

The thousands of hours that many people spend playing these games often pay off in improved risk-taking abilities, a conclusion documented in the book *Got Game: How the Gamer Generation Is Reshaping Business Forever*.[112] I once asked a young player age 10 or 12 what he thought he had gotten from playing video games. He didn't even need to think about it: "To move faster and to take better risks," he blurted out. Many observers, such as writer Steven Johnson *(Everything Bad Is Good For You)*,[113] think that playing so many of these games is leading to brain gain among humans in the area of risk-taking, and I agree.

The U.S. military agrees as well. They create and use more risk-based games and simulations than any other group. And they see the results of this risk-taking practice on the battlefield: When one group of soldiers was asked why their tank unit attacked in a certain way—with a highly risky move that paid off big—they replied, "We did it [before,] in simulation."[114]

Digital wisdom requires, I believe, thinking about and practicing risk-taking in these new, technology-based ways. Digital wisdom lies not just in taking more risks, but in taking more *prudent* risks, thereby increasing the probability of payoff. Another aspect of digital wisdom in this area lies in the increasingly sophisticated construction of models, in testing them against reality, and in training people in their use.

But the most digital wisdom comes—as in every case we have looked at—in how we combine the new technological capabilities we create with our human judgment. Overreliance on either models or humans provides more risk—and less digital wisdom—than the wise combination of the two.

Are we wiser if we combine our minds with technology
to base more decisions on evidence?

That a term such as "evidence-based medicine" even exists is, to me, both surprising and disconcerting. What it implies is that medicine, up until now, has been based less on continuous evaluation of all the current evidence and more on "received" wisdom, that is, what doctors were taught in school.

But it is not the doctors' fault. Up until only recently, much of the "evidence"—that is, the statistical analysis of current conditions, treatments, and results—was not available to them. There was published research, of course, which good doctors kept up to date on, but even the biggest, most sophisticated studies were limited in scope compared to all the existing patients in the world, and they represented conditions only at the time the studies were done.

Of course, much of this "best-practice-based" medicine works. The world, despite the terrible setbacks of AIDS and other conditions, is, on trend, getting healthier.[115] But there are many patients for whom the "gold standard" treatments of the past either don't work or are not the best option. As I observed earlier with the APACHE system, there are a great many instances in which statistical information is not only helpful but *required* for an optimal solution.

Large numbers of technological tools are now being produced to give doctors and other medical professionals access to the totality of the evidence relating to whatever decision they need to make, and to do it in as close to real time as possible. One of the most important is the current computerization of health records, which finally allows us to take information out of doctors' handwritten notes and to put it into databases—we are finally reaching the point where this is becoming, at least in much of America, a reality. The tools to analyze these millions of records and trillions of data points are, thanks to tools that were developed for national security being repurposed to medicine, advancing quickly as well.

Having these sophisticated analysis tools (along with the relevant data) in individual doctors' hands (and, increasingly, on devices they can carry around and ask questions of, as is the case at Yale medical school[116]) is definitely a form of brain gain.

Is it digital wisdom as well? The wisdom resides, as always, in the application of the technology—including that the data be accurate, appropriate, sufficient, and reliable, and that the analyses be appropriate and timely—and in the symbiosis of the technologically produced results with the doctors' judgment and experience. In the best of cases, this will lead to the digital wisdom of putting things together in new ways, such as when doctors use Google Health or Twitter to track the spread of disease and take preventive action.

The term "evidence-based" is also heard more and more these days in conversations about education. But the brain gain from introducing statistical analyses into school data has been far less helpful, I believe, than in medicine, because much digital wisdom is missing in doing it. Unlike medicine, where all the data is appropriate and relevant, the data currently being collected and analyzed in education—which consists almost entirely of test scores—is often *inappropriate* to our real educational needs. And, in what can only be described as a deliberate rejection of digital wisdom, this incomplete (in terms of the overall educational picture) data is often used to supplant, rather than complement, the human judgment of educators.

Are we wiser if we combine our minds with technology to encourage and increase entrepreneurship?

More and more educators and business people are coming to the realization that new skills are needed for the twenty-first century. In particular, entrepreneurship—the ability to start and run a successful business—will likely be a key skill and factor in many of our young people's future success. Additionally, as more and more of our traditional jobs shrink or disappear, many individuals who in the past would have been content to remain salaried "working people" are becoming interested in running their own businesses.

Entrepreneurship is not an easy skill to master—most new businesses fail within a year or two of getting started. Can technology provide brain gain that helps improve these odds? Is entrepreneurship a skill that resides purely in the human mind, or can technology partner with humans to help develop it? There are indications that it can.

Technology is now playing a bigger and bigger role in entrepreneurship in a variety of ways. These include (but are certainly not limited to) using technology for raising capital, creating and sharing tools for running businesses, creating databases of good practices, rapid prototyping of products, creating business models, and many other things.

We have already explored some of the new ways technology is being used to raise capital when we looked at the brain gain and digital wisdom of new business models. The fact that any potential entrepreneur can now post an idea and, if it finds supporters, quickly raise capital (often in unexpected amounts) is, if not technology-based brain gain, at least a tremendous head start. More brain gain in entrepreneurship comes from the kinds of connections and information the Internet now provides—the ability to gather all this information in one place is crucial to starting businesses successfully and helping them grow. One of the reasons that startups in Silicon Valley are so successful is the vast reservoir of knowledge and advice that is available to those who work there. Today much of this advice is now available online to those considering entrepreneurial ventures—how to write a business plan, what to do, and what to watch out for—often industry by industry.

Brain gain in entrepreneurship also comes in the form of technical tools, many of which are free. Budding business owners can use Google analytics to measure the traffic to any web site they set up. Technology now allows them to accept micropayments—they can even add a credit card reader to their phone. They can download databases of business leads and use software tools like salesforce.com to manage their customers. Software entrepreneurs can also benefit from a host of new development tools, such as rapid prototyping tools and methodologies. Because of technology, starting a business successfully has become easier than ever.

And where is the digital wisdom in entrepreneurship? It lies, to a large extent, in knowing about these tools and using them well. This is what is now taught in the many new entrepreneurship classes and programs starting up around the United States and the world. For example, students at the Harvard Business School are now required to start a business as part of the first-year program, something that in my time at Harvard was considered "trivial" and "beside the point" for future "captains of industry."

No matter what kind of business a person wants to start, his or her chances of success will be increased many fold by either learning to use these technology tools themselves, or by hooking up with someone—often much younger—who is adept at using them. It is the combination of the traditional human entrepreneurial drive (the so-called "fire in the belly") with sophisticated modern technological tools that today very often leads to business success.

Are we wiser if we combine our minds with technology to access alternate perspectives?

You have no doubt encountered the optical illusion whereby you can either see in a single image an old hag or a young lady, or a cup or two faces, but you cannot see both images at once. Our limited capacity to see and incorporate multiple perspectives at the same time has always been one of the barriers to successful decision making. It is hard to see (and live with) someone as both an enemy and a friend, or as both a competitor and a supplier.

Increasing humans' ability to simultaneously keep multiple perspectives in view and balance them would be a form of brain gain. The recent entry into our vocabulary of terms such as "frenemy" and "copetition" indicates that this might be getting easier for some (or at least becoming a goal). Technology can contribute toward building and strengthening this increasingly useful human capability.

Computer modeling, for example, is a technology that allows multiple scenarios and multiple changes in assumptions to be made and evaluated, often side by side. In addition, modeling and game technologies allow decision makers to play out scenarios with real people to gauge real-world perspectives and reactions. The U.S. military has used massive multiplayer games to see whether new perspectives and tactics emerge for friendlies and enemies in real time as the games are being played. These games improve upon something the military has long done, often known as "red-teaming," that is, having some of its own members role-play the enemy (the "red" team) and see the world from its perspective, while fighting against our own forces (the "blue" team). Warfighting games created from different perspectives (such as from the perspective of Arab or Palestinian fighters) are used by both military and civilians to see the world differently.

There is digital wisdom in decision makers' use of as many of these modeling techniques as possible. Doing this enables them to see the situation—and the potential results of their decisions—in a much broader way before actually making a decision and acting.

Are we wiser if we combine our minds with technology to have better judgment?

Having good judgment, in the opinion of many, lies at the core of what it means to be wise. Yet good judgment, as the saying goes, comes from experience, and experience comes from bad judgment. What this means is that developing a level of judgment that most would consider "good," in whatever situation, requires a great deal of experience and feedback. Can technology help in this process? Actually, it can.

Providing large quantities of experience and feedback—at least simulated experience—is something that technology is extremely good at doing. Simulators can hold a limitless number of real examples in their database, incorporate new ones on an ongoing basis, and present them to users in useful order, based on the users' reactions, strengths, and weaknesses. Think of the airline simulator. Most pilots will (thankfully) never encounter in their real flying the extreme conditions that they face in the simulators, and there would be no way, in a real plane, for them to learn about and practice dealing with such emergencies. Yet the simulator can replicate them all, over and over in different contexts, with great fidelity and precision.

Such simulators produce brain gain in several ways. Obviously, they extend the experience of the pilots to situations, such as wind shear or water landings, that they may not have experienced in actual flying. But just as powerfully, they extend the minds of the individuals training the pilot. Those people, whose job it is to present the pilots with unexpected challenges that test their capabilities, can, at the push of a button, select particular situations and conditions for the pilot, and change them on they fly. The simulator, by itself, is not the digitally wise experience—it is the combination of the simulator and the instructor that provides this.

Since the early days of digital technology, both military and business instructors and trainers have been putting together a huge number of technology-based simulations, in a wide variety of areas where success requires development of the good judgment that comes from a great deal of experience. What these simulations allow people to do, in the words of one military expert, is to compress what used to be a career's worth of experiences into a very short amount of time.[117] Unlike some educators, who are just getting used to the ideas of using simulation, the military is far beyond the point of just studying this. They feel they already have ample evidence that it works. "We don't understand the educators who call for 'more studies,'" says one Pentagon official. "We know it works. We just want to get on with using it."[118]

Role-playing has, of course, always been a way of extending people's minds, and it doesn't necessarily require outside technology. Making lots of judgments while playing the role of the decision maker in real-life historical business situations is the principle behind the famous "case-study method" used at Harvard Business School and many other places. It is now the preferred learning method in many medical schools.

But the use of technology extends and enhances human minds greatly in this area. For one thing, by putting the cases online, it allows the case-study methodology to be used far more widely than in just elite university classrooms. Simulators are being incorporated into more and more classrooms, industries, and jobs. In some cases, the simulators are stand-alone, but in the best cases there is still a real instructor testing the user's capabilities to their limits. Whenever the pilot in an airline simulator begins to feel comfortable, the instructor adds new problems—like wind shear, or another plane close by—unexpected but plausible examples that the pilot might some day experience (and will be better prepared for).

Is the use of such simulators brain gain? Most would say yes. For millennia military and other leaders have been using the non-technological predecessors of these simulators (such as sand tables) to increase their brain power. Technology now provides immensely more powerful ways to build and use these tools, in almost every field and job.

Where is the digital wisdom in such tools?

Part of it lies in building models that faithfully reproduce the effects of real life. This is much more easily done with simulators for machines, like airplanes or cars, than with people simulators. The human mind and human behaviors are still far too complicated and difficult to predict to allow anything but crude simulations of human behavior (although some of these, as we saw previously with Bruce Bueno de Mesquita and others, can be remarkably accurate under the right conditions).

Part of the digital wisdom in designing simulators includes looking for situations and solutions that may run counter to natural instincts. For example, there are some flying situations in which a pilot's instinct is to pull up, but the right thing to do is to point the plane's nose further down, in order to provide more lift. There are interpersonal situations as well where the right thing to do is to overcome one's natural instincts to fight, say, or to run. Digital wisdom comes in recognizing and highlighting such counter-intuitive situations and in getting users to practice them so many times that the mind will override the body's instincts in the actual emergency. One of the lessons the military learned from World War II is that a large percentage of the (conscripted) infantry *never* fired their rifles in battle, because they couldn't overcome their natural instincts not to kill, even when it was required. Doing so, when appropriate, is now a part of combat training.

Digital wisdom also consists of understanding that some situations fall outside the parameters of what has been modeled, and therefore not trusting any simulator technology completely. Only recently some airplane designers mistakenly assumed that because they never lost their plane's tail under extreme conditions in the simulator, it couldn't happen in real flying—until it did, with deadly results.[119] Such hard-to-forsee events are what Nassim Taleb calls "Black Swans." Digital wisdom requires including their possibility in our planning.[120] As always, it is the human-machine combination that provides the digitally wisest solution.

BRAIN GAIN AND DIGITAL WISDOM FROM COMBINING MIND AND TECHNOLOGY TO INCREASE OUR CREATIVITY

Are we wiser if we combine our minds with technology
to create better music and art?

"Creating a work of art," writes Lev Grossman in *Time* magazine, "is one of those activities we reserve for humans, and humans only. It's an act of self-expression. You're not supposed to be able to do it if you don't have a self."[121] This is, I believe, a widely held opinion. Yet technology is making big inroads into creating new music and art.

Although some may prefer to think of the domains of artistic creativity—music, art, and literature—as the unique province of the unenhanced human mind, creators in those domains have always maintained an intensely symbiotic relationship with technology. As just one obvious example, the materials and tools technologically available to an artist at the time a work is produced are typically very much a part of his or her artistic creation.

But with today's technology, the parameters of that artist-technology symbiosis are now shifting drastically. Today technology can do more and more of the actual "creation" (in the sense of imagination) of works of art—writing and composing music, writing, and images. If technology cannot yet create finished masterpieces, it can certainly provide helpful inspiration and parts.

In 1965, very early in his career, engineer Ray Kurzweil appeared on the TV show "I've Got a Secret," playing the piano. His "secret" was that the piece he played had been composed by a computer, something novel at the time. Today computers can do this easily—and, by analyzing what intervals, harmonies, and kinds of melodies composers favor, create original music in the styles of individual composers, living and dead, without the composer's intervening at all. Machines can compose, even on your own computer or smart phone, original pieces in any style. Stephen Wolfram (whom we heard about previously for his Wolfram Alpha analytical software) has also created a program known as WolframTones, which composes original music with parameters (length, style, instrumentation, scale, etc.) chosen by you. WolframTones works by "taking simple programs from Wolfram's computational universe, and using music theory and *Mathematica* algorithms to render them as music. Each program in effect defines a virtual world, with its own special story—and WolframTones captures it as a musical composition." It is, as one writer put it, "beautiful music created by algorithms."[122] "The nice thing about WolframTones is you don't have to be a computer science graduate to appreciate the beauty of composing melodies based on computational processes," says this reviewer. "The user interface is fun and easy, and the WolframTones magic really shines when you add more variations to your creation. Another great perk this experiment offers is a free download of your music creation which can be applied as a ringtone."[123] But is this art? Try it at tones.wolfram.com and judge for yourself.

Art or not, is it brain gain?

I think we'd get a lot of dispute as to whether it is either art or brain gain. But, according to Wolfram, many professional composers use the computer-generated pieces from WolframTones as inspiration. So for their brains, at least, it is gain.

A different kind of musical brain gain is coming—at last—from a technology that I have personally been waiting for for years: the midi voice controller. This technology lets any person (you, for example, or me!) express, with whatever naturally given voice we have or don't have, the musical ideas in our head by humming into a microphone. The computer then corrects pitches and enhances our voice, turning it, if we wish, into any instrument. Even though I was a professional guitarist earlier in my life, I have always dreamed up in my head all sorts of melodies and accompaniments that I lacked the "chops" (i.e., technique) to play. The controller, though, provides a direct connection between my thoughts and their expression. For me, at least, this is true brain gain.

Many other programs, such as the WI Orchestra app on the iPhone and iPad, can provide similar abilities for non-players to perform on what sounds like instruments using physical gestures. I will always remember a beautiful, soulful, cello solo played by media teacher Marco Torres on the iPad during a lecture.

But is this digital wisdom?

An interesting question. To me, the ability to express my deepest emotions is a kind of wisdom, and the inspiration of other composers might add to their wisdom as well. But this is certainly debatable.

Visual artists' brains can be enhanced as well by modern technology, leading them to new ways of seeing the world. Some of these new enhancements are tools and media for artistic expression—artists have been using video for some time now, and many more use computers to generate their images.

One interesting direction is what is known as "procedural art." In this technique, the artist creates by using computer algorithms (i.e., equations and programs) to generate visual images on the computer—without the artist's ever taking a brush, pen, or even stylus to hand. Images generated in this way can be quite stunning: You may have seen some of the beautiful, abstract images generated algorithmically by so-called "fractal" algorithms. But the images generated by algorithms can also be quite realistic and life-like, generating, for example, realistic-looking grass, trees, and clouds. While Disney's professional animators used to draw all their backgrounds and characters by hand—cell by cell—today's high-end animation houses, such as Pixar, do it increasingly with equations (although sketches may still be used at first).

Is this art? Again, the jury is still out. But more and more people are accepting computer-generated images, still or moving, into that realm.

Is it brain gain? The ability to see "art" in sets of numbers and equations (similar, perhaps, to the way a sculptor might see a statue inside a solid block of marble) is a particular gift, and nurturing that gift leads, I believe, to a kind of brain gain. "When you can use technology like a paintbrush," says Peter Semmelhack, the founder of Bug Labs, "we'll see artists invent new ways to use these tools."[124]Artist and TV show host Jason Silva makes the interesting point that "technology increasingly shrinks the lag time between what we can imagine and what we can create in the real world."[125]

It is digitally wise to create art in this way (i.e., by combining the mind with technology)? In the end, there may be no other way to do it. Technology (old or new) is what gives artistic ideas expression and allows them to be shared.

Are we wiser if we combine our minds with technology to innovate better?

Innovation has become, in our times, a very hot topic. Everybody seems to want to get better at it. Some see it as the only lasting competitive advantage among companies, and even nations.

Does the combination of minds and technology help us become more innovative? I would argue yes, because technology (i.e., things that people have already creatively innovated) helps, in a virtuous cycle, spur innovation ever faster. Technology helps the human mind innovate by providing a base to innovate upon (i.e., providing databases of building blocks and prior art), as well as by offering new data, providing useful creation and innovation tools, helping evaluate and choose among alternatives, providing needed capital, enabling research and development, and protecting and incubating nascent ideas.

First the base. One of the toughest things about innovating these days is that so many are trying to do it. The "technium," Kevin Kelly's name for the entire human-created technological universe in his book *What Technology Wants*, is expanding so rapidly and exponentially, and knowledge about what is going on is now so easily and widely shared via the Internet that the same innovative ideas often occur to several people, independently, at once. This is not totally new—many of our greatest technological innovations, from radio to TV to electricity, were made independently by more than one person, with only quirks of fate, such as who got to the patent office first, determining the innovator we remember. The same is true even in intellectual innovation—Charles Darwin was not the only person to figure out natural selection, only the first to publish. That said, this process has now greatly intensified. Innovation typically stands on the shoulders of previous work, that is, innovations in both ideas and technology, and the more we have access to the world's ideas and technology, the more innovation we are likely to see.

This is particularly true of what are known as technology "platforms": hardware and software on which others can build. Each of our modern technological platforms, from the multipurpose computer, to Microsoft Windows and the Apple graphical interface, to the world wide web and Facebook (to name only a few), unleashed huge waves of innovation from people who saw those platforms, rightly, as a way to more easily get their ideas out. This has always been part of the function of "infrastructure," but today's technological platforms are so much more versatile than the infrastructures of the past that the innovations they enable are orders of magnitude greater.

The data to innovate with, and around, are also increasing exponentially. There is an immense data surge in business today coming from increasingly detailed computer tracking of shipments, sales, suppliers, and customers, as well as email, web traffic, and social network comments. The quantity of business data now doubles every 1.2 years, by one estimate, and that is bound to shorten.[126] According to a study from the McKinsey Global Institute entitled "Big Data: The Next Frontier for Innovation, Competition and Productivity," creating new ways to analyze this enormous amount of data will be a big source of company innovation over the next decade.[127]

Tools for analyzing this data and for other types of innovation are also improving, often at an ever faster pace. Most of these tools are easily accessible, and many, because of their government-sponsored origins, are in the public domain. One of the most well-known tools for dealing with large data sets is Apache's Hadoop,[128] a spinoff from early work at Google. IBM, Oracle, and others offer proprietary tools.[129]

Software tools also exist for managing the innovation process: that is, creating an idea pipeline and picking the most promising ideas, and setting up rating and review engines, prediction markets, and methods for taking innovations to market, "separating the gold from the gravel" as one innovation tool supplier puts it.[130]

Technology has also combined with human minds to produce new innovation patterns and culture, of which California's Silicon Valley is the best known and most successful. "The business of the Valley today is less about focusing on a particular industry than it is about a continuous process of innovation with technology, across a widening swath of fields," writes Steve Lohr in *The New York Times*.[131] "The newer model for starting businesses relies on hypothesis, experiment, and testing in the marketplace, from the day a company is founded. That is a sharp break with the traditional approach of drawing up a business plan, setting financial targets, building a finished product, and then rolling out the business and hoping to succeed. It was time-consuming and costly. The trend reflects the steady march of that most protean of technologies—computing—as it makes further inroads into every scientific discipline and industry. Clean technology, bioengineering, medical diagnostics, preventive health care, transportation, and even agriculture are part of the mix these days for the Valley's technologists and entrepreneurs."[132]

The preferred formula today, says Lohr, is often called the "lean start-up." The approach emphasizes quickly developing "minimum viable products," low-cost versions that are shown to customers for reaction and then improved. Flexibility is the process's other hallmark: test business models and ideas, then ruthlessly cull failures and move on to Plan B, Plan C, Plan D, and so on— quickly "pivoting," as the process is known.

Is all this brain gain? It is almost certain that all these new tools, combined with the kind of innovation culture that is now establishing itself in Silicon Valley, is causing brain gain among the innovators and entrepreneurs there and elsewhere in the world.

Is it digital wisdom?

In general, I think it is. The more people are exposed to this culture, the more excited they become, and the more innovation increases. Issues about digital wisdom arise, however, around what particular innovations are (some may be digitally wiser than others) and the extent to which the process, while making some innovators wildly successful, may hurt others. Digital wisdom is also needed, I think, in deciding who should benefit from all this innovation. Is it just the innovators, just the already wealthy (like the venture capitalists), or should it be society in general? Should the most successful innovations in some areas be appropriated—in a process similar to eminent domain—into public ownership (as we already do with important military innovations) or into the public domain? Does the answer to those questions differ for particular fields such as education or civics? The increased innovation arising from the combination of human minds and technology leaves us many important questions to ponder.

Are we wiser if we combine our minds with technology to design and play better games?

Games have been played by humans for millennia, if not all of history. They are, according to some, nature's preferred way to teach and learn, providing engagement, goal-seeking behavior, and instant feedback. "How do cats learn to hunt?" is the way one game developer puts this.[133]

Today games have been integrated with technology to an extraordinary extent. At one time computer and video game makers imported technologies from other fields; now it is often technologies invented by the game industry—such as some types of chips and artificial intelligence—that are used by other fields, even by the military. Technology-based game development has proceeded in two overall directions. On the one hand, game companies have produced a (relatively) small number of extremely complex games, like Civilization, Call of Duty, The Sims, or World of Warcraft, that require enormous skill and can take years to master. On the other hand, game developers have produced thousands and thousands of "mini-games," such as Bejeweled or Angry Birds, that are limited to one particular type of gameplay or skill. As both of those types of electronic games have matured, games have also begun entering a new stage—often referred to by labels such as "serious gaming" and "gamification"—that is less concerned with entertainment and more with using gaming for real-world results. Many game players and designers, now entering adulthood, are trying to apply their hard-earned knowledge and skills to create games that will positively impact the world, motivating players to do "good" things, both while playing the games and because of them. Game technologies—honed over the last several decades to provide engagement, learning, and feedback and to motivate players to continuously struggle to win—are being pressed into new causes: social change, business results, health care, and education. This new phase has not yet replaced (or even seriously dented) entertainment games, but it aspires to.

The case has now been effectively made that game technologies can produce a great deal of learning and positive effects. (I discuss this more in Chapter 6.) Yet the results of the serious games movement so far have been mixed, despite a lot of hype from the games' makers, and despite strong cases for games' worth being made by people like James Paul Gee (*What Videogames Have to Teach Us about Learning and Literacy*) and Jane McGonigal (*Reality Is Broken*). Recently even the U.S. government has gotten into the act, with one office of the Department of Education trying to spur what it calls a "national conversation" about the value of games for learning.

The problem, though, is the games themselves—few of the serious games produced so far live up to the hype. To a large extent, this is because designing a "great" serious game is extremely hard—these games require not only all the many difficult elements that go into a great entertainment game, but must adhere to and communicate the "serious" content as well. The only "serious" (if you want to call it that) game that has so far had success with millions of users is America's Army, a military recruiting game designed to teach players about army life and warfare. America's Army is currently played by tens of millions around the world. But very few other games have even broken the one million mark in terms of users. (A hit entertainment game franchise can sell more than 100 million copies.[133]) Still, many more people, some with great experience, are now trying to change this and produce effective "serious" games millions want to play.

Is the application of game technology to business and society issues brain gain? I would argue yes, because it increases both skills and motivation.

Is it digitally wise to introduce games in more "serious" contexts? I believe it is as well, as there is much to be gained, and most of the objections raised to doing so are based on either old information (e.g., games are solitary pursuits) or claims that have been proved false (like all games lead to addiction, or violent games have major long-term negative effects). Still, while games are an important way many of today's young (and increasingly older) people learn, do things, and get motivation, they are not the only way. Digital wisdom requires not denying games a place at the table, but also creating really good games and figuring out when and where they do the most good.

Are we wiser if we combine our minds with technology to make better creation tools?

Creativity often takes off when people are given new tools to create with—think of oil paints or electric guitars. Our twenty-first-century technology is providing us with new, powerful tools in enormous quantities. We have already considered the many new platforms that are being developed for software innovation. Now let us look at some more physical tools.

Among the most promising of these is a technology known as additive manufacturing, or 3-D printing. Because it has been difficult in the past for creators to produce new, complex objects, both large and small, in three dimensions (despite being able to visualize them in their minds), creating such objects has often posed difficulties for designers. Such creation long remained the province of highly trained sculptors, architects, and engineers. But a number of technology developments have changed this. Technologists developed 3-D modeling software (computer-aided design [CAD] software) capable of designing and rendering, in three dimensions, any object from a cell to an airplane. These tools, which originally cost tens of thousands of dollars per user, quickly came down to only thousands and even hundreds of dollars. They extend 3-D design capabilities to anyone who can master the complex software, even college and high school students. By incorporating game-like interfaces, the use of these software tools has become much easier and more widespread.

But what technology now provides as well is the ability to output electronic data from the software specifying precisely how the three-dimensional product, or object, should look. This type of computer output had previously been applied to control machines, in a process called computer-aided manufacturing (CAM). Today, with this control, machines can easily produce any designer's ideas physically, in three dimensions.

Industrial model creation (and three-dimensional art creation) has been, in the past, mostly done subtractively, that is, the way a sculptor in stone does it, starting with a solid block and cutting away the unwanted parts. The sculpture, or model, is physically "liberated" from the solid material. (Michelangelo's "Awakening Slave" and "Atlas" sculptures, in which he leaves part of the original block intact as the figures emerge, artfully highlight this "liberating" subtractive process.) Doing subtractive manufacturing industrially, however, can be very wasteful. In some cases, in order to subtractively produce parts they need, manufacturers must throw away as much as 80 percent of expensive materials like titanium.

The technology that solves this problem is known as "additive," or 3-D, printing and manufacturing. In 3-D printing machines, the output from 3-D CAD software is used by the CAM (i.e., printing) machine to build up a product by depositing tiny layer by tiny layer of material just, and only, where it is needed. The technology is enormously flexible and can produce an infinite variety of complex shapes. (This is similar to what a sculptor in clay does, but in far more detail. In some cases the layers of built-up material are as little as one atom thick.[135])

Today 3-D printers are used by almost all professional designers to create and evaluate prototypes, and to see and feel many of their ideas as three-dimensional objects. 3-D printing is used for designing everything from cell phones, to cars, to medical instruments, to airplane parts. As is usual with technology, the prices for these machines have come down steeply, even as their quality has vastly improved. In fact, 3-D printers are now available to students in many K–12 schools and even to hobbyists at home. In manufacturing, 3-D printing has taken off rapidly. Although traditional manufacturing techniques remain, for now, the most cost-effective way to produce parts or products in very large quantities, for creating small quantities or customized and "one-off" products, additive manufacturing is increasingly the preferred process. In coming years, it is likely that more and more of the products we use will be printed (i.e., built up in a machine layer by layer) rather than manufactured subtractively. In a 2011 demonstration that made the cover of *The Economist* magazine, engineers designed and 3-D printed all the parts of a violin, which they then assembled—the instrument played well.[136] This means that we can now send physical products, such as violin (or airplane) parts over the Internet—as just data—to be printed out at the receiving end. Think of how this will change the replacement parts business!

Still another great advantage of 3-D printing is that it can produce forms that human minds can readily imagine, but that traditional manufacturing techniques cannot produce, either easily or at all. This is liberating designers' creativity in many fields. Buildings, such as those of Frank Gehry, take on fantastical shapes.[137] Even clothing is now printed in 3-D, producing fanciful designer creations.[138] 3-D printing output has been incorporated into games like Will Wright's Spore, enabling players to print out as 3-D models the fantastic creatures that they create.

Perhaps even more interesting—and certainly more useful than models—is the 3-D printing of replacement human body parts, such as artificial muscles.[139] Replacement blood vessels and skin are now being printed as well.

An interesting technology tool for creation recently developed and released is the low-cost, low-power, microcontroller board known as "Arduino." As described by its web site, Arduino is "an open-source electronics prototyping platform based on flexible, easy-to-use hardware and software. It's intended for artists, designers, hobbyists, and anyone interested in creating interactive objects or environments."[140] Arduino can sense the environment by receiving input from a variety of sensors and can affect its surroundings by controlling lights, motors, and other actuators. The microcontroller on the board is programmed using the Arduino's own programming language and development environment. Arduino boards can be built by hand or purchased preassembled; the software can be downloaded for free. Arduino projects can communicate with other software, such as Flash, running on a separate computer. The hardware reference designs (CAD files) are available under an open source license, so people are free to adapt them to their needs.

The Arduino controller allows amateurs in many fields to electronically control, quickly and inexpensively, a wide variety of displays and devices. Among the first to put Arduino to use were museum curators, who used it to build interactive electronic exhibits.

A somewhat similar creative tool, but this time aimed directly at students, is Lego Mindstorms.[141] This commercially available "toy," which can be used by some kids as early as kindergarten, is an excellent preparatory tool both for using Arduino and for building "real" robots as well. The Mindstorms kits contain Lego parts, a microcontroller brick (similar to Arduino, but simpler) and various sensors. Mindstorms grew out of MIT professor Seymour Papert's work with children and the Logo computer language he invented for them to learn to program. The microcontroller block at the heart of the kits can be integrated by people of almost all ages into a wide variety of robots by adding the sensors, servo feedback motors, and external parts.

And to all of this we can add the many new tools available to amateurs for working and doing research in scientific fields like gene sequencing, neuroscience, drug development, and astronomy.

Is all of this brain gain? I would certainly think so. When ordinary people, without a lot of money or fancy degrees or labs, can, because of the technology tools now available to them, do cutting-edge design, creation, and research, one would have to say that their brains have been enhanced. Creating new objects and designs is also a form of brain gain. Putting technologically printed body parts, such as muscles, to use in new ways thought up by inventors and doctors is, I believe, a particularly good example of brain gain.

Is all this digitally wise? Why would we *not* give people these tools? It would almost certainly be digitally unwise not to do so. Of course it is digitally wise as well for us to monitor in some way the uses to which these tools are put, and their output, to be sure that no harm is done. But compared to the gains for both humanity and individuals, the risks of these tools, I believe, are infinitesimal.

Are we wiser if we combine our minds with technology to connect more ideas?

One of the key technologies fueling the suddenly enhanced dissemination and sharing of creative ideas of the Enlightenment, claims author Steven Johnson in *Where Good Ideas Come From,* was coffee. That is, coffee was consumed in eighteenth-century coffeehouses where people, amped up by the caffeine, frequently met and talked, connecting their individual ideas. Connecting ideas is important, because few of them—as good as they may be—change the world on their own. It is a process of adding, subtracting, refining, and building up ideas that eventually produces what becomes a world-changing proposition.

Digital technology is enhancing human abilities in the area of idea connection rapidly and fundamentally. Once books, previously each separate, are scanned and in a database, they can be searched, compared, and analyzed together. Verbal comments and exchanges, once ephemeral, can be videotaped and shared online. Search and other linking software is becoming much better at understanding ideas rather than just words, and in finding examples of connections in various places. So, by using technology to supplement human efforts, common ideas and threads can be found, and new connections are made much more easily.

Connecting ideas via available technology is not, itself, a new idea: People have long invented technologies for connecting ideas they come across. One that has been written about by several authors is the "commonplace book," a small blank personal notebook into which people in earlier centuries copied by hand passages of interest to them as they found them, using a simple indexing system. Writer William Powers refers to this early technology, metaphorically, as "Hamlet's BlackBerry."

Today, of course, there is no longer a need to copy passages by hand into a book—they can be cut and pasted into software, and ideas can be added by voice and video as well. Software programs allow people to search for and easily retrieve such connections between the many thoughts on passages they have recorded over time. One is Devon Think, for Apple computers, which writer Steven Johnson reports using to write many of his books.

The greatest promise for connecting ideas may be the "semantic web," which I discussed previously. Although complex to implement (it requires a great deal of scanning and tagging of text), the semantic web will hopefully be up and functional in your lifetime, and it will certainly be there in your children's lifetime.

Is this brain gain? The ability to connect ideas has always been considered a "brain" activity, and the ability to do more of this, faster, has to therefore be brain gain.

Is it digitally wise? It is hard to imagine how connecting ideas better would *not* be wise. But there will doubtless be a need for digital wisdom in figuring out how we do it and who has access.

BRAIN GAIN AND DIGITAL WISDOM FROM COMBINING MIND AND TECHNOLOGY TO INVOLVE OUR WHOLE PLANET

Are we wiser if we combine our minds with technology
to combine the minds of many people?
Suppose we could connect the minds of the smartest people on the planet? Of course now, with the Internet, in some sense we can. Is this brain gain? Does that make us collectively smarter? Does it make us digitally wiser? Clearly, the answers depend on how we use these capabilities.

One group very interested in the answer to the question of whether crowds can produce wisdom—or even just better answers—is the U.S. intelligence community. It is currently sponsoring, through the Intelligence Advanced Research Project Activity (IARPA), a number of technical attempts to extract wisdom from large, random samples of people. The program sponsoring this research is the Aggregative Contingent Estimation (ACE) Program. Here is how the IARPA web site expresses the aims of the program:

> Intelligence analysts are often asked to forecast significant events on the basis of limited quantitative data. It is common for such events to be contingent upon earlier events or actions. Generally, forecasts are prepared using expert judgment by individuals and small groups. Empirical research outside the intelligence community has shown that the accuracy of judgment-based forecasts is consistently improved by mathematically aggregating many independent judgments. The goal of the ACE Program is to dramatically enhance the accuracy, precision, and timeliness of forecasts for a broad range of event types, through the development of advanced techniques that elicit, weight, and combine the judgments of many intelligence analysts. The ACE Program seeks technical innovations in the following areas:
>
> - Efficient elicitation of probabilistic judgments, including conditional probabilities for contingent events.
> - Mathematical aggregation of judgments by many individuals, based on factors that may include past performance, expertise, cognitive style, metaknowledge, and other attributes predictive of accuracy.
> - Effective representation of aggregated probabilistic forecasts and their distributions.
>
> The ACE Program will build upon technical achievements of past research and on state-of-the-art systems used today for generating probabilistic forecasts from widely-dispersed individuals. The program will involve empirical testing of forecasting accuracy against real events.[142]

The first ACE contracts have been awarded, but as of this writing, no results have been made public. Stay tuned.

Assuming this works, is it brain gain? Absolutely. Already, the number of brains accessible before making a decision (even about whether to read a book) has gone up exponentially.

Is it digitally wise? There is no doubt that this makes us wiser in some ways. Researching a potential hire on the Internet is a wise thing to do. Angie's List lets us do this for contractors. We no longer have to bring people together from all over the United States or the globe to do a Manhattan-type project (except, possibly, in order to maintain secrecy). Today the people can all collaborate, with varying levels of security, online.

The big danger, though, is that the "crowds" that we access may turn out to be, in fact, self-selected, and therefore biased. It is very easy to be influenced only by those who have made the effort to put something online and to ignore the equally valid positions of those who didn't.

At a time of easy crowd access, the digital wisdom may lie in a combination of being sure one's own opinion is fully expressed (online or off), remaining vigilant about biased influence, and working to prevent undue influence by making as transparent as possible who and where online thoughts and opinions are from.

Are we wiser if we combine our minds with technology to solve problems collaboratively, and do collaborative improvement?

There are problems in the world—such as how to deal with climate change or nuclear waste, for example—that are just too hard for any individual to solve on his or her own. Such problems exist not just in the sciences, but also in mathematics, the social areas, and even in practical situations such as how to prepare our children for the future. Many of these very-hard-to-solve problems revolve around the best ways to cope with our new and changing world context. These types of problems cry out for new tools, one of the most powerful of which is collaboration.

Large-scale collaboration at the world level is relatively new, and we are still learning how to do it. Much of our collaboration in the past happened either at the tops of hierarchies—heads of state collaborated, elected representatives collaborated—or at the "few individuals working together locally (or at longer distances via letters)" level. Today vastly more opportunities for collaboration are open to us. Today if we put our minds to it, we could easily gather—probably on very short notice, using forums, listservs, Facebook, Google Plus groups, and other tools—all the specialists, all those who are interested in, and all those who want to learn about *any* topic in the world, or any issue or problem.

We have already begun to do this in some ways. Among the great success stories of the Internet so far are Wikipedia, how-to videos, and open source software. What they all show is that a great many knowledgeable people are willing to contribute to collective efforts, not because they are paid but just to make the result better. Better for themselves, of course, but also for others.

Wikipedia now has almost four million articles in English and more than 10,000 articles in more than 100 languages. There are dozens of how-to video sites with millions of videos. Open source software exists in almost every domain as a free alternative to commercial software, and it has even gone commercial: IBM now sells a version of the open source Linux software that runs much of the world's computers. The open source Android smart phone operating system from Google now runs more than 40 percent of the smartphones in the world.[143]

Is this brain gain? Absolutely. Big problems have already been solved in this new collaborative way. Very hard mathematical problems have been solved by the collaborative Polymath project on mathematician Tim Gower's web site.[144] Difficult protein-folding problems have been solved by people using the online Fold-it program. World scientists have collaborated to produce what is called the HapMap (short for haplotype map), completed in 2007, which charts how and where different human beings can differ in their genetic code.[145] Enormous data sets, such as the data collected in the search for extra-terrestrial intelligence (SETI), could not be analyzed in any other way than collaboratively (through parts being distributed to many individuals' computers). More than 200,000 amateur astronomers are currently collaborating on the web site Galaxy Zoo to help astronomers classify galaxy images taken by a robotic telescope, and they have made several new discoveries.[146] Even better, most of this information is freely shared by scientists and citizens alike.

Everyone is better off having potential access to free information on all topics—especially current ones—information that is compiled by the collective contributions of many interested people, and that can be accessed by anyone from a pocket device or from publicly available computers. Another way this leads to potential gain is that our children are now having to learn to evaluate information for themselves, rather than just trusting an editor or source, as in the past.

Is this kind of collaboration digitally wise? I believe so. In fact, the more we harness this collective and collaborative energy in the world for positive uses, the better off we are.

But humans are just learning how to take advantage of this enormously powerful collaborative capability and to understand how to collaborate well. Digital wisdom lies in our learning how to do this most effectively, and in teaching all our children to do so. Digital wisdom includes teaching and learning the collaboration lesson, for example, that just hurling invectives at ideas, or comments, or people we don't like, is not an effective (or even an acceptable) form of collaborative behavior.

Are we wiser if we combine our minds with technology to match needs with solutions?

A great many of our traditional jobs have involved matching things up: matching people, matching buyers and sellers, matching providers of services with those in need of them. The people who do this type of work are known—officially or unofficially—as "brokers." Brokers have long been a feature of human society. They include people who help find mates (marriage brokers), houses (real estate brokers), investments (stockbrokers), companies (merger and acquisition brokers), recreation (travel brokers), and beauty (art brokers). Many other industries and fields have brokerage functions as well.

The brokerage function has two components: One is market search—the ability to find parties who have something to offer and other parties who are looking for that same thing. The second is market knowledge and expertise, to find the best matches for each party, to negotiate a price acceptable to both sides, and to make the deals happen. Good brokering has traditionally been a "people" service, with a high degree of personalization and human-to-human contact.

Brokerage, though, is one of the areas in which technology has caused the most change.

This is because in many cases, technology can do the first brokerage function much better. It can cut out the often expensive broker, or "middle man," by establishing and presenting lists of potential buyers and sellers and allowing the parties to browse for themselves. (The jargon word for this is "disintermediation.") eBay started in just this way—people who had something to sell posted their wares (often secondhand items that were not readily available) and others searched for them. People quickly found that with the reach of the Internet, the number of buyers and sellers was much larger than any broker could possibly keep track of—the much easier and more economical solution was to use technology to let people do the matching for themselves.

The second function of brokering, making *good* matches, has also been influenced by technology. One way in which technology has helped is through the establishment of what are known as "reputation sites": Angie's List is a good example, as are complaint/review sites like Yelp. Buyers and sellers can check reputations and reviews and decide for themselves whether they have made a good match. Ebay shows the reputations of all buyers and sellers in providing a good experience. Computers also help with matching by offering questionnaires, as is done on each of the many dating and matchmaking sites, each site having its own proprietary (and secret) algorithm for analyzing the answers and making the matches.

The brokerage function of establishing a fair price was nicely enhanced by technology in the form of online auctions, also pioneered by eBay. Auction software made price setting not only fun, but better. Auctions, it turns out, do the pricing function so well that they have quickly spread to business, eliminating brokerage jobs entirely in some industries. In other industries, sites continuously scour the Internet for the best prices available; consumers can in many cases get the comparison shopping advantages of technology as well.

Because matching unusual problems with good solutions is one of the hardest things to do, the use of technology for matching can, and will I believe, be taken much further. It is easy to find a doctor for a condition that is well known, but if your diagnosis is not obvious and the easy-to-find doctors and specialists are baffled—that is, if something unusual is going on—you are often forced to just travel around from doctor to doctor, hoping to find one who knows what to do. But if the world is taken as a whole, any non-unique condition, no matter how rare, has almost certainly been seen before by someone—it is just difficult to locate that person. In situations such as this, it is very useful to have technological help to match up needs with solutions and questions with answers.

Is using technology for brokering a form of brain gain? I believe so, in that it extends what was always a human capability much further and lets ordinary people do a job once reserved for specialists. Technology has not completely taken over or eliminated the brokerage function, as the many travel agents and stockbrokers still around attest. But it has changed their business in fundamental ways.

Is technology-based brokering digitally wise? I believe so as well. It enables many matches of goods and people that were impossible before because of either geographical distance, lack of market knowledge, limits on sizes of transactions, or other reasons. It offers customers the best prices. However, some types of computer-based brokering, such as "fast trading" financial applications, work so fast that a human can't follow them in real time, and this can often lead to trouble. Brokering technologies can at times be manipulated and don't offer everything the best human brokers can. As always, the digital wisdom lies in wisely combining the human and technology roles.

Are we wiser if we combine our minds with technology to live on the whole planet?

As we saw earlier when discussing Wolfram Alpha, if we do a quick, "back of the envelope" calculation dividing all the arable land available on our planet by its seven billion inhabitants, it will show that, if we were to spread out evenly, there is still plenty of room—almost two and one half acres, in fact—for each of us. And "arable land" does not, of course, include the oceans, which take up the majority of our planet's surface.

Humans' current tendency, though, is not to spread out evenly but rather to agglomerate in cities, where the combination of people, infrastructure, and interaction of ideas is most fertile. But space in cities, of course, is limited—which is the reason for taller and taller building technologies.

Now suppose we could, through technology, establish a great many more cities, with all their advantages, in new places, thus lowering the burden on each? Or suppose we could, through technology, bring the greatest advantages of cities to people anywhere, eliminating the need to congregate in the squalor of slums? Would that be a form of brain gain?

Technologists are currently exploring creating new cities in the middle of the ocean by building man-made islands and habitats, a process known as "seasteading." Aside from more space and the availability of natural resources like minerals and seafood, there is an important technology-related reason for doing this: One of the limitations we run up against as our communications technologies get faster and faster is distance. Because the speed of particular cables (and eventually of light) is fixed, a communication that has a longer distance to travel will always arrive later, an issue known technically as "latency." Latency is undesirable in a great many situations, such as having to wait minutes or hours for a large electronic file to arrive, or having a bullet arrive after the target has already moved away in a game.

Latency is particularly troubling in today's financial transactions, which often take place at the highest possible speeds. Any data that has to travel via a longer route can arrive too late to be included in a trade or bid, which can result in losses of multiple millions of dollars. So there is value in building communications links (i.e., laying cables) along the most direct routes between financial centers. A quick glance at a map or globe shows that many of these direct routes go across oceans. This could make certain ocean-based locations, and the "real estate" (if it can be called that) built there, particularly valuable.[147]

And while physical proximity clearly still matters—which is why cities are getting denser—this is not necessarily the case for all groups of people. In fact, the more a group is technologically enabled, the easier it is for it to survive and thrive in a more spread-out way. People with excellent communications technology can work from home, or from anywhere, and often prefer to do so. Online technologies—written, oral, and, increasingly, video- and virtual community–based—allow such people to be in constant contact with their colleagues. I believe that to the extent that people are enabled to connect well virtually, there is digital wisdom in doing so, and in using criteria other than physical proximity to determine the best place to live.

Of course it is not just communications technologies that make it easier for humans to live on different parts of the planet; a host of technologies do too, and will continue to do so even more. Desert areas, like parts of the Middle East and even parts of the United States, have been opened up to humans by technology in ways never thought possible. It is hard for many to imagine that our modern air-conditioning technology, for example, is only roughly a century old; before that many of the places we now consider wonderful were uninviting and largely uninhabited.

Being able to cope with one's environment better because of technology counts for many as brain gain. If we can squeeze enough brain gain from our combined communication, climate, homebuilding, materials, insulation, clothing, and energy technologies, we will be able to help even poor people live well everywhere. If this should happen, it is even possible that the current population agglomeration trends will reverse.

Would making that happen be digital wisdom? Possibly. But this is not entirely clear. People make decisions about where and how to live for a wide variety of reasons, mostly social. Technology plays only a part. We all—particularly optimists like me—need to be careful to look at things as they are and not how we wish they would be.

BRAIN GAIN AND DIGITAL WISDOM FROM COMBINING
MIND AND TECHNOLOGY TO DO NEW, WISER THINGS

As I began to propose my potential categories of digital wisdom to various people, one suggestion I received from many was that brain gain comes not only from doing things that overcome deficiencies in our healthy human brains (as most of the human-technology combinations I have described do). Brain gain—and digital wisdom—also come from inventing entirely new things for machines and humans to do together that we haven't previously considered. Along those lines, some additional large categories of brain gain, I think, also constitute a large piece of digital wisdom. Here are two of them.

Are we wiser if we combine our minds with technology to control our machines?

Our machines—computers and everything else—are now increasing in power so rapidly that with the doubling of technology power roughly every year (a phenomenon of combining Moore's law of processor improvement with increases in storage capacity, increases in transmission capability and speed, plus new developments like quantum computing), we can calculate that in just 40 more years, which is well within the working lifetime of almost all of our children, our machines will be over *one trillion* times more powerful.[148] So an important question is, "Will humans control this technology, or will it control us?" This question is taken up by Douglas Rushkoff (among others) in a book entitled *Program or Be Programmed* that I will discuss more in Chapter 7.

I believe that knowing how to make machines do what we want them to is crucial to the acquisition of digital wisdom. This skill is known, generally, as programming, and it can take place at many levels, some accessible to all. Unfortunately, we have already created, de facto, a separate tribe of people who *can* make machines do things they want: programmers. Just as it was with the powerful scribes of old, most of us who need a program's capabilities cannot write that program ourselves, but are forced to go to the tribe. When it comes to programming, most of us are illiterate, just as in the Middle Ages.

Of course with machines as complex as they now are, there will always be a need for professionals and specialists in this area. But is it digitally wise to leave this ability to only a few? Or is programming an area in which we should all become to varying degrees proficient? I believe digital wisdom requires the latter, and I discuss more about how to do this in Chapter 6.

Would learning to better use and control our technology, and particularly our machines, be brain gain? I believe so. First, because it empowers us. Those who can do no more with technology than push the "start" button will be disadvantaged in the future, as those who now have to pass our gadgets to our children to get them working already are. Today, most of the technology-based tools we currently use in business—word processing, databases, spreadsheets, web sites—all require some level of programming (known often as "scripts" or "macros") to be used to their full advantage. The business tools of tomorrow—such as complex interactions between multiple media in online communities—will require much more programming skill.

In fact, individuals who can program already enjoy great advantages in society. They can earn lots of money—look at Bill Gates, Pierre Omidyar, Mark Zuckerberg, and other programmer-billionaires. Even discounting the unusual level of success of those few named above, learning to program is a sure route to well-paid employment (for life, if one stays current)—programming is a skill that the United States and the world will always need.

Would teaching all our kids to program be digital wisdom?

Is it wise to know, at least to some degree, the tools of your time? Is it wise to continue relying on tools that are outdated and have long passed their prime of efficiency? In a world as highly dependent on machines as the world of today's young will surely be, do we want our children to have no understanding of how to make their machines work for them?

Not everyone will go, or needs to go, to the deepest levels of machine programming, because between just pushing a button and writing assembler machine code there are a great many intermediate programming "levels" of varying sophistication and complexity. Each person needs to find his or her own comfort zone along that gamut. But controlling machines is an area where I think it will be extremely digitally unwise to be illiterate. Despite the many problems we will have in getting people up to speed in this area, I really do not see, as I discussed in an article published in 2005, any way around this.[149]

Are we wiser if we combine our minds with technology to educate people better?

And it's not just programming skills that our children will need to survive and thrive in the future. We must rethink, in the twenty-first century, *all* of what we currently call our "education" in order to adapt to the digital future. This will not be easy, because we are tied so strongly to the education of the past. People have a very hard time letting go of things that were once truly very important to learn—but no longer are.

I spend an entire chapter of this book, Chapter 6, discussing education, focusing on how and what to teach our kids (and adults) to achieve the maximum brain gain and digital wisdom in the future.

Will changing our education in these ways actually produce brain gain? I am confident not only that it will, but that *not* doing so will lead, inexorably and inevitably, to *brain loss,* in ways that the people who today criticize technology—or education—can hardly begin to imagine.

Is it digitally wise to rethink our education? Again, with all the change in the world, it is digitally unwise not to.

To summarize this long but important chapter:

Brain gain and digital wisdom are already with us today in a great many ways, although they may not yet be evenly distributed in the world. But there is still a lot more brain gain and digital wisdom that we can find and achieve.

The next chapters discuss how to do this.

FOUR

LESS DESIRABLE PATHS

Digital Cleverness and Digital Stupidity

People are not born digitally wise—in fact, it is certain that most of us, much of the time, are digitally *unwise*—at least for now. But there are dangers in not *trying* to be digitally wise in everything we do with technology, that is, dangers in using technology in other ways, ways that are less thoughtful and less well considered than wise.

In this chapter, I consider examples of these "lesser" uses of technology, placing them into two categories: "digital cleverness" and "digital stupidity." Both categories can be benign or dangerous. Although most forms of both digital cleverness and digital stupidity (also known as "being digitally dumb") fall into the "benign" category, there are real dangers in both of these categories. I talk some about those dangers here, and I go into them in much more detail in Chapter 7.

I offer these characterizations ("digital cleverness" and "digital stupidity"), which admittedly are quite subjective, less for their ultimate "correctness"— you may disagree, even violently, with some of the examples I choose and the bins into which I put them—but rather as a framework for your thoughts and for public discussion.

In some cases, it is the technology itself that is dumb or merely clever. In others it is how the technologies are used. In both cases, this framework is not typically the way technology gets looked at and evaluated—except colloquially, in people's minds, when they hear about some new technology or use and think to themselves, "That's pretty clever!" or "That's pretty dumb!"

I offer here a variety of examples of digital cleverness and digital stupidity, to which, I expect you, the reader, can, and will, add many more of your own (I hope to collect these on the book's web site). And I hope that you will agree with my overall contention that these "less-than-wise" examples and uses of technology are different—in important and meaningful ways—from the technologies and uses that are digitally wise.

"DIGITAL CLEVERNESS"

Digital Cleverness That Is Benign and Even, Sometimes, Useful

Most of the digital technology and digital products in the world fall into the area of "digital cleverness": They do not make us wiser, but they are often inventive and do no real harm. This goes for mind-related technologies as well.

Into this category fall all those technologies and gadgets that we like, want, and often buy, but don't really need. This includes much of our latest television technology: flat-screen TVs, super-size TVs, 3-D TVs. Although it might make a person happier, it is hard, I think, to argue that a bigger or 3-D TV makes anyone wiser.

The same goes for many other gadgets that come onto the market, such as electronic cork-pullers, talking luggage scales, water-squirting remote-controlled cars, or weed-whacking golf drivers. (All of these can be found in the fun-to-browse catalog of the Hammacher-Schlemmer company[1]—some of whose products I myself own.) It is even more true of new features added to differentiate products within a category from one another, for example, audio cables made of gold, cameras with extra screens and modes, and the many consumer robots, from Sony's Aibo robotic dog to the voice-activated R2D2. Some are things companies do, seemingly, just because they can, or because they think it will buy them some publicity (like Toyota's amazing trumpet-playing robot Toyotashi, whom we met in Chapter 3[2]).

Digital technology has inspired a great deal of creativity in these features, but most of them are not very worthwhile and don't last. David Pogue, the personal technology reviewer for the *New York Times*, points out that most of the gadgets he reviews "don't last a year." This is because the ideas behind these products are not, I believe, digitally wise, but merely digitally clever.

So a useful way to evaluate the technologies in our lives, and those that we come across, is to ask, are they digitally wise? Or are they merely digitally clever?

Is it digitally wise, for example, to have a "digital presence," or a Facebook page, or to use Twitter? Just having these things adds nothing to our, or others', wisdom; any digital wisdom comes from how these social tools are used. In 2010, David Pogue and his publisher, Tim Reilly, put together a digitally clever book of Pogue's many followers' tweets of answers, comments, and reactions to questions he posed.[3] The result is amusing. However, some are using Twitter to track the spread of flu and other diseases or epidemics: This is digitally wise.[4] Figuring out ways to get huge numbers of friends on Facebook is merely clever. Extracting emerging trends from the complete database of Facebook posts is digital wisdom.

Making an analog product, such as a camera, digital is an example of extreme digital cleverness on the part of engineers. It can make things much easier for users: no more film to buy and develop, no more severely limited exposures to count and run out of at awkward times. But it offers no more wisdom than a film camera. But add the ability to connect that camera directly to the Internet so that it can instantly upload images and videos to YouTube, and the democratization of photojournalism that that creates (a development that can change the world, as it did in Tunisia) becomes digital wisdom. (Of course the uploading feature can also be used unwisely.)

Me-too products, of which there are, unfortunately, a great deal, are typically just digitally clever (and sometimes hardly that). Makers may add a clever feature, such as a folding viewing screen, that differentiates their product but offers but little new wisdom to customers. But adding certain features, such as a forward-facing camera so that people can see each other as they communicate, is digital wisdom. Using multiple monitors for advertising displays might be clever, but using them to increase efficiency and productivity in offices, a growing trend, is digitally wise.[5]

Like digital wisdom, digital cleverness can be found both in the ways we use the technologies available and in the new technologies we create. Consider, for example, the iPad. Is the iPad—or owning one—digitally wise? Many of the technologies in the iPad are extremely digitally clever: the touch interface, the flat size, and the magnetic cover, for example. But at least for me, all the digital wisdom in the iPad already came in the iPhone, which put together a collection of technologies that had not been combined before and enabled a small device to become infinitely extensible via apps. Merely making that wise collection bigger, while it clearly appealed to many, was more digital cleverness than digital wisdom. There may be some digital wisdom in making a device that is more accessible to those with disabilities, but that was not, I believe, Apple's main goal.

So it is important to distinguish between enviable sales volumes and digital wisdom. Just the fact that something sells well does not imply that it is wise (think, for example, of McDonalds' calorie-filled burgers). Sales volume implies only that some marketer has successfully tapped into a human desire.

One possible criterion for discerning a digitally wise technology is how quickly and thoroughly it becomes truly ubiquitous. When technologies truly are digitally wise, not only do all who can quickly adopt them, but those who do, often find themselves asking the question, "How did I (or how did people) ever do this before?" By this yardstick, word processing is wise, because it so beats handwriting in terms of clarity, speed, and distribution that a great percentage of the world, particularly the business world, has adopted it for almost all of its writing. (Just as a reminder of the totality of these changes, I keep on my wall a large framed diploma from the "Palmer School of Business Handwriting.")

But some of the features of word processing—like the ability to include a huge variety of fonts, colors, and sizes—are only, I would argue, digitally clever, and the random use of multiple fonts and sizes and colors, with little relationship to any useful standards of communication, fits more easily into our next category—digitally dumb.

Is the recent digital transformation of the automobile digitally wise or just digitally clever? Some of the technological features that have improved cars over the last century—non-shatter glass, seat belts, airbags, additional side and back lights, for example—are wise in that they save lives. New digital features that also do this, such as automatic traction control and sensors that turn on lights automatically, are digitally wise as well. In contrast, features like automatic parallel parking are merely digitally clever.

Computer-based spreadsheets, because they allow necessary and useful calculations that used to take armies of people large amounts of time to be done much more quickly by single individuals, and with fewer errors, are, I would argue, a digitally wise invention. That is why they are used almost universally by businesses with access to computers. But certain features of spreadsheets, such as "flippable" rows and columns, are really just digitally clever.

And Nassim Taleb points out (in *The Black Swan*) that some of the ways they are used for forecasting are digitally dumb.[6]

Search engines provide another illustration. The *idea* of search engines, that is, creating filters that let us narrow the huge quantities of information on the web to things that are relevant, is certainly digitally wise. So is the idea of extending the search to images. But features that some search engines have added, such as Ask Jeeves's "natural language" searching,[7] have been merely digitally clever. That feature may be wise when machines reach a certain level of understanding of human language (Wolfram Alpha is already doing it better), but on Ask Jeeves, it was just a clever addition that didn't add enough wisdom for the search engine to really take off. In contrast, a feature like Google's "I'm feeling lucky" button, which returns only a single result, obviates the whole concept of multiple sources and is just digitally dumb.

"Benign" digital cleverness is rampant on web sites and apps. A great many of these do clever, even useful, but not very wise, things—such as the app, for example, that counts down the number of days until Christmas or your birthday.

Of course, the distinction between wise and clever is not always clear-cut, and in some cases it depends on a user's needs. Are games, for example, digitally clever or digitally wise? There are probably some of each. What about WikiLeaks?

My point here is that we should look at the technologies in our lives with a critical eye and decide for ourselves how much each piece really adds to our understanding. We don't really need most of the digital cleverness that is constantly being foisted upon us, and we can ignore much of it. But that should not prevent us from trying to decide which technologies, and uses of technology, are digitally wise, and taking advantage of their benefits.

Digital Cleverness That Is Dangerous

There is another kind of digital cleverness, however, that we cannot ignore and have watch out for carefully. Many creators and users of technology do not have our best interests at heart, but rather are out to scam and take advantage of us. And some of them are enormously clever. Even though some of their schemes are relatively well known, people still fall for them, and new snares are being developed all the time.

Some of the cleverest people in the world are, unfortunately, hackers who deliberately use technology to cause harm. Malware (such as viruses, Trojan horses, and zombie computers) is often easier to create than to protect against.

Digitally clever ways to rip us off include phishing schemes (i.e., sending "You won the lottery!" or other emails in the hope of getting people to send back personal information), fake identities, identity theft, and many others. Their digital cleverness consists, often, of creating fakes that fool unsophisticated computer users—and even sometimes sophisticated users—into doing unwise things, such as divulging personal information to strangers. Despite wide publicity, their cleverness allows them to continuously, with newer schemes and twists, rip off innocent people.

The practice of "typosquatting" is one of these dangerous, digitally clever ways of tricking people. Scammers acquire sites that are typical misspellings of frequently searched-for terms or companies and use the traffic that mistakenly comes to those sites to do nasty things.

The development of financial trading software technology that opens up trading to a much larger number of people—and allows many of them to do it at home—may or may not be a wise thing. But the development of "fast trading" technology, that is, programs that take advantage of second-to-second fluctuations in prices, unnoticeable by humans, to make quick profits, is digitally clever only in the negative sense—it changes the entire playing field of trading exchanges, giving unfair advantages to those capable of making such trades. Similarly, frauds that digitally send a tiny fraction of each dollar traded or earned by a business (say .0000001 cent) to a scammer's personal bank account may be clever (the individual amounts can be hard to notice) but can add up over millions of transactions to a lot of stolen money.

And those are hardly the biggest dangerous, digitally clever schemes. Bernie Madoff's highly destructive Ponzi scheme would hardly have been possible without the digital technology he used to create his false reports.

The law, and law enforcement, is typically far behind in trying to keep up with nefarious digital cleverness. That is why governments and law enforcement organizations try hard to find digitally clever, destructive people and "turn" them, whenever possible, to help them prevent fraud and catch criminals. Whenever I hear educators complain about students hacking into school data systems or doing other nasty but digitally clever deeds, I always suggest that instead of expelling those students they instead make them the head of the school's computer security squad. In so doing, they could potentially, much like a Jedi knight, turn those students away from the "dark side" and into the "light."

Businesses use technology to do many things that, while often within the letter of the law, seem more clever than wise to many of us. Technology, for example, enables variable pricing methods—that is, allowing airline tickets, highway tolls, and other fees to change frequently based on demand. These fluctuating price systems are certainly clever and, from the company's point of view, may appear wise in that they increase revenue.

But are they always digitally wise from a customer's perspective (assuming that matters)? I was recently told, for example, that if you go to some sites and search for airline tickets, but then decide to wait before buying, and you later go back to those same sites on the same computer and search for the same flights, the prices will have gone up—based solely on the fact that the computer had recorded your interest. That is certainly digitally clever. But is it digitally wise, especially if it is not disclosed?

Not disclosing what is really going on is a big piece of dangerous digital cleverness. Are your movements online being tracked? Are they being sold? Are they being compared and put together to make profiles of you without your knowledge or consent? Absolutely.

Understanding that these kinds of technologies and technology uses are mere cleverness, and not wise or even smart things to do, may help in persuading some people not to do them. I certainly hope that is the case.

DIGITAL STUPIDITY

Digital Stupidity That Is (Relatively) Benign and Forgivable

And then there is digital stupidity. A lot of people do a lot of things with technology that can't even be described as "clever"—they are just plain digitally dumb. Some of these things are relatively benign and to some extent forgivable, at least the first time. But digital stupidity is not just a "beginner's mistake" made by people who don't know better—it often comes from relatively experienced people who should know better (including, for example, me). Unfortunately, no one seems immune to digital stupidity—it's something we all have to watch out for.

One of my favorite cartoons from the digital past shows a woman with an iron in her hand standing over an ironing board on which sits a key ring. The caption reads, "It said to 'press any key!'"

Our language has already changed because of digital technology. There are new words ("podcast"), new meanings for old words ("press," as in the cartoon), changes to old words ("email," "phishing"), changes of nouns into verbs ("texting"), and the anachronistic retention of old words for new things ("dial" a number). This changing language is one of the confusions that led me, in the past, to distinguish digital immigrants from digital natives. When I once suggested using the computer language Unix for a project, an older colleague thought I meant "eunuchs." (I can still remember her shocked face.)

But that was then, and this is now. We are already a reasonable way into the twenty-first century. When misunderstandings like this happen, it is becoming digital stupidity on our part, rather than just ignorance.

That doesn't, of course, make it go away. Some other kinds of digital stupidity that I and others have engaged in include:

"Forgetting" to back up. As the saying goes, "There are two kinds of people in the world—those who back up and those who will." Seemingly, no matter how much this is talked about and emphasized, people—even highly intelligent people—don't do it. And not just the "old" people who might have the excuse of being "digital immigrants," that is, those with a late-in-life start in using digital technology. I know an extremely bright high school senior, with a 4.0 average, who, the night before all his college applications were due, lost all of his essays and other application material when his computer crashed. (I am now pausing my writing to back up this book draft in several places.)

Hitting the send button on an email that you knew *was too dangerous to send.* We all compose nasty emails from time to time in our heads in response to provocations. The wisest thing to do is to not even type them. But if you do, the next wisest thing to do is to not include the email address of the intended recipient in the "to" box. But many of us do so and, on occasion, because we are upset, mistakenly hit the send button. (I have done this—hopefully you haven't.) This is just digital stupidity, as there is no way to take this back. (The "recall" function, if used, only highlights the mistake.) I have learned that if I do write such emails, to be sure the "to" box contains only my own email address. That way if I do stupidly hit send, the only one who will see my mistake is me!

Of course this is just a specific instance of a more general digitally dumb activity, that is,

Hitting the wrong button. Once, perhaps. But do we then learn? If not, it's digital stupidity.

Particularly when it leads to:

Purchasing things we didn't intend to buy. Yes it's dumb, but we are often being set up by the merchants as well. A great many digital items are sold today not just though clearly identifiable "shopping" sites, but also through what are known as "in-app" or "in program" sales. While we are in a non-sales-oriented program, or site, or game, a pop-up often appears offering the option to buy a virtual good or to buy some virtual cash to spend. My six-year-old son understandably gets confused many times as to whether to hit yes or no. But we adults?

Of course when we do get this wrong, we often resort to one of the most digitally dumb things of all, that is,

Blaming (#$%!) Microsoft—or some other software developer—for our own mistakes. "It wasn't my fault—they put the [x] button right under the [y] button!" is a frequently heard user complaint. True, perhaps, but the buttons do have names or icons, and there are plenty of things that are next to each other that adults don't confuse. Companies like Microsoft spend a great deal of money, time, and energy to optimize the placement of controls for the majority of users of their product. Not to mention, of course, that many of these controls can be moved to different places by the user. So that excuse is, in my view, digitally dumb, and we all have to learn—as I often do—to live with our own stupidity.

Exposing an entire list of sensitive emails to all recipients. Unless your intention is for everybody to see them, lists of recipients' email addresses belong *not* in the "to" or "cc" box but in the "bcc" box below. That way they are not exposed to all recipients. This is a particularly common piece of digital stupidity among otherwise intelligent people. (Yes, I have been guilty of this myself.)

Making rude comments. Many of us are frequently appalled by not just the ferocity of expression in online comments but also the language. Yet the feelings of anger and frustration when we see things online that we strongly disagree with are in all of us. Digital wisdom demands that we all learn to exercise great restraint in our commenting.

Which is closely related to:

Texting or responding when drunk (or angry). This has become so common that there are names for it among young people, such as "drunk dialing" and "drunk texting." Dialing or texting while under the influence of a powerful emotion such as anger can be just as dangerous.

Forgetting things you have access to. I now have so many capabilities in my digital devices, particularly in my iPhone with all its apps, that I often forget I have them with me or don't connect them to the situation at hand.

I've often wished I'd recorded an interview (I sometimes ask reporters to send me their recording, which they never do), forgetting that I had a recorder in my own pocket. I've searched in multiple drawers for a flashlight, forgetting that I had one in my phone. I once came across an elevator door cleverly painted as an opening and closing curtain, and I was happy I took a photo of it until someone pointed out to me that I could have (and should have) taken a video (Duh!). I've bemoaned not having partners to play musical duets with when I could have recorded the other part myself and played it back. Ditto for finding partners for chess and Scrabble—there is always someone online willing to play. After much digital stupidity, I have finally realized that many of the things I search for (such as timetables, tickets, and addresses) are online and available by just asking Siri, but my wife still laughs at me for many of the old ways and places I search. I still often put in accents by hand when I write emails in French instead of just switching to a French keyboard and dictionary. I still think I can't read things in languages that I don't know. I still wonder, outside at night, "what planet is that?" rather than pointing my iPhone app at the sky.

I'm sure I'll be digitally dumb in many of these ways for the rest of my life. Thanks goodness for my six-year-old, who doesn't forget these things and often reminds me to use them.

Losing stuff. One reason that the promised "paperless office" hasn't happened is that people like me lose things in my computer in digitally dumb ways. "I know it's in there," I say, "but damned if I can find it." Some of this I can legitimately blame on the software—despite great improvements, we still rely on an outdated file-cabinet-metaphor-based system and need better ways to search. But much is my own digital stupidity in not knowing all the existing ways to find what's there.

Responding to phishing. Okay, once. (Or even twice.) But I get emails regularly from people I know that say, "I hope you didn't send any money in response to that email I supposedly sent"—many of that person's supposedly digitally wise friends did. Yes, we all have big hearts, and there have always been effective scammers. But come on—most of this stuff has received wide publicity.

Misspelling an email address. Teachers are fond of telling students not to "just cut and paste," but there are places where *not* cutting and pasting is, in fact, the digitally dumb thing to do. How many times have I transposed two letters in an email address and waited and waited for the return email, which never came? Too many digitally dumb times to count!

Not realizing something was not sent. Akin to the above is hitting the send button on an important email (or text) and sitting back satisfied, not realizing that it never went out. This has often happened to me because of my multiple email accounts, some of which don't "send" on certain systems (including my home one). It can also happen when I shut my computer down (say to get on a plane) before an email actually makes it out. I do have an indicator right in front of me that shows me the number of unsent emails in my outbox. But still. . . .

Hitting "reply all." Have you ever meant to say something "privately" to only the one person sending an email, but mistakenly sent your response out to the whole listserv or cc list? Most of us have. Have you done it twice? Digitally dumb.

Not plugging in. Hard to believe, but this is still a huge source of help desk questions. If your toaster or other kitchen appliance wasn't working, the plug would be the first thing you would check. But computers?

Forgetting to charge a battery. Okay, from time to time we are too busy. But I have woken up in the morning, ready to head out the door, with my phone at 16 percent. Can I blame the battery life? I also carry two batteries for my computer for long trips where there is no power outlet. How many times have I plugged in the second only to find it was empty? Digitally dumb, Prensky.

Using someone else's login. This one, at least, is a little more sophisticated. It is easy to sit down at someone else's laptop, or a public computer, and proceed as if you were logged in to your own. This, however, is certainly digitally unwise and, at least the second time you do it, digitally dumb.

Revealing your password. Passwords are a pain, so no matter how many times many of us hear it, we still use passwords that are easy to guess, too weak, not changed frequently, etc. Digitally wise, or . . . ?

Not checking your spam. The *New York Times* ran an article about a guy who missed an email from someone who wanted to buy his company because the email went into his spam, and he didn't check it. I've missed invitations to speak. Digital wisdom is remembering spam filters are imperfect. I once found in my spam box several emails from a person who listed her degree in her email signature as Ed.D. He emails were being rerouted because the spam filter interpreted the Ed. as "erectile dysfunction." Not reviewing your spam before deleting it is digitally dumb. Check it.

Not using "protection." It doesn't feel any better to use your computer without protection against viruses and other computer malware, and it will almost certainly make you feel worse. The basic programs are free and typically come with the computer's original software. Those programs that are sold bombard you with reminders to renew until you do (and, if you don't, bug you even more). Going without it is really, really digitally dumb.

Deleting something you meant to save. Deleting stuff you didn't mean to is so common that software makers all add an "undo" button whenever they can and a trash file from which you can recover things. But the supposedly "sophisticated" users among us (like me) often choose not to "clog up" our trash and delete directly, using a bypass key. Anyone think this is digitally wise?

Not saving. Ditto for saving. Happily, most of my programs auto-save—until the moment I lose power. 'Nuff said.

Not bookmarking. I can't be alone in opening multiple browser windows with sites I know I will need later but neglect to bookmark. I bet there are automated solutions, but I'm too digitally dumb to find them.

Counting on connectivity. After more ruined presentations than I care to remember, I finally have established a rule for myself: Do *nothing* that requires a live connection to the Internet. Even if the effect is far poorer than I could get with a live connection, the state of connectivity in the world—particularly when you need it—is still far too unreliable. You can try it in rehearsal, for example, and have it work fine. But then, when the 1,000 people in the room all go online at once to check your website. . . .

Not syncing. Some of the best pictures I ever took on my iPhone are gone because I didn't sync it up before the phone was lost or stolen. At the start of 2012, a person wrote in the *New York Times* that even though she had recently seen a friend lose all her work, music, photos, and email when the friend's phone went dead, "I watched my glitchy phone finally die—and take with it almost every photo I had ever taken of my daughter since the day she was born." The writer lists all the reasonable-at-the-time reasons she had not backed up her phone and can't mentally accept that her photos are gone. But they are. Digitally dumb.

Not realizing stuff will be seen. This is the Anthony Weiner thing. Stuff online *will* get seen. For sure. By people you may not want it to. Assuming you or anyone else can keep online information secret is digitally dumb.

Giving your kid the OLD computer. We talked about this before—your kids need the newer equipment and know how to put it to good use; you most likely don't. Sorry, but buying yourself a new computer (or iPad) and giving an old, outdated one to your kid is almost always a digitally dumb move.

Not assuming you will always need more. Along the same lines, if you do anything up-to-date with your computer at all, it is digitally dumb to think you can get by without the largest amounts of memory and storage you can afford, even if you have to sacrifice other things, like weight or upgrading to the fastest processor, to get a price you can pay. Digital stuff takes more space these days, and we tend to keep more of it.

It is worth mentioning one more time that old people by no means have a monopoly on digital stupidity. Young people, particularly students, can be just as guilty of digital stupidity as oldsters, something that teachers see all the time. I have heard many teachers tell of students' downloading papers from the Internet (already not digitally wise) and handing them in electronically. One could, perhaps, characterize this as "digital cleverness of the nefarious kind." But when the downloaded papers have the original author's name on them, and the students do not even change that name to their own before they submit them, that is pure digital stupidity.

Digital Stupidity That Is Dangerous

While the kinds of digital stupidity we just looked at are relatively benign (though often annoying) and are often causes for chuckles, some kinds of digital stupidity are deadly serious.

On 9/11, New York City firemen who went up in the World Trade Center Towers found that their radios did not work properly in those spaces. Was the fact that their superiors had not tested this capability in such conditions— whether or not they were "required" to do this—dangerous digital stupidity? You decide.

Is restricting access to parts of the Internet—as some countries and leaders are currently trying to do—dangerous digital stupidity? People will almost certainly find a way around the restrictions, making the limits stupid, even if they work in the short term. It is also dangerous for the leaders, because their people will resent it. On the other side, just handing very young children unrestricted access to the Internet may be dangerously digitally dumb as well.

Another example of dangerous digital stupidity (at least dangerous in the financial sense) is over-investing in quickly changing technologies. The large investments by colleges and universities in hardware and software to provide their students with personal ".edu" email addresses was quickly made mostly worthless by the mass movement of college students to texting and Facebook, and the students' resulting lack of interest, in many cases, of ever checking their emails. Was this investment dangerous digital stupidity on the part of those running the schools? I believe so. Not because those particular shifts in technology could have been anticipated by the administrators—they almost certainly could not have been. But rather because they did not think that there *would be* rapid movements in technology, and invest more flexibly, they were not digitally wise or clever, but digitally dumb.

A MATTER OF TIMING?

Sometimes, though, whether something looks digitally wise or digitally dumb can be only a matter of timing.

Many decisions seem digitally dumb in hindsight. Was Rupert Murdoch's purchase of MySpace for $580 million (and later selling it for $35 million, losing a net of more than a billion dollars in the process[8]) a huge case of digital stupidity (a.k.a., "business misjudgment")? It certainly seems so with hindsight, but it was hailed a digitally wise move at the time. So we can't always tell.

The opposite also holds true. When my ex-colleagues Philip Evans and Tom Wurster of the Boston Consulting Group—both extremely bright guys—wrote their book *Blown to Bits* in 1999 about how digital technology was changing business dramatically, it was marketed widely around the country as great wisdom.[9] Unfortunately for them, there followed, shortly after the book hit the stores, the "dot.com crash." Whoops. "What was blown to bits was us," I remember Philip saying. But what was actually wrong was not their ideas, but their timing. The profound changes they described are indeed coming, but the transition is taking longer than they imagined it would.

NOT RELYING ON THE PAST

Which brings us to perhaps the most dangerous kind of digital stupidity of all—relying too heavily on the wisdom of the non-digital past as a guide to the digital future. A very interesting question is how much of what happens in the world is, in fact cyclic: Those of us who have lived for a bit and have studied history know that some patterns seem to repeat themselves in reoccurring cycles. Interest rates and stock prices rise and fall, civilizations are born and die, often with many interesting regularities. The received wisdom, of course, is that we can and should learn from these cycles. "Those who don't learn from history are bound to repeat it," said George Santayana. ("—next semester," as the history teacher's joke goes.)

The most interesting judgment call, and the one that requires the most digital wisdom, is deciding how much will repeat and how much will not, and getting the answer right (at least more often than not). One thing we can be certain of as we move into the digital age is that the answer is changing. With today's rapid advances in technology, it is shifting toward more of the new and unexpected happening. Which is why avoiding digital cleverness or stupidity, and finding true digital wisdom, is so important.

FIVE

THE TRADE-OFFS

Cultivating Brain Gain and Digital Wisdom

I f you believe—as I do—that digital wisdom is important for humans and citizens to have and to grow, we need to think about how we can cultivate digital wisdom in our population, that is, encourage more and more people to join, voluntarily and eagerly, the quest for digital wisdom in their lives.

Cultivating digital wisdom, to a large extent, involves making trade-offs. To do so we must give up some things that were considered valuable in the past and balance the benefits gained against the dangers from gaining them.

In this chapter, I examine two sides of life—personal life and work— where I believe digital wisdom can be cultivated and enhanced—and I try to suggest ways that we can do it. As you read, I strongly suggest that you reflect on your own life, and the lives of those you know, and consider how everyone's quotient of digital wisdom can be expanded.

CULTIVATING DIGITAL WISDOM IN OUR PERSONAL LIFE

Digital wisdom is important and can be cultivated and increased in several areas of our personal lives. These include (at least) our communications, our use of devices and apps, our personal health, and our personal finances.

Cultivating Digital Wisdom in Our Communications and in Using Our Devices

Cultivating digital wisdom requires being on the Internet—being connected to the world in this way is the hallmark of the twenty-first-century *Homo Sapiens Digital*. With almost one-third of the world's population online at the end of 2011(see Table 2 below), we are well on our way, and it is becoming digitally unwise *not* to be connected. Many parts of the world, particularly Africa, are still behind and need to catch up—with improved technologies, falling prices, and government and private help, at some point soon they hopefully will. The world goal is to have 50 percent connected by 2013, and our children, if not us, will almost certainly see close to 100 percent in their lifetimes.

But cultivating digital wisdom increasingly requires not just a connection to the Internet, but getting the fastest connection you can possibly afford. The Internet provides not just information, but also, if you want or need it, company. Not only is it the medium for most video calls, and for Facebook (now at roughly one billion subscribers[1]), but it is also the way many people play games such as Scrabble with each other.[2] Fast broadband is increasingly important for web-based activities, and digital wisdom includes working to make sure the place where you live provides it. Unfortunately, the United States is far behind many parts of the world in this regard.

Cultivating digital wisdom means making a trade-off of exploring new forms of communication (and entertainment) vs. sticking only with old ones. Today's digitally wisest Internet users have already installed an RSS reader and have subscribed to as many feeds as they can find relating to their particular interests, using it to read online many news sources daily, from multiple parts of the world, with different points of view, including both professional sources and amateur blogs.[3] They have found and subscribed to a number of email listservs and other online groups relating to their personal and professional interests.[4] They regularly search and browse the Internet. They select their entertainment from a much wider variety of choices than are available on television alone—even cable television. (Many of today's young people already spend more time watching YouTube, for example, than watching their TVs.[5]) They learn about things they like, or need to know, from YouTube and other video sites. They also spend a great deal of time online sharing with their family and friends what they have found and doing online activities together, such as playing games or doing homework. This is often traded off for couch-potato time, which digitally wise people typically have less of.

WORLD INTERNET USAGE AND POPULATION STATISTICS
DECEMBER 31, 2011

World Regions	Population (2011 Est.)	Internet Users Dec. 31, 2000	Internet Users Latest Data
Africa	1,037,524,058	4,514,400	139,875,242
Asia	3,879,740,877	144,304,000	1,016,799,076
Europe	816,426,346	105,096,093	500,723,686
Middle East	216,258,843	3,284,800	77,020,995
North America	347,394,870	108,096,800	273,067,546
Latin America/Carib.	597,283,165	18,068,919	235,819,740
Oceania/Australia	35,426,995	7,620,480	23,927,457
WORLD TOTAL	6,930,055,154	360,985,492	2,267,233,742

World Regions	Penetration (% Population)	Growth 2000–2011	Users % of Table
Africa	13.5%	2,988.4%	6.2%
Asia	26.2%	789.6%	44.8%
Europe	61.3%	376.4%	22.1%
Middle East	35.6%	2,244.8%	3.4%
North America	78.6%	152.6%	12.0%
Latin America/Carib.	39.5%	1,205.1%	10.4%
Oceania/Australia	67.5%	214.0%	1.1%
WORLD TOTAL	32.7%	528.1%	100.0%

© 2000-2012, Miniwatts Marketing Group. All rights reserved.
Source http://www.internetworldstats.com/stats.htm
Copyright © 2001–2012, Miniwatts Marketing Group

Table 2

Cultivating digital wisdom means being intellectually curious and active, continually expanding one's online universe rather than sticking with the same things, and continually bringing more of the new world into our lives. One of the best ways to do this is to find partners. Ideally, they should be of two sorts—partners our own age (for sharing and comfort) and partners who are far younger (for information and learning). Cultivating digital wisdom means getting good at finding help, when you need something, in the most efficient, technology-enabled ways.

Cultivating digital wisdom includes—even for the most advanced technology users—frequently reexamining our habits to be sure the mix of online and offline activities in our lives is both appropriate and satisfying. Digital wisdom suggests that the balance and mix is different for each individual, and that there is no one-size-fits-all prescription.

Digital wisdom suggests helping others cultivate their own digital wisdom as well. If someone does not have, in this day and age, an email address (as some of my older friends in the United States and in Europe still did not until recently), it is certainly digitally wise for any advanced user who knows the person to assist him or her in getting one, and to help him or her understand the value of trading off electronic isolation—which some still mistakenly call privacy—for this connection.

Digitally wise people are often intense communicators, with many more, and easier, communication tools at their disposal than in the past. Cultivating digital wisdom involves constantly being on the lookout for, and being open to, new and better digital tools for communicating, and suggests that the digital communications tool one uses vary according to the situation and the person (or people) one is communicating with. (People have always used communication tools situationally, of course, but the range of options is now much wider.) Many have already abandoned phone calls in favor of texting and adopted Twitter as a preferred means of communicating certain things.

Cultivating digital wisdom means trading off sticking only to the forms of communication we have always known and are comfortable with, versus adding new ones as they become widely used, often with some discomfort. While I use Skype and Face Time regularly with my family, I am just becoming comfortable with clients video-Skyping me unannounced from around the world. I am often at home during the day and quite informal, so video calling is not always my first preference, but I would be digitally unwise to reject it—it is now digitally wise to share your Skype address with others just as you would your phone number.

It is digitally wise to have multiple email, Twitter, and other addresses, each one used for different purposes (e.g., one for public consumption, registering at online sites, etc., and another for personal communications with family and friends). In some places, even second or third graders have up to half a dozen email addresses.[6]

Cultivating digital wisdom means thinking through and working out our own personal relationship with Facebook, Twitter, Skype, and other new tools—and not rejecting any new tool before trying it and thinking carefully about where it can potentially help us.

Since cultivating digital wisdom means continually searching for ways to communicate better, we should also ask: Is turning off all our devices periodically, and communicating only in person, as some recommend, a digitally wise way to behave? Perhaps for some people, but not necessarily for everyone. All situations and people are different in this regard, and we should certainly reject anyone who would force all of us, "for our own good," into "required" digital breaks. These can, at times, result in a lot of people sitting around bored—a situation I remember quite well from rainy days at my non-electronically-enabled shared beach house.

Technology changes remarkably quickly, and cultivating digital wisdom requires staying abreast of it. One good way to do this is to regularly read the technology columns in a number of newspapers and periodicals, either on paper or online (many periodicals have RSS feeds). I find the *Economist*'s excellent technology coverage particularly helpful in this regard.

I can still remember a time when using email in large companies was considered totally nerdy—real businesspeople sent on paper, via people who ran around delivering office mail (I both sent and delivered memos). While many adults now complain about too much email, that medium is already considered passé by much of our youth—useful only as a way to communicate with "old people."

But since email is still (for now) the preferred method for communication in most business and other professions, it is important to cultivate "email digital wisdom." This means learning how to keep one's emails and attachments as short and small as possible, so that they won't clog up mobile devices or slow connections, and so readers can quickly get your point and know what response is needed. Email digital wisdom includes knowing how to make effective use of the subject line—such as by using "EOM" (end of message) to indicate that what you've written in the subject line is the entire message (making it unnecessary for receivers to open it), and by keeping subject lines current and specific. There is no digital wisdom in a subject line such as RE: RE: RE: RE: Yours.

While cultivating digital wisdom does require finding your comfort level with social media like Facebook and Twitter, this doesn't mean, necessarily, becoming a big user of those services. What cultivating digital wisdom does mean is *knowing when each is an effective means to do what you want to do.* This is often far from obvious—those who can afford to, such as celebrities, often hire consultants to help them find this digital wisdom.[7]

Cultivating digital wisdom means abandoning any lingering prejudices one still may have about how much better "in-person" is, trading these off for more fruitful online interactions. But this does not mean trading off, as some wrongly insist, "quality" of interactions versus quantity. Cultivating digital wisdom means constantly thinking about how to make our electronic communications more meaningful and higher quality—"deeper," as some would say. It also requires not investing ourselves too deeply in any one form of communication—whether in person or online—so that we can remain open to newer forms.

Cultivating Digital Wisdom With Our Smart Phones and Apps

Since more than 50 percent of new phones sold in the world are now smart phones,[8] we need to cultivate digital wisdom for these devices as well. Certainly, with prices now as low as zero (with a contract) for earlier models, and with market shares quickly growing, a smart phone is a digitally wise thing to own. But digital wisdom also involves finding the combination of features and price that works for you, and not necessarily always running after the newest models. I quickly upgraded my iPhone, for example, to get Siri and 4G, but I still haven't seen enough additional value for me from the (larger) iPad to purchase one.

Cultivating digital wisdom requires being continuously on the lookout—in print and online—for new apps. Finding new apps does not even necessarily mean trading off "people time" for "screen time." One of the preferred in-person activities of digitally wise individuals with smart phones is comparing and trading apps—an activity that is fun and makes both parties more productive.

Finding an app that works well in your life can immediately make your life better. Because it is an app in my phone, I now always have a camera with me—I have a wonderful archive of my son's life that I would never have had if I'd had to carry around a separate camera. I now always have with me a way of recording ideas that come to me while I am out shopping, exercising, or doing other things—thoughts that I used to just forget. (Many of the ideas in this book were initially recorded on my iPhone.) For me, an important piece of cultivating my own digital wisdom is training myself to remember and use all the various apps I have on my phone—I am continually forgetting about tools I am carrying that could be helpful to me, to my detriment.

One does need to cultivate digital wisdom in selecting the apps and capabilities one installs on one's smart phone, trading off things we want (or need) immediate and constant access to, against what we can, or prefer to, save for later. This trade-off depends very much on the way you choose to conduct your life. For some, having email on their smart phone is important and even crucial. For others like myself, who don't actually need to look at email minute to minute, it may be preferable not to have it on one's phone, as I don't. The same "it depends" answer is also true for other apps, like Twitter. Following too many people, and reading all their tweets as they are posted, is probably of little value. But it is almost certainly digitally wise to follow individuals whose ideas, communications, or whereabouts are important to you—which might include family members and, for some, colleagues or politicians—where knowing immediately what these followers have said is quite useful. Sending out tweets yourself is wise if they help you achieve a goal, such as informing people of your thoughts and whereabouts or marketing yourself or your products, and it is increasingly valuable for sharing one's opinion with particular groups by using what are known as hashtags.[9] But it may be digitally wise to learn to restrain yourself from sending out too many tweets, particularly at once, because getting a long series of tweets from the same person can often turn people off.

Cultivating digital wisdom also involves learning not to spend too much time finding (and especially using) apps that are just digitally clever (or dumb)—particularly apps that will just clutter your phone, taking up space, after you have played with the "new toy" for a bit.

Cultivating digital wisdom means learning (and accepting) a lot of new ideas that come with technology. Many features that may initially strike you as silly, or even bad, can on further inspection be seen as digitally wise. For example, the abbreviations many use while texting ("u" for "you," etc.) may seem awful, ungrammatical perversions to some when they first come across them (complaints are often heard about how they are destroying our language and our kids' ability to write). But once a person begins to text, those abbreviations make things go so much faster that not using them is digitally unwise. The trade-off here is speed and productivity against traditional grammatical correctness, but "correctness" depends very much upon context. So cultivating digital wisdom means keeping a close eye on context. Language perfectly acceptable in a texting context, for example, is unacceptable in a formal context, such as a government or business report—and vice versa. This is what we need to teach our kids—not that texting, with all its "funny" language, is bad, but rather that "good or bad" depends on the formality (or informality) of the context. Digital wisdom lies in knowing what is appropriate to use when.

Similarly, people new to texting, or who text infrequently, often find that using "predictive text" (where the program suggests your next probable word, based on initial letters and context) slows them down and gets in their way. But if you text frequently, making the trade-off of taking the time to master this system pays off handsomely in time saved while texting and is therefore the digitally wise thing to do.

Cultivating Digital Wisdom in Personal Health

An important area of life where it is important to cultivate digital wisdom is personal health care—taking care of ourselves and our bodies. Cultivating digital wisdom here generally involves doing more work ourselves (such as online searching) versus leaving everything to health professionals, as most of us did in the past, but this has a large payoff as well. In some cases, having the digital wisdom to find information about diseases and nutrition can, as we saw with the case of Larry Smarr, prolong our lives.

Cultivating digital wisdom in this area means learning about and exploring sites like WebMD, which provides accurate and trusted medical information. It means finding the email addresses of as many of your healthcare providers as possible—often you need to ask for them directly—and even selecting, when possible, only health providers who let you communicate with them in this easier and more direct way. Today many doctors—although far from all—are willing to give their patients their email addresses to be used in appropriate circumstances. Doing this involves new trade-offs for both parties:

for the doctors, trading off personal privacy (and possibly lifestyle) against patents' ability to reach them; for the patients, trading off increased access against respect for doctors' busy lives. Cultivating digital wisdom involves learning to discuss these trade-offs with your health providers directly.

Cultivating digital wisdom also means learning to use the Internet, when conditions warrant, for deeper medical research, by accessing a wider base of information than any single healthcare professional may have time to pursue. It is often a worthwhile trade-off to invest your own time and thought in doing this versus just trusting whatever "experts" you happen to have access to. A father told me the story of his young son who, when he heard that the father's mother needed surgery, found online published success rates of every local surgeon doing the operation she needed and recommended to his grandmother the surgeons with the highest success rates. Needless to say, the father was pleased. He was also surprised that this was possible, even though he worked in the computer industry—we can always get digitally wiser.

Cultivating digital wisdom means making all your trade-offs in favor of being an informed and a proactive health consumer. Should you or someone you know develop any serious medical condition needing treatment, it is digitally wise to spend time searching the Internet for options that your own healthcare network may not provide. This can often be done by connecting via the Internet with people who have already had various treatments—online communities exist for almost any serious disease. It is wise to talk with such people—online or off—before making any irrevocable decisions, as I did, very helpfully, when I was diagnosed with a disease for which there are multiple treatment options. (I'm now fine, by the way.)

Even when you are not ill, there are, as we saw in Chapter 3, many digitally wise ways to monitor your own body and health. More and more digital devices measuring heart rate, blood pressure, blood-sugar level, and other parameters have become inexpensive and easy to wear (e.g., while exercising). Many connect easily to smart phones and Internet databases.[10] Using these is digitally wise in that they can provide signals and early warnings of possible danger.

Some things that are difficult for many people to do, such as losing weight, are also made easier by the wide use of digital technology. Using an Internet-connected scale to compare your weight online with others of similar age, height, and health and/or competing—via smart phone apps—to see who can lose the most weight safely are among the many digitally wise ways to do this.

Finding and exchanging healthy recipes online, and getting online support in difficult medical and emotional circumstances, are also digitally wise things to do.

Cultivating Digital Wisdom in Managing Our Money

A third personal life area where cultivating digital wisdom can be of great benefit to many is in managing our money and finances—something almost all of us struggle with. Increasingly, digital wisdom is required to do this well. Almost all bank and brokerage accounts can now be monitored online, and it is digitally wise to do so, and to know what to look for. Cultivating digital wisdom means, for anyone who is still uncomfortable with monitoring their finances and paying their bills electronically, becoming adept at doing so—it is digitally wise, with the help of knowledgeable people, to learn to use the many available—and now quite sophisticated—money management tools. Some fear trading off their privacy for these online capabilities, and although it is certainly worth trying to protect oneself against, some loss of privacy is one of the trade-offs required to get modern financial benefits. Despite Madoff, and other stories we hear about, the occasions of actual harm are, statistically, quite low. Most taxes in the United States are now filed online—many are required to be.[11] Refunds now show up electronically—and much more quickly and securely—into more and more people's bank accounts. This is digital wisdom—the days of people showing up in a financial advisor's office with a shoebox full of paper receipts are, mercifully, coming to an end.

Cultivating Digital Wisdom in Our Other Personal Activities

It is also important to cultivate digital wisdom in our leisure activities, such as vacations, sports, and hobbies, and to always look for digitally wise trade-offs. Examples of opportunities to do this, which increase every day, include using the Internet (and apps) to find the cheapest airline tickets and hotel rooms, to locate the best camping and fishing spots, and even to finding the fish, using digital locators. Many of the trade-offs involve using our own time versus paying someone else, such as a travel broker—a broker's useful expertise now gets traded off against your own self-knowledge of your particular preferences, and against the opinions of the many people who report their good and bad experiences online.

Cultivating digital wisdom also involves building connections online to others who share even our narrowest interests. From my days studying the Japanese language, I am part of a small but worldwide community of people who practice an obscure Japanese incense ceremony. We rarely see each other, but we are in frequent contact online. My 7-year-old son recently increased his important (to him) knowledge of taxicabs by finding a web site that sold scale models from all over the world. Assuming his interest continues, a digitally wise next step once he gets a bit older would be to try to connect with some of the site's customers to find others around the world who share his passion.

Cultivating Digital Wisdom Through Video

I want to emphasize one particular tool that is crucial in cultivating digital wisdom. That is the important new role that short video (and, more generally, self-directed online learning) now plays in our becoming digitally wise. The number of "how-to" videos online is now so vast that people can learn not only particular tasks but also whole new tools and professions, particularly digital professions, by watching appropriate videos. Many computer programmers, digital artists, and, increasingly, app makers now learn or build their skills in this way. The creator of one site that offers such videos for learning app making—appdevsecrets.com—claims you can learn skills that will allow you to earn money, and perhaps even a living, without ever leaving your house. Doing this type of digitally available learning can, in many cases, be digitally wise. But cultivating digital wisdom also means carefully investigating for scams before investing any money, and it certainly requires trading off our desire for relaxation and leisure at home for what can often be some pretty hard work.

CULTIVATING DIGITAL WISDOM AT WORK

We all live in an increasingly digital work world, and it pays to become a digitally wise worker. This is not just true in so-called "white collar" jobs. I have observed beverage delivery men carrying around company-provided tablet computers on which they keep their route and all their records. Package delivery employees carry tracking devices and bar code scanners. And many waiters and waitresses today—even in Paris cafés—have computers strapped to their belts for taking payments and, in some cases, for ordering. Some Salvation

Army Santas who ring bells in the streets at Christmas time have begun using new cell-phone technology to accept donations by credit card.

Cultivating Digital Wisdom in Business

Anyone who resists the computerization and digitization of their own business or job is almost certainly fighting a losing battle and is very likely being digitally unwise. Cultivating digital wisdom in business means trying to understand as much as you can about whatever technology is provided to you by your employer: how it works, what its shortcomings are—and in trying to improve it. Whether you are a factory worker, journalist, salesperson, or in any other job, the digitally wisest course is to try to be the most digitally savvy worker that you can.

Of course while technology at work can be a tool for great productivity, it can also be a great way to goof off. Cultivating digital wisdom at work lies in figuring out the difference and acting accordingly. Companies, bosses, and supervisors are increasingly concerned with employees using their work time and technology to pursue personal interests, such as online shopping or gambling. Much digital wisdom in the workplace lies in figuring out how to achieve the proper balance in your own setting.

We need more ways not to waste our increasingly powerful business tools, but to put them to a variety of good uses to increase both business and personal productivity (this even includes unused computer cycles).[12] More and more managers are learning to trade off letting workers use technology to pursue personal interests, within limits, for higher productivity overall. Google has found, for example, that giving employees one day a week (i.e., as much as 20 percent of their time) to pursue their own interests—using all of the company's technology—makes them, overall, far better and more productive employees.[13] Technology, when used with digital wisdom, helps Google and other companies and their employees work smarter, versus just working harder.

Is the trend that we increasingly see in business of the merging of people's business technologies and tools with their personal ones—things that have heretofore typically been mostly kept separate—digitally wise? To the great dismay of many technology managers, employees increasingly want to use their own personal tools—including computers, iPads, smart phones, and others—as their work tools as well. (This new office-based trend is not surprising to workers in fields such as construction or medicine, who have long preferred to—and been allowed or required to—bring their own tools.)

In the case of electronic tools, the reasons for bringing your own can include that your own tools are better (which they are in many cases) or that you just prefer them. But in the digital world, everyone bringing their own tools brings with it a whole host of problems, including security, backup, privacy, and many other issues for businesses to deal with. Companies certainly need to cultivate digital wisdom to do so. They must learn to make new, digitally wise trade-offs—business security versus employee access, more productivity from familiar tools versus more opportunities for distraction on those tools, and more recent and expensive technology that employees own versus older technology the business might have.

Interestingly, as technology advances it often solves its own problems. For example, a great many technology managers were at one time losing sleep over how to trade off their need for security of information in the "cloud" of remote—but unsecure—data centers against their need for having variable capacity available to deal with load peaks—each required a different cloud solution. But then a technology called "secure cloud bursting" was developed that allows managers to have the best of the two worlds, private and public, and avoid making the trade-off altogether.[14] This is typical of the way technology advances—we have issues and we find digitally wise solutions. The digital wisdom lies on the part of both the people who develop such problem-solving technologies and those who quickly move to use them. It should be cultivated.

Top-level executives, who in the past prided themselves on not having a computer in their office (or who had one in there, unplugged, just for show—I actually saw that), are needing to cultivate more and more digital wisdom as well, particularly for developing business strategies. Companies, from start-ups to giants, now require a "digital strategy"—that is, a way to construct and manage an online presence, keeping it always up to date. Top executives now need to cultivate digital wisdom about things like search engine optimization (SEO) and the use of social media as important pieces of their strategy and tactics. As a result, all sorts of new business jobs and professions are emerging for the digitally wise.

For example, with the rise of sites on which customers can comment—often anonymously—on any product and service, companies must carefully monitor what people are saying about them online. They now require the digital wisdom to successfully manage their reputations. This goes for the smallest companies as well as the largest: I recently searched the Internet for a long-lost friend who was, I knew, a custom homebuilder. The only thing I found online about his business was a horrible screed from a dissatisfied customer telling anyone who would listen that my friend was a crook and to never use his business under any circumstances (leading me to wonder whether my friend had gone out of business or even moved to another country). But when I finally located my friend—via Facebook, of course—and talked to him, I found that he was doing fine, and that the writer was just one of my friend's extremely few unsatisfied customers out of hundreds of happy ones, a customer who, my friend said, was "impossible to deal with." But anyone searching for my friend's business would come away with a totally wrong impression, as I did, so my friend would be digitally wise to repair this. Cultivating digital wisdom in business (and even sometimes personally) means trading off spending time and money to actively manage your online reputation against the dangers of just letting that reputation happen, often to your detriment. Some refer to searching for yourself or your business online as "ego surfing." But whatever you want to call it, it is digitally wise to do this frequently. Doing so can often be beneficial: A writer I know found an incredibly positive review of his book that he had totally missed—a review that he now features prominently in his marketing.

Cultivating digital wisdom is also needed by executives, as I discussed in Chapter 3, to find good and appropriate new, online business models. In more and more industries, the traditional business models that have worked for generations, and even centuries, are being shaken up and changed by technology. Think of Michael Dell's shaking up of even the "new" (at the time) personal computer industry by starting to build to order, instead of to inventory. Or think of music. Or publishing.

The industries that have already been digitally transformed are only the tip of the iceberg, as technology enables more new possibilities and channels for earning customers' money. Finding a good business model is one of the hardest and most important things for any company to do—without it a business, no matter how innovative, will die. Many traditional models, such as advertising support, are becoming more targeted with digital technology. Individually targeted ads, which technology now permits, are worth more, which is how Google and Facebook make so much money. The combined purchasing power of large numbers of online buyers, along with the elimination of expensive retail stores, allows companies like Amazon to lower prices dramatically, also changing the competitive landscape.

Huge court fights erupt around tiny elements—such as the use by others of Amazon's trademarked term "1-click"—because such seemingly trivial features can be worth billions of dollars to a company. I use "1-click," for example, to buy every interesting book I ever come across, and I always use Amazon—something I would not do if it weren't so easy—every vendor wants to copy that. The fact that the books can go directly to my Kindle device (in my case to the Kindle app on my iPhone) in seconds also makes me want to spend more. Cultivating digital wisdom also means being the first to implement these technological advantages. It also means understanding all the legal, financial, security, and other issues in doing this.

In expanding successively and successfully from the online iTunes store to the online app store to the online Apple software store, and by tying those stores into devices people wanted, Apple became the largest technology company in the world. There is still much opportunity to find new, technology-based business models like these, and cultivating digital wisdom in business lies, to a great extent, in looking for them—entrepreneurs, venture capitalists, and others who spot the good models early can become extremely wealthy. According to Professor Clayton Christensen of Harvard Business School, author of *The Innovator's Dilemma*, a constant struggle goes on between older, successful companies that tend to extend their current technologies and innovators who offer new technology in a "disruptive" fashion to leapfrog and reach customers in different and often cheaper ways. With the pace of technological innovation increasing, we are seeing such disruption in a great many fields, including health care, education, and even manufacturing. Cultivating digital wisdom includes looking for and implementing such disruptive technologies, whether as an entrepreneur or an existing business. The trade-offs include investing in new business models versus continuing to incrementally improve old ones, finding new ways to get customers to part with their money versus annoying them, lowering prices versus maintaining local relationships with customers, and continually providing new kinds of value versus just charging more for old stuff. The struggle between local book stores that cater to local customers' needs (but at higher prices) and large online booksellers like Amazon and Barnes and Noble is a good example of this this trade-off and the continuing search for digital wisdom

Entirely new roles, jobs, and professions are being created because of digital technology, and those who cultivate digital wisdom will be the first ones to design and fill them. There now exists, for example, a job (perhaps even a profession) of "Twitter coach"—one of the first to hire one of these was the basketball star Shaquille O'Neal, who realized that he lacked the digital wisdom to use Twitter effectively, on his own, to promote himself and his career. The person Shaq hired was so successful she has now moved on to be a Twitter consultant to a great many businesses. Her digital wisdom resides in knowing how, when, and how much to tweet for maximum effectiveness.[15] So-called "social media consultancies" are opening up, seemingly, on every digital corner, and established PR firms are also adding these capabilities to their roster, creating a growing demand for such people. Another brand-new job is "app developer," expanding on—and in some cases already replacing—the now old programmer and "web developer" professions of the last decades.

Digital wisdom in the use of social media has become, in a very short time, a lucrative capacity to develop. Cultivating such digital wisdom requires continually preparing yourself to move into emerging and growing new jobs and professions, trading off the effort and cost required to do this against remaining—perhaps no longer so securely—with those you have. It often involves taking time off to invest in getting retrained.

Cultivating digital wisdom certainly involves being a continual learner, versus having your learning come to a halt when you leave school.

Digital wisdom is increasingly required in management at all levels. As new digital tools get created, employers must decide whether to buy them and/or whether to help employees learn to use them. Managers must now have the digital wisdom to find the right answers to questions like: Should my company's salespeople be using customer relations management software, such as Salesforce.com? Which software (with so many competitors and innovators in every field) is the best to purchase? When do I change or upgrade? When should I switch my factories from machines controlled by individual people to digitally controlled machines?

More and more businesses are finding that newer, younger "digital native" employees differ, in many ways, from workers of the past, often in terms of their backgrounds, preferences, and capabilities. This requires cultivating new, digitally wise management approaches, something that many companies are still searching for. In the digital world, young new hires who traditionally had to "pay their dues" before making meaningful business decisions and contributions can now often, if managed right, start adding enormous value from day one—particularly in technology-enhanced areas of the business.

Cultivating Digital Wisdom in the Professions

People who currently work—or aspire to work—in what we call "the professions," that is, fields such as medicine, law, and teaching, have a particular need to cultivate digital wisdom. On the one hand, more and more technology is being used in all aspects of the professions—technology that it is digitally wise for a new or experienced professional to learn how to employ to maximum effectiveness. At the same time, professionals who are, or have become, digitally wise are finding and creating more and more opportunities to use digital technology (and their digital wisdom) to leverage what they do and to increase the effectiveness of their practices. It is important for people in these professions to trade off things like having humans do tasks versus automating them, using only highly paid professionals to do tasks versus allowing more technology-enhanced people with less training or experience to do them, and adopting more efficient technology practices versus billing more hours.

Budding lawyers and paraprofessionals, for example, now need to acquire, as part of their training, a great deal of digital wisdom, including how to wisely use the many legal databases available for searching case law, and how to wisely make use of digital forensics. Law schools are struggling to cultivate digital wisdom to keep up in these areas. Many firms and lawyers are now using the technology of "e-discovery" to cull through thousands, or even millions, of documents and records in a short time—this was done in the Enron case, for example. Using these digital tools wisely can, in many cases, give an individual lawyer or small practice the search power of a large firm—and a big competitive advantage. Digital wisdom is needed to decide how and when to employ these tools—whether to buy them or in some cases rent or lease them; whether to hire new people who know how to use them, or invest the time to learn them and retrain existing employees.

In the legal profession—as in most other professions—digital tools do not—at least for now—replace the professionals for everything. Lawyers are still needed to think, strategize, and produce written and oral arguments. But as digital tools become increasingly available to help with higher-end tasks such as research, they often allow some of the work previously done by higher-paid lawyers to be done by lower-paid paraprofessionals and assistants.

Researching past legal cases and precedents used to be a laborious task of look-ing in the large volumes that traditionally fill lawyers' library shelves, one often done manually by incoming first-year lawyers. Since the advent of LexisNexis, an online database of all these cases, this type of research has become largely computerized. Since good legal research can often provide an edge, having the digital wisdom to buy and use the best search software is important—no mat-ter who uses it.

And in many cases, things that used to require hiring a lawyer no longer do. Legalzoom.com and other online sites enable ordinary people to complete previously lawyer-requiring tasks, such as setting up wills, incorporations, and even simple divorces. This removes some of the easy, high-paying work that made the legal profession an attractive one in the past. However, technology (and digital wisdom) puts human lawyers' knowledge effort and ingenuity back on the most complex and difficult legal cases, where it belongs.

A big need in cultivating digital wisdom is to invest in more up-to-date training for professionals that takes into account modern digital developments and tools. Recent calls for more "real-life" training of legal students reflect this; one of the best ways to provide more life-like experience is through the use of computer-based simulations, which, as I previously noted, some law schools are now using.[16]

Digital wisdom is also becoming indispensable for doctors and all medical professionals, as medicine and health care become both more evidence-based and complex. I discussed at the start of this book the APACHE system that helps doctors decide whether patients should remain in an ICU. More and more of these so-called "expert systems" now exist in the medical area; part of cultivating digital wisdom for doctors is becoming aware of all the systems that apply to them and fully understanding those systems' strengths and shortcom-ings. Some expert systems, such as those for detecting drug interactions, may be available to patients as well, and digital wisdom for doctors increasingly includes knowing how to deal with patients who arrive in their offices techno-logically pre-informed.

Another part of cultivating digital wisdom in health care is making sure that all the new digital tools being developed actually work as advertised. Technology is creating new medical tools and prostheses almost daily, from digitally printed bone replacements to custom-grown skin, blood vessels, and other body parts.[17] Recently, a type of technological hip joint was pulled from the market after being used in hundreds of operations. Could more digital wisdom have prevented this? How do we trade off care and risk in deciding which technologies are digitally wise to use, as both doctors and patients?

A huge and increasingly difficult part of every doctor's job is keeping up to date with changes in medicine, overall and in their own specialty and sub-specialty. Even if doctors find the time to read through their piles of paper journals to keep current, that is no longer sufficient. In most cases, doctors need to use new technology-based tools and filters to enable the important information in their field to come to them quickly and directly, in the formats and timeframes that are most useful to each of them. One example of such a tool is Cyberounds (cyberounds.com). It's an online quiz for doctors providing very serious and intense online medical training, even offering continuing education credits to doctors for successful completion. Cyberounds's information—created by high-reputation doctors in a variety of specialties and extremely detailed—is set in the engaging and competitive scoring context of golf and other games. Part of cultivating digital wisdom for doctors (and all professionals) is knowing about, and using, these forms of technology-based continuing education effectively.

Digital technology is being used more and more for diagnosis and treatment, and new machines are appearing in all medical and healthcare fields with higher and higher frequency. Which ones should doctors and other medical professionals learn about, train on, and/or purchase for their practice? How should they interpret the results? Which technologies are easiest and most worthwhile to make mobile (like ultrasound technology)? Much digital wisdom needs to be cultivated in these areas.

And as medical records become increasingly computerized—and indefinitely stored, in many cases—the amount of data for researchers to analyze is rising exponentially. This is certainly a good thing in terms of increasing statistical sample sizes for evidence-based medicine. But how to best manage, analyze, interpret, make sense of, and make effective use of all this data requires cultivation of a great more digital wisdom on the part of both doctors and developers.

Dentistry, too, has also become more digital. In addition to dental school training simulators using haptic (i.e., feel-based) technology, digital dental x-rays are now routinely viewed on the examining room's computer screen by doctors and patients together, an instant after being taken, with all the doctor's notes in view. One patient commented that this technology gives her more confidence at the dentist—clearly a positive benefit that digital wisdom suggests all dentists provide!

Cultivating Digital Wisdom in the Humanities

I noted in Chapter 3 that many practitioners in fields like literature, history, philosophy, language, and religion often favor approaches that are critical and speculative, rather than empirical and quantitative, and have been laggards in using technology in their work (other than as writing tools). Many have been strong resisters of technology. Just to give you some idea of the strength of resistance to digital transformation of our universities and colleges, an article I recently wrote for the *Chronicle of Higher Education*, suggesting that some colleges might want to consider—voluntarily—using only digital books and no physical books at all, provoked more than 100 very nasty online comments, including, a "God help you."[18] Stories abound in academia of older professors rejecting the introduction of technology into scholarship. One recently minted Ph.D. told me that, although all the old manuscripts that she used and cited in her doctoral thesis were scanned and online, she was not allowed to link to any of them. The humanities are an area that could stand to cultivate a lot more digital wisdom.

And this cultivation is already happening in many places. In 2012—the year this book was written—"Digitizing the Humanities" was the cover story of an issue of *Harvard Magazine*. Harvard has started a research program, called metaLAB (a part of its Beekman Center for Internet and Society), to chart out "innovative scenarios for the future knowledge creation and dissemination in the arts and humanities."[19]

Computer-based tools such as statistical and linguistic analyses, historical geography using new exploration and visualization techniques, interactive, participatory multimedia databases about historical events, the use of scanners, x-rays, spectral analysis in art history, and a variety of other technologies—most originally developed for other purposes—are enabling professionals and workers in these areas to move in many new directions. Some departments are experimenting with allowing doctoral theses in multiple media.

Cultivating digital wisdom can enhance scholarship in many ways, including the temporal and intellectual scope of research and of publications as well.[20] It is particularly important in these types of fields—characterized by slow change and high resistance—that the trade-offs be discussed. These include trading off new, easier ways of doing things versus traditions, modern versus old ways of learning, and even new versus old definitions of scholarship. No field, including the humanities, should reject technological enhancement out of hand. Fortunately, through the work of younger professors, the creation of new research centers and online journals, and the establishment of new, technology-assisted processes of accelerated online peer review more digital wisdom is beginning to emerge in these fields. Cultivating digital wisdom means encouraging these initiatives.

Cultivating Digital Wisdom in the Arts

Artists—perhaps because their work revolves around creativity and connecting with the current world—often embrace new technology quickly. Artists have been incorporating digital technology into their work for some time, ever since its first appearances—works incorporating video, recorded sound, multimedia, along with live-action can be found in museums, galleries, and studios in all parts of the world. Electronic music has been with us for more than half a century.

Still, we need to constantly work to cultivate even more digital wisdom in the arts. Composers, visual artists, and performance artists often need to master many technological tools—think, for example, of how Broadway musicals and even circuses have changed their technology dramatically. Photography and motion pictures have already gone, to a large extent, digital. In fact, in almost every artistic field, digital tool creators are making it easier and easier for people with non-technological backgrounds to use technology to create: The range of music and video that it is possible for almost anyone to produce with an iPhone or iPad is staggering. The digital wisdom in the art fields resides both in the development of new tools for maximum usefulness and expression, and in the ways professional artists (and teachers and ordinary people) use the tools and put the pieces together.

Today even live performance requires much digital wisdom. How should voices be best enhanced and amplified? Different theaters, for example, do this in different ways. Should opera translations be provided on the backs of seats or over the stage? Technology increasingly is used to enhance live artistic experiences—the world of popular music concerts has become a technology wonderland, with acts competing to include the most spectacular effects as part of the performance. Think of how incredibly dull the opening and closing ceremonies of the Olympic Games would be without ever-improving (and ever more creatively used) technology. Of course, digital wisdom comes in assessing not only the artistic value of this technology, but also its safe and cost-effective use.

Non-digitally enhanced music is already practically an anachronism. Amplification is used even for so-called "acoustic" instruments, and new concert halls are built incorporating the latest digital sound-enhancing technologies. Some of the people with the greatest digital wisdom in music are not the artists but the technicians, the engineers, and the so-called "roadies" who design, build, and maintain the technology. Many of them are among the most digitally wise among us.

We have already seen the technology-based matching of human voices and animated drawings. In addition to technical wizardry of "repurposing" long-dead actors into modern commercials and films via technology, this generation is now witnessing the emergence of totally artificial (yet artful) actors, often called "synthespians."[21]

Wherein lies the digital wisdom? This question is being asked and explored at many artistic levels. One interesting phenomenon that creators have found is the "uncanny valley"—a strange space between caricatured characters of cartoons and human actors in films. There appears to be a point at which, as technology-created characters become more and more lifelike, they begin to make many people feel uncomfortable and "creepy"—it is hard for humans to accept characters that are almost human, but not quite.[22] Digital wisdom, and art, lies in exploring this uncanny valley and other phenomena like it that emerging technologies create.

Given the ephemeral nature of many, if not all, digital technologies, many artworks already only run on computers, or exist only on hard drives, that have already become obsolete. One of the key places where digital wisdom is needed is in preservation of many of these new artistic works. In order to continue to exhibit older technology-based art works, the technologies they run on—which may have long gone out of use (and lost their technical support)—have to continue to work. Maintaining old hardware has become a major problem for museum curators around the world, and we are in need of digitally wise solutions. (Creating so-called "emulators"—which create the old computers' capabilities on new ones using software—is one such solution.)

It is also digitally wise to develop new artistic technologies that require as little digital paraphernalia as possible to be experienced: Eliminating the need for 3-D glasses is an example of this. Many movies are now 3-D, and the era of viewing our characters and stories as holograms is close upon us. Will the Star Trek Holodeck, long a holy grail for visual and storytelling artists, show up in our children's lifetimes? Digital wisdom suggests it very likely may.

Speaking of which, storytelling is yet another art that has been greatly influenced by digital technology. I have already discussed how technology is helping make many things shorter and more concise—YouTube, television commercials, and "Kindle Shorts" e-books are examples. Technology is also now transforming story content, particularly by making it, in many cases, interactive (i.e., user-controlled). This happens, for example, in story-based video games such as Halo and World of Warcraft—storytelling itself takes on new meaning in these technological settings. It will take much digital wisdom to create the kinds of masterpieces in these new media that were created in poems, novels, and films. But anyone who bets it won't happen, and that the old media and forms of storytelling will continue to dominate forever, is not showing, in my view, nearly enough digital wisdom.

For all artists, digital wisdom means employing new digital technologies in service not of novelty (although that may often happen—particularly in entertainment) but rather of communication of powerful and lasting ideas. Digital wisdom lies in finding new ways, through these technologies for artist to express—as they have always done—their ideas, feelings, vision, and comments on our human condition.

Cultivating Digital Wisdom in Other Spheres

There are, of course, many other spheres and walks of life in which digital wisdom and important trade-offs are required. Without the space to go into those in detail here, I invite you, on your own, to consider digital wisdom in such fields as sports, architecture, safety, law enforcement, environment, and others.

CULTIVATING DIGITAL WISDOM IN EDUCATION

A final area where I believe an enormous amount of digital wisdom will need to be cultivated in coming years is education. Many of our young people— even though they may be "digital natives" who were born into the digital age and quite comfortable with much of the new technology—are not necessarily digitally wise. It is up to us to help our young people cultivate and acquire digital wisdom as they grow up to live in the digital, twenty-first-century world. Cultivating digital wisdom in our young people is so important that I devote the entire next chapter to it.

SIX

TEACHING DIGITAL WISDOM

How Do We Lead Our Kids to Develop It?

N
ot only is it wise for us to teach digital wisdom to our young people, but it is imperative that we do so. Digital wisdom certainly can be learned, and we need to teach it profoundly.

Unfortunately, this is not easy. But we need to figure it out.

Digital wisdom—the idea that future wisdom *requires* that we integrate our minds and technology—is a new concept, one that is just developing. Most of today's older adults—a group that includes many of our teachers—did not grow up with technology and find it deeply uncomfortable.

I described the issue a decade ago using the metaphor of "digital natives" and "digital immigrants."[1] Digital natives are the people born into the digital world who (while they may not know everything about it) are very comfortable with its use and consider it a foundational part of their lives. Digital immigrants are those who grew up in a pre-digital world and often regard technology with fear, suspicion, and mistrust.

Over the decade, a great many people found this metaphor very useful, but recently there has been a backlash. Some professors have interpreted the digital native concept as meaning knowledge of *everything* about technology, rather than referring to a comfort level with technology by virtue of having grown up with it. Observing that their students didn't know every detail about technology, these academics have wondered if the concept of a digital native is a myth. Seeing many older people now comfortable with technology and many young people who are not, they ask whether age is still the best criterion on which to base a distinction. Some also worry that the digital native/digital immigrant concept divides people, letting each group retreat into a corner of "I'm right" or "I'm comfortable here" rather than working together.

In general, the digital native/digital immigrant distinction has become far less useful than it was a decade ago. I believe it is now time to move on from this decade-old metaphor. Expressing this, a recently published collection of my essays was titled *From Digital Natives to Digital Wisdom.*[2] It no longer serves our best interests to just describe our differences; we need to find ways to work together to solve the future's problems. Many of today's adults, as we have seen in previous chapters, already possess and exhibit digital wisdom in their lives and work.

Technology, as we all know, plays a huge part in more and more of our young people's lives. Many are already deeply involved with cell phones, computers, and other technology in their daily activities. And most of the young people around the world who are not currently involved with technology would love to be. I have heard this personally from kids in many countries, including the Middle East. We also know this from innovative undertakings such as the Hole in the Wall project in India, where Sugata Mitra embedded computers in a wall and children were allowed to use and play with them as they wished, and the One Laptop per Child (OLPC) program started by professors at MIT, which has provided computers costing $100–$200 to children in many underdeveloped nations. Nicholas Negroponte, founder of the OLPC project, reports that it takes only 20 minutes for the typical child who has never laid hands on a computer to get connected to the Internet and begin doing useful work on it. Both of these projects showed that even the most impoverished kids can and will learn to use technology extremely quickly if they are just given opportunity and access. And those kids, moreover, are excited about doing so.

In many cases, kids first connect with technology through games: In the United States, for example, more than 90 percent of households with children have at least one game machine.[3] Many of these machines have more computing power than the machines that took us to the moon.

So the willingness and ability of young people to use technology is not the problem—on the contrary. And even the problem of equal access, which is still an issue, has more and more initiatives addressing it.

So we no longer need to communicate to kids how, or even why, to use technology, as we had to do to many of their digital immigrant parents. Our most important educational need now is to communicate to our young people a strong sense of *when their use of technology is wise,* when it is just clever, and when it is dumb. This knowledge will be critical to the success of all young people: from the digitally privileged youth who grow up with technology from their infancy, to the digitally disadvantaged students who are just beginning to use technology or are still waiting.

But how do we teach something that we don't yet, in great measure, all know? A big problem is that because digital technology is still something that many adults are uncomfortable with or even afraid of, our initial attempts to "teach" our kids about digital technology have focused excessively on that technology's potential risks and downsides, rather than on its positives and benefits. This is typical of any new technology—think of our initial teaching about electricity or microwave ovens: It was mostly "be very afraid."

Today this same knee-jerk reaction to focus mainly on the negative can often be seen in adults' "educational" behavior toward their kids regarding technology, both at school and at home. Many parents do not let their young kids touch or play with much of the technology they have—their laptop, smart phone, or tablet—particularly when those items are new. Yet there is little reason not to. Most of this technology poses no more risk to kids than other electricity or battery-using gadgets they use. It's also pretty hard to break these devices if they're not played with excessively roughly. With proper safeguards (including programs limiting the ability to accidentally delete things, see unwanted images, or acquire viruses or malware), kids can explore their parents' digital technology and learn—something that they typically love to do—with few downsides.

The same thing holds true in schools. I recently surprised a group of inner city principals, each beaming because they had been given a new iPad (paid for by a grant), by suggesting to them that those iPads were not for their own use, but for their students', and that they needed to get them into their schools' classrooms and make sure that every student got to spend some quality learning time with them. Some were disappointed, but they all knew I was right. Many technology items that schools have purchased, such as electronic white boards, have signs taped on them saying, "Students don't touch." The signs should, in fact, say the opposite: "Teachers don't touch: Our technology is to be used by our students."

The communication problem actually goes far deeper. Many wonder today why so many of our kids avoid the "STEM" fields of science, technology, engineering, and math. Well, all these fields are technology based. While politicians like President Obama are expressing positive messages about these fields, many of the adults actually in the kids' lives—including many of their teachers—are continually broadcasting to them the unconscious message that technology is hard to use, not helpful, and best avoided.

So what *should* we want people, young and old, to learn about digital wisdom and about technology?

The most fundamental lesson of all is cultural, not technological. It is that these digital tools and technologies are now used fruitfully in every walk of life and cannot be rejected, but must be rather embraced. Digital technologies are part of our young people's (and our own) twenty-first-century lives, and we all need to get comfortable with our lives being enhanced by them. Just as more and more people in the world now have difficulty conceiving of a world without television (a technology that, unfortunately, we never succeeded in using to its maximum advantage), digital technology is now among the givens of twenty-first-century life in more and more places. One could even say it is the birthright of those born into the early twenty-first century. This is particularly true of game machines, cell phones, and, increasingly, video. I often point out to teachers that if they feel uncomfortable appearing in a video, they have to work to get over it, because video is one of the most important ways in which twenty-first-century people communicate. Teachers need to get comfortable so they can teach their kids to be comfortable.

Of course even though kids do need guidance, the lesson that technology is an important part of their lives is one that young people generally absorb on their own. "For us, technology is a foundation," explained one high school student. "It underlies everything we do."[4] A great many of our young people are already teaching themselves to get along in the symbiotic, man-machine, extended-mind world of their future. Our job now is to coach them and teach them to do that wisely; our job as adults and teachers is to be sure they are helped, and not held back, by today's many technological extensions and advantages.

But to teach digital wisdom to our children, we need it ourselves, and so we must all remain continually on the quest for digital wisdom and focus on teaching in a way that is digitally wise.

What does that mean, practically? It means we must stop focusing primarily on technology's dangers, as we currently do. An enormous part of the "computer" education offered today tends to be of the "this-is-a-bad-web-site" or "don't-put-a-naked-picture-on-the-Internet" kind. Many adults think they are extremely clever when they discover something "bad" about the Internet that they think their students might not know (such as the now-famous Martin Luther King, Jr., web site actually run by a hate group). But instead of dwelling on this, as is too often the case, what they need to tell kids is, "Yes, these exist, go find more of them to prove the point, and then let's move on to something positive we can do with technology."

One terrific technique for teaching both the positive benefits of technology and the digital wisdom in using it is what I call "imag-u-cation" (or sometimes just "imagining"). It is a technique for teaching about technology that requires neither devices nor money at all but, rather, a great deal of useful—and educational—thought on the part of educators and students. The "technique" (perhaps too fancy a word) consists merely of a teacher or other educator frequently asking the class (which could be in any subject at any level) a couple of important questions such as, "If each of us had an iPad (or a laptop, or an iPhone, etc.) at this moment, or if our class had access to a supercomputer, or any other kind of technology, what could we do with it that would enhance our learning in a major way? What would be the digitally wise way to use these technologies? What uses would be merely clever, or dumb?"

This is the real learning we want our kids to have. Not to just "do" computer-based exercises or lessons—that is trivial—but to know *why* they are doing them, that is, to figure out how to use the tools to produce brain gain.

I also recommend that adults put the students' focus (and keep their own focus) on what I call the "verbs" of education, rather than the "nouns." "Verbs" are the ongoing, important skills we want our students to acquire: to understand, communicate, do critical analysis, persuade, and so forth (there are many of these, and they vary—and their mix varies—in different subjects). Verbs do not vary much over time—they were the same in the past as they are now, even though we may use them differently. The "nouns," in contrast, are the technologies that we use to learn, practice, and master these skills: the hardware, software, computers, phones, tablets, Word, PowerPoint, and the millions of programs and now apps out there.

What has changed radically—and what needs to change radically in education—is not the verbs, but the nouns. We used to have essentially one noun for learning: the book. Now we have a huge number, and they change rapidly. Books become e-books. Blackboards become smart boards. Overheads become PowerPoints. Notebooks become notebook computers and then become smart phones and tablets. All of these tools will continue to evolve, and many others will be added.

Digital wisdom means using all the twenty-first-century tools we can, while always keeping teachers' and students' focus sharply on the skills these tools enhance. Digital wisdom demands that educators first begin by asking themselves, "What are the verbs (i.e., the skills) that we want our students to learn, practice, and master?" And only after they have answered that question can they ask, "What are the latest, most up-to-date nouns (i.e., tools and technologies) that we can use for our students to learn these verbs in a twenty-first-century context?"

The many fights that educators and parents have over what technology tools students *can't* or *shouldn't* use certainly don't help our kids' education or teach them any digital wisdom. This is the real (and unfortunate) lesson that kids learn today from too many adults: that technology is harmful and distracting, and that it gets in the way of "real learning" and of doing things that are important. The dangerous subtext and underlying message about technology from most adults to most children in most places is that all the "really important" things can be done—and in most cases are better done—*without* technology. This is why, even when technology makes its way into schools (and our homes), it is so incredibly under-used compared to the possibilities it offers. It's not that adults can't, in concert with the students, figure out how to use technology for brain gain. It's rather that deep down, I believe, many of them really don't want to. This, unfortunately, is not digital wisdom, but its opposite.

Thankfully, many educators are beginning to see the light. They are introducing iTouches and iPads, integrating blogs and online writing tools into English and other subjects to allow and encourage kids to express themselves and communicate in twenty-first-century ways. One master teacher has created "Cyber-English" classes, in which students use and program digital tools to do all their work.[5] Other educators are integrating social media, such as YouTube, Facebook, and Twitter, into subjects like current events and language learning, letting students communicate with real people—both their peers and experts, in real places, often in real time (as they do in real life). This is all good.

But true digital wisdom lies not just in introducing or allowing the technology into our classrooms (although there is some benefit in doing that), but rather in combining the technology with human minds to create new ways of teaching and learning that our new technology enables.

For example, technology enables teachers to record all lectures for students to watch on their own. Doing this provides, among other benefits, the ability for students to choose the lecturers they like best and to repeat as often as they need the parts they don't understand. Salman Khan, a former investment banker and founder of the widely touted and now well-funded (by Bill Gates and others) Khan Academy (www.khanacademy.org), began doing a lot of this recording for math: He has personally created 10-minute video lectures of much of the U.S. math curriculum, available to anyone on his site or on YouTube for free. He and his organization are now starting on other subjects as well. That it took so long to take this simple yet powerful step—and that it required a non-educator like Khan to do it—is a powerful indictment of our educational system.

But the true digital wisdom, as Khan himself realizes, lies not just in the recordings, but in how they are used. The digital wisdom, as Khan suggests, is for learners to view these lectures *before,* and not during or after, class. (They can also, of course, review them after.) The digital wisdom is in reserving all class time for what the human minds of well-trained and experienced teachers do best: diagnosing student problems and giving them individual attention and support. This is now known as "flipping" the class, and it appears to produce better results.

Additional digital wisdom lies in finding other effective ways to use this technology, such as when teachers ask their questions the day after the students have watched the recorded lectures, *not just telling students the right answer.* Instead, Professor Eric Mazur of Harvard asks his students to "find another person nearby who got a different answer" and to "try to convince each other of whose answer is correct." What Mazur gets from this digitally wise approach is better, more student-centric explanations; what his students get is better understanding for having had to defend their reasoning. Mazur uses technology in several ways to facilitate the process, for example, flipping, having students submit answers via their computers or cell phones, and recording student explanations. He and others also add digital interactive simulations to the mix. But the real digital wisdom comes in combining the technology with better pedagogy to produce the best result. If we continue to use our digital tools wisely and appropriately in ways such as these, our teachers and students will, I believe, get the message that this is a better, more mind-extended way of doing education.

But to truly achieve digital wisdom in our education, that is, to truly prepare our children and students for their digital future, we must still address many fundamental questions about *what* we teach.

When I went to school, half a century ago, I was taught to write letters, reports, and essays. All of these were at that time important and widely used. But today, if a student were to go to work, none of those would likely be needed. The worker would write emails, PowerPoints, and blog posts. So is that what we should teach instead? Yes, to some degree. But by the time many of today's kids are working, those skills won't be important, either. What skills will? I believe we can already foresee that among the most important ones will be working in virtual communities, making videos (on both sides of the camera), and programming our increasingly powerful machines. So these are skills we should be teaching today.

In continuing to teach old, rarely used techniques, we waste a great deal of our educational time, which is, after all, limited. Not that the old techniques weren't useful for developing certain mental habits and skills. But if we believe the habits and skills are valuable, we should find useful, modern ways to develop them.

Is it digitally wise, for example, to spend large amounts of time teaching skills that *practically all adults* now offload to machines? These include, for example, adding, subtracting, multiplying, and dividing large numbers? Do students really need to spend years learning the old methods for doing this (which, by the way, are really just paper-based shortcuts)—even as backup? Wouldn't it be digitally wiser to teach our young people to use spreadsheets and other widely used mathematical tools—and to use them well—from the earliest grades?

Many would be loathe, for example, to see "mental arithmetic" go. But if we are still going to teach it—along with the fundamental lessons of what math is and means, which are still important—we must figure out how that skill helps twenty-first-century people, enhanced with digital tools. One of the only times where the ability to do quick math in our head is truly important is when we are negotiating: A person who can quickly figure out in his or her head the value of something proposed can have an advantage over someone who must pull out tools to calculate. So I'd be for teaching some mental math to our kids in a modern negotiating context. But is it digitally wise to spend years and years of their schooling—which should be a useful and inspiring time—forcing kids to practice long division and multiplication solutions to problems that they can easily do in other ways—solutions, moreover, that many of them will never master? (And it is not even clear how long the negotiating advantage of mental math, assuming there is one, will last. More and more people now sit at the negotiating table with their tablet, or whatever will replace it, in front of them.)

Actually, as Conrad Wolfram noted, in the modern context, we get mathematics teaching backward. We spend almost all our time teaching calculation—the part that machines are much better for. We should be putting our focus instead on the setting up of problems in mathematical language and in interpreting the machine-calculated solutions.

Similar issues exist with writing. Is there anyone who works for a living who still writes most things out in longhand? Yes, there still are some novelists and some doctors—including mine—who do, but are they being digitally wise in doing so, or would their writing of non-fiction books, medical records, and notes be enhanced by being done digitally? (Artistic writing can, of course, be done in whatever way the artist prefers.)

Again, when it counts, we get it backward. Instead of *making* our kids use keyboards to write, which is clearly the best twenty-first-century way, we not only allow them to do it the old way but in many cases even require that they do it by hand. Why?

People have all sorts of explanations for this. I have heard some worry about keyboards changing. Perhaps, they say, we should not teach and require kids to use QWERTY because it might be replaced. *Of course* it will be replaced—it is an awkward technology. But it's unlikely to be replaced by another keyboard. Numerous attempts to change have shown that despite its inconveniences, QWERTY is too embedded in our culture for it to be replaced with another, even better, keyboard—in some cases it's far worse to have two systems than one that is universal. Although it has its flaws, the keyboard is the best text-entry technology humans currently have. It is the one that all businesses use, and the one that all our kids should master—perhaps even before handwriting—so they can write closer to the speed at which they think.

But I do think all keyboards will go away in their lifetime. Humans are in desperate need of a better technology than a keyboard for entering text into a computer. I am confident that a technology will emerge that is universally acknowledged to be so much better than keyboarding or voice that we will all just switch to it in the same way we all quickly switched to automobiles for travel and Google for search. Some still think voice will be that technology, but even when voice-to-text is perfect, there remains the problem of unwanted noise from many talking at once that we already experience with public cell phone calls. The best candidate I have heard about from people working on this problem is something called "sub-vocalization." But the eventual winner remains to be seen. Digital wisdom, though, demands that we solve this particular problem as quickly as possible.

If we really bothered to look at our kid's curriculum carefully, we would see that much of what we teach is not to our kids' benefit at all. A lot of it is really for our own nostalgic pleasure—teaching them to do old things because those things once worked for us. (Worse, we sometimes deliberately make students suffer through whatever we had to suffer though—this is typical of Ph.D. programs.) Today there exist *better ways* than the ways in which most of us learned to write, read, calculate, and do scholarship. The ironic truth is that while we still teach the old ways to our kids, most of us have abandoned those ways and adopted the new ones ourselves.

But we do still insist on teaching the old ways of writing, calculating, and researching to our kids. Not that the old ways aren't fun sometimes, or even attractive or useful, but they have effectively become, in the digital context, little more than a hobby for enthusiasts, like writing with a quill in Chancery Hand. Nothing completely goes away—there are still people in the world making flint arrowheads.[6] But is that (metaphorically) what we want today's kids to be doing?

Some do offer serious rationales for continuing to teach the old ways. They make the (valid) argument that the technology we use influences how we think. Writing by hand, some believe, can influence students' thinking in positive ways.

But even if that's true, so what? Our kids are not going to think like people in Shakespeare's time, who wrote with quills, nor do we want them to. They are not going to think like people in the twentieth century, who wrote with ballpoints. They are going to think like people of the twenty-first century, influenced *by the tools of that century,* the tools of their time. And we should all want and expect them to.

We certainly wouldn't say to a kid who loses his pen or pencil, "Oh, just write the essay in your head!" It is hard to think of a job or profession where the wise interplay of mind and technology is not important. Medical school without technology, anybody? Even the most menial tasks, such as garbage collection, recycling, or sewage treatment, rely on computers to schedule, report issues, and more and more, to automate the process. We need to teach kids to think and work in this way. Digital wisdom also consists of helping kids understand *why* we use technology, which is something we can and should teach not as separate subject, but integrated into all our lessons and classes, just as reading and writing are. They should learn in school not to solve puzzles like Sudoku, for example, but to write the program that creates (and solves) all Sudoku puzzles in one shot.

The questions I believe we should always ask ourselves when deciding what to teach—and when to change over to newer technologies—are, "Is this a digitally wise move?" and "How can we be digitally wiser about it?" It is not always the case that just introducing technology into classrooms *is* digitally wise, which is why so much of it sits unused. Potentially, it is a very good thing, for example, that Mark Zuckerberg plans to give $100 million to the Newark, New Jersey, schools—*if* it is used in a digitally wise way. That way, in my view, would be to imagine and plan for at least a year (and maybe more) before any technology gets ordered. Doing it the other way around—that is, purchasing and *then* planning, as too many educators do—means that by the time people finally figure out digitally wise ways to use the technology, it is already a generation or more old and well on its way to becoming obsolete.

Some worry that valuable skills—particularly "thinking" skills—get lost when we integrate technology. I disagree. This may happen in some instances, but it by no means has to be the case. To prevent it from happening, we must ask, for those skills we consider important: "What are ways to use technology to *better* learn and build these skills?" What we need to find are ways to learn, practice, and master these skills that do not take our young people backward into the past, but rather move them forward into the future? To teach logical thinking, for example, we no longer have to make our kids spend large amounts of time doing 2,000-year-old geometrical proofs; we can offer them programming, which teaches the same skills *and* prepares them for twenty-first-century jobs.

There is no time to teach—and no point in teaching—all the curriculum we taught in the past to our kids. We can't do that in the time we have—or even if we add more—and still prepare our kids for the future. Why is there not more interest in developing a new, twenty-first-century curriculum and not just adding on new skills to the old? If we could all suspend our personal preferences, prejudices, and nostalgic thinking for a bit, it wouldn't be that hard to do.

As parents, we must also become digitally wiser in deciding what technology our kids can use and have. When do we buy our kids their first device? When do we let our kids go online? What games can they play? When can they get onto online communities? When can they go onto Facebook? When, if ever, do they get their own cell phone and unlimited texting plan? These are all decisions parents must make in a digitally wise way. Parents should consider all the technologies' *benefits* before the supposed dangers, many of which, it turns out, are far more theoretical than real. (Even the Public Safety Council cautions that "risk" is not the same as "harm.") And most important, for all parents, is talking with, interacting with, and knowing their own child.

Most children, in my experience, understand requests for balance, and even restrictions—when they see that our admonitions contain what the children instinctively perceive as digital wisdom. If all that parents (or any adults) do is blindly follow fear-inspired advice, such as that often offered in the press, and limit kids beyond what is balanced and reasonable, the children will feel unfairly treated. A high school student expressed this to me in an unforgettable way when I asked her if she had played video games growing up. "No," she responded, "my parents deprived me." The danger we face is that too much of our parenting and education is depriving our kids of important digital wisdom they need for their future. We need to ask ourselves: What benefits do these technologies bring to our kids' lives? Do they make them better communicators? Wiser people? These conversations can, and should, be had with children directly, as soon as they are capable of having them.

Most parents understand, I believe, that at some point kids should have their own technology (assuming the parents can afford it), although there is great disagreement on when to give devices to children. Unfortunately, when many parents decide it's time for their kid to get a piece of technology, such as a computer or a cell phone, they do it in a way that is digitally unwise: They merely give their device to their kid and buy a new one for themselves. "I'm the adult, after all," their internal rationale goes. "I deserve the best and newest. I will treat it better and use it more wisely."

But this is not digital wisdom. Today such thinking is, in fact, backward. Relatively few adults use, or need, the full capability of today's personal machines and tools. But most kids do. They use them for games, for videos, for movies. They constantly push the limits of what the tools they possess can access, download, and do for them, in ways most adults never do. So, hard as it may be to swallow, the digitally wise thing for a parent to do is to buy the latest and greatest technology for your kid, and not for yourself. You, the adult, should keep the technology hand me down (or, perhaps we should call it the hand me up). This may seem like a mistake when you find yourself sitting, as I have, in a room full of colleagues with iPads and you pull out your old laptop. But you are wise to ignore the social pressure and give that iPad (if you only can afford one) to your kid. Chances are excellent that she or he will make much greater use of it than you will.

As schools and educators around the world struggle to find the wisest ways to integrate technology with their instruction, perhaps the digitally wisest thing they can do is to listen carefully to their students—and let the best ones demonstrate just how much they can do. I regularly include panels of local students in the presentations I give to educators, in which the young people get to respond to questions from their elders about what technologies they prefer and about how their learning and performance can best be technologically supported. In most cases, it is the first time that these questions have been asked of the students, and the first time that such discussions have taken place. Audience members always say they find this valuable, and panelists universally find it worthwhile as well. We can learn much digital wisdom from our young technology users.

Another fear often heard relative to technology in education is that using technology will "dumb down" our teaching. This needn't be the case, and, in fact, it ought to do the opposite. For example, teacher and author Howard Rheingold offers a technology-filled course entitled "Introduction to Mind Amplifiers," delivered through his totally online RheingoldU.[7] In it he focuses on the learning potential of mind enhancement and on the ability of new tools to "augment what you can do online." The course is hardly what one would call, in the lingo of students, a "gut." Rheingold requires all students to learn and use many tools, post regularly, and even sign a pledge that they will do all of the extensive work the course requires.

A related fear is that machines will take over the teaching function entirely. If this could be done—and done well—it might not be a terrible thing (the current generation of teachers' jobs aside), but it cannot. Today the digitally wise thing to do is not to let computers do all of our teaching—even though for some types of learning computers may be more efficient or better. Digital wisdom comes rather from a learning partnership among teachers, students, and technology. Such a partnership is, in fact, something that technology both encourages and facilitates. I discuss the partnering process in great detail in my earlier book, *Teaching Digital Natives—Partnering for Real Learning.*

And what technology is it digitally wise for educators to buy and provide for their students? Digital wisdom here, I believe, requires maximum flexibility. One piece of digital wisdom that many educators have acquired the hard way is that it is digitally *unwise* to buy expensive technology, or infrastructure, with an expectation of using and amortizing it over many years. Unfortunately, a great many educators (having finally learned what "amortization" means) are still getting caught in this trap. In an age when technology changes extremely rapidly—with some of it having a life of only months before it is updated or superseded and, at the same time, prices dropping equally quickly— the digitally wise thing to do is generally to purchase new but not too expensive technology (a good example, as of this writing, is the iPod Touch at roughly $150), and to change it every year so that students are continually using the most up-to-date tools. The old educational wisdom of "use it until it breaks or falls apart" and "even though the books may be old, the information is still good" needs a digital update. There is no digital wisdom in trying to educate our kids with old (or even last year's) technology.

More and more people are using technology in digitally wise ways, on their own, in what are now referred to as "informal" learning situations. These out-of-school learning situations are becoming a bigger and bigger part of our total learning, and taking advantage of them is increasingly seen as digitally wise. Some have nothing to do with school or even kids. The *New York Times* recently published a front-page article about a 50-year-old physician—a pathologist—who takes bagpipe lessons from a master teacher more than 1,000 miles away, via Skype. It is likely that this doctor uses much technology in his work, and, being digitally wise, he now integrates it into his play as well. It is now easier than ever, thanks to technology, to learn to play an instrument. The web is awash in how-tos, tablatures, and lessons from experts—resources totally unavailable in my own guitar-learning days. Music learning and appreciation is certainly one domain that technology has opened up, and we should encourage it.

In fact, the digitally wise way to learn almost *any skill* not taught in school has become almost the exclusive domain of technology, via the hundreds of thousands of short how-to videos that can be found on YouTube, Videojug,

Sclipo, Sutree, ExpertVillage, ViewDo, HelpfulVideo, TeacherTube, Vidipedia, and other sites.

Although they typically don't use the term "digital wisdom," a number of academic programs and institutes have arisen, over the past few years, to study and provide more digital wisdom in the world.

One of these programs is the Institute for the Study of Collective Wisdom at MIT. Director Tom Malone describes the key question they are using to organize their work as: How can people and computers be connected so that collectively they act more intelligently than any individual, group or computer has ever done before? "New technologies are now making it possible to organize groups in very new ways" he says, "in ways that that have never been possible before in the history of humanity. And no one yet understands how to take advantage of these possibilities."

"We certainly don't have all the answers yet," he continued. "We're just beginning to ask the questions. We hope that in the long run the work we do in this center will help contribute to scientific understanding in many different disciplines and help us understand new and better ways to organize businesses, to conduct science, to run governments, and—perhaps most importantly—to help solve the problems we face as society and as a planet."[8]

Another academic program related to digital wisdom is the Center for Game Science at the University of Washington. It is directed by Zoran Popovic, creator of the previously discussed protein-folding application, Fold-it. The Center focuses on "solving hard problems facing humanity today, most of which are thus far unsolvable by either people alone and by computer-only approaches." They pursue solutions with a computational and creative symbiosis of humans and computers, attempting to evolve a symbiotic problem-solving engine that is game-based. Their belief, says Popovic, is that while "people have to learn to adopt to new technological tools, the technologies also have to learn to better assist humans." Working on both of these things simultaneously will, he says, produce the best human-machine symbiosis.[9] The center has produced a game for leaning fractions (Re-fraction) and is working on other learning games embedded in virtual worlds.

Computer games are a technology that is being increasingly associated with learning, and that association already is a source of digital wisdom. The case has now been made conclusively, by academics and others, that game technologies can produce a great deal of learning and positive effects.[10] Important skills that games have been demonstrated to develop include collaboration and working in teams, working effectively with others, making effective decisions under stress, taking prudent risks in pursuit of objectives, making ethical and moral decisions, employing scientific deduction, quickly mastering and applying new skills and information, thinking laterally and strategically, persisting to solve difficult problems, understanding and dealing with foreign environments and cultures, and managing business and people. And this is true, in varying degrees, of *all* types of well-designed games, including single-player, head-to-head, multiplayer, "massively multiplayer," virtual persistent worlds, "alternate reality" puzzles, and even many mini games. The principles are established—even the federal government has begun promoting computer and video games as a digitally wise way of learning. Now the challenge, as I said in Chapter 3, is to create enough good games that students want to play and learn from.

Whether their learning happens though school, through informal routes, though mastering games, or through other means, the world's young people already know that they will need to work with technology in the future. If our goal is to prepare those young people and help them succeed, it is now imperative that we educate them to do this: first, by helping them imagine and understand how to use technology; second, by giving them access to the most up-to-date technology we can afford, even if they have to share; and third, and most important, by helping them achieve digital wisdom.

SEVEN

ARE THERE REAL DANGERS?

What Should We Be Wary Of?

Yes, there are clearly dangers with technology, and with the mind-enhancing technologies that concern us here—dangers that are real. We need to take great caution with some relationships with these technologies, and, others, perhaps, we ought to avoid entirely.

Yet, as with fire, these dangers must always be balanced carefully against the positives. As we saw in Chapter 5, digital wisdom comes from making the right trade-offs.

For all but the most extreme purists, the issue is never *whether* to use technology, never *whether* to enhance our brains and minds when appropriate, but rather *how*. It is how to create and use these enhancements in a digitally wise way. And at this point, despite identity theft and hacking, many of the dangers remain more "potential" (i.e., risk of harm in the future) than actual harm being done today.

But that doesn't mean there aren't arguments and varying points of view as to what is, in fact, digitally wise. In particular, many people these days who feel their lives are becoming more stressful, complicated, or hectic attribute their problems to technology itself, or to what they see as its excessive use (or misuse). Many of these people, when they observe the kind and extent of enhancements we are talking about here, often scream "stop!"

Proponents of "turning off" technology, either periodically (through "digital sabbaticals" or "digital Sabbaths") or even permanently (by "going off the grid") proselytize their position widely, and many listeners welcome their message.

William Powers, for example, a journalist, wrote a book called *Hamlet's Blackberry,* in which he advocates taking days off from technology in order to have what he calls "deeper" relationships. Powers spent more than a year on a book tour speaking at colleges and other places to promote his ideas. He (and others) claim wide support for their cautionary position ("When I ask who agrees, many hands go up," says Powers).

Of course we also know that a great many people would *never* want to turn off their technology and would feel lost without it. (Have you ever forgotten your cell phone? How did you feel?)

But thinking about this does makes some sense. As these technologies enter our lives so rapidly, at some point *any* smart person would sit back and ask him or herself, "Is this wise?" "Is our quickly advancing technology helping or hurting us as individuals? As humans? Or are we being led downhill, toward dystopia, and perhaps even toward domination by our machines?"

We've certainly heard plenty about technology's supposedly negative effect on us. We've seen it in movies from *Blade Runner* to *The Matrix.* We've read about it from authors from Ray Bradbury to George Orwell to Arthur C. Clark to Octavia Butler.[1] It fills books from *The Dumbest Generation* to *The Shallows.*

Most of the critics start out, of course, by acknowledging technology's "great benefits." But then they go straight to the "Yes—but . . ." and the dystopia.

Whether we call the effect of technology on human minds outsourcing, enhancement, extension, amplification, improvement, or liberation, the fear of it is real. A huge number of the books, articles, and talks that have appeared about technology, not just today, but over the ages, portray a dystopian future. From Plato's *Phaedrus* (where Socrates complains about the negative effects of writing) to *Fahrenheit 451, Brave New World, The Terminator,* and *The Matrix,* people seem to delight in watching technology cause society to break down. Why is this? we should ask. Why is dystopia so much more compelling, as both story and entertainment, than its opposite? Why do books and articles like Nicholas Carr's "Is Google Making Us Stupid" in the *Atlantic*[2] and his follow-up book *The Shallows* (to choose but one oft-cited example) sell well?

Underlying it all, I think, is a deep human fear of change.

It takes time for us to understand the world around us and to acclimatize ourselves to it. We humans invest a lot of effort in doing so, and in creating frameworks for understanding in our minds. As we mature, our brain switches from creating these frameworks and learning about the world in general, to fitting what we learn into the frameworks we have created.[3] We tend to get "set in our ways" at some point or another. We form strong opinions on what is, what is important, and how we like things to be. We learn that things, and people, can go bad, and that this can in some cases happen quickly—the world can turn, as they say, "on a dime." We learn to like things (or at least accept them) the way they are and shine the best light on them. We often become more conservative because, as a colleague once put it to me, we have more to conserve. Few if any of us escape this, at least in some areas. But we all get as comfortable as we can.

Technology, though, disrupts our comfort. It often require us to change the way we work and use our time. It may cause us to spend our money on new things. Worst of all, it may mean we have to change our thinking—particularly about what is good, bad, right, or important. Some of this thinking is deeply ingrained, and changing it can be painful.

Some of the major shifts in thinking in the past, and the disruption and resistance they caused, are well known: That the world was not flat. That the sun didn't revolve around the earth. That disease wasn't caused by "bad air." That "bleeding" sick people didn't help them. People fought strongly, in all these cases, before finally giving in and accepting the wisdom of these ideas.

Today we hold many false ideas of equal strength. For example, that "longer" equals better and "deeper." That the ways *we* learned are the "best" ways to learn. That the "basics" of the past are the "basics" of the future. That simplicity and lack of technology equals "more human." An entire publishing industry and an army of writers and speakers support these myths, but myths they are. I discussed many of these in Chapter 2.

It is myths like these that make the dystopian views so popular and attractive. "Change and you'll be sorry" is a strong belief, even in America, supposedly the land of change and progress. Add to that the schadenfreude when those people who do change and later regret it, and we have a powerful anti-change lobby. We assign pejorative names like "geeks" and "nerds" to early or big technology adopters (although several are now billionaires). We see our children spending time with technology that is often far more compelling to them than we are and accuse them of being "addicted' to screens or media. We ignore that a huge percentage of our human-to-human conversation and interaction—so highly prized by many—is, and always has been, about nothing more important or interesting than the weather.

I believe it is wrong to fear change, because change is what makes humans better. It is, in fact, the only thing that makes us better, because without change, we would remain just who we are. "Our evolutionary lineage," said astronomer and science writer Carl Sagan, "is marked by mastery of change."[4] Technology—human invention—is a big part of that change. It is therefore silly to resist all technological enhancements.

But that doesn't mean that change doesn't upset us as individuals. And dystopian thinking—and literature—may actually be, in some way, a cry for help. At some level, people may be thinking to themselves, "I see humanity out there busily adapting to change, becoming something new and getting better, but what about me? I am still mourning the loss of all those pre-new technology things I used to love. I need help!" From there it is only a short step to "A pox on all your technologies!"

Are some technologies actually bad? Of course. The atomic, or hydrogen, bomb is a human invention—and certainly technology. Blowing all of us up would not be progress, at least in any human sense.

But other than weapons of war, it is hard to find technological progress that is in the long run negative for humans. And people typically find ways to overcome whatever negatives there are—to detect and neutralize bombs and missiles, to prevent nuclear accidents. Potentially harmful technologies get put to more positive uses, like energy generation.

Technology is not the only route to human progress, but it is certainly the fastest and most immediately effective route (unless you believe we can all suddenly start meditating, or thinking more critically or creatively, or having better, more significant conversations, or coming to a better understanding of others, on our own, or through traditional forms of education).

It is imperative for human progress, therefore, that we embrace technology and focus more on its positive effects than on its dangers. "Dissing" all technology in a blanket way, or even just the mind-enhancing technologies we are discussing here, is like indicting democracy because of its many flaws. What is important is to acknowledge the flaws, while emphasizing, to both ourselves and our children, the overall positive direction. The press—useful to society in many ways—is not necessarily our friend here. They are too often much more interested in showing us the negatives and dangers than in the positives, because that is what they think we want to hear.

As an example, take the Internet. It is, perhaps, one of the greatest human achievements and mind enhancements of all time. Yet the stories we hear and read about in the press are almost all about its use for bullying, theft, fraud, and deception. These stories may be true, but compared to the Internet's advantages, they are so minor—even Madoff's Ponzi theft is minor compared to the positives of our technology-based financial system—that it makes little sense to overly dwell on them.

We acknowledge the problems, fix them, and move on. This is progress, and we all welcome it.

Video games present a similar situation. I discussed in previous chapters the many benefits of these games—attested to by a large and growing number of academics and scientists.[5] But the press (and as a result many parents) still obsesses about this technology's minimal danger to their kids.

A fear-inducing science fiction image for ages has been the cyborg—the person who is part human, part machine. The concept strikes terror into many of today's adults, who ask, "Is that what our children are destined to become?" "Isn't that *less* than human?" they wonder. "If cyborgs are what our kids are becoming, aren't we going backward?"

We should, of course, have no illusions—in one way or another, cyborgs, that is human-machine combinations, are what twenty-first-century humans are fast becoming. For a long time I thought I was alone in feeling a "phantom vibration" in my leg even when my iPhone was not in my pocket, but then I heard others talk about it, and apparently this phenomenon is widespread. As we noted, people are already thinking and saying "cyborgian" things like, "If I lose my cell phone, I lose half my brain" and "My phone is my third hand." While our phones are not yet implanted under our skin, they soon might be, just as tracking chips are already under the skin of pets and kids. And it's only going to become more true as our technology—particularly in areas like medical implants, nanomachines, and mind-improving interventions—continues to advance rapidly. Some already embrace this. Neil Harbisson, for example, calls himself the "first human cyborg," and that title has also been accorded by the press to Kevin Warwick, whose work I discussed in Chapter 3.[6]

Still, as our minds continue to be enhanced, extended, and amplified, and as our emerging mind-technology symbiosis develops, we would do well to have some guidelines to help us understand when we may be going off the "digitally wise" path.

There are some dangers in making "rules" for this, as the authors of *Practical Wisdom* point out and as I discussed in Chapter 2. Behavior guided purely by rules is not really wisdom at all and often leads to counter-productive results. Laws requiring mandatory sentencing terms, for example, actually take judges' natural wisdom out of the picture. Incentives, too, have problems as a path to wisdom—they often encourage behavior that achieves some of our goals and unwisely ignores others. Giving teachers (or students) financial incentives to maximize test scores, for example, may result in less useful, or valuable, learning.

This doesn't imply that we shouldn't have rules or incentives, but that we should carefully examine the effects they produce to be sure they are helping. Any guidelines, for example, need to be both simple enough to be understandable and implementable by most people and complex and nuanced enough to take into account as many variables as possible. Setting an absolute rule limiting a kid's screen time, for example, is a very unsophisticated approach to making their use of technology wiser—they might miss something very useful. Even just suggesting "balance" in using technology (as it is always politically correct to do) is probably not that useful either. Balance what? Some uses of technology, even in large amounts, mostly enhance us (listening to recorded music may be one of these). There are other technologies we are not entirely clear about. We know that extreme amounts of book reading can affect people's eyes, but we know less about how reading on screens affects them.

Writers with their own agendas often draw our attention to particular issues and problems with technology, all of which should be considered. But to make their case, they often sensationalize and exaggerate the dangers. For example, a great preponderance of evidence suggests that playing video games—even in large amounts, and even violent games—has little if any permanent negative effect on healthy young people, said *The Economist* in 2011.[7] Yet we still hear the contrary.

It is, as I said earlier, all about trade-offs. The difficulty is that the trade-offs today, for ourselves and especially for our young people, are not the same as they were when we grew up—or even as they were earlier in our lives. Technology advances so quickly that we must be careful not to deny our children—or ourselves—something that could be really useful. Hopefully, none of us wants to prevent our kids from learning about and using tools that will be necessary to ensure their success in the future. Digital wisdom comes in understanding which tools those are and how to best use them.

Digital wisdom comes also, though, from a clear and open-eyed understanding of what the real dangers in the mind-machine symbiosis actually are. I try to indicate in the following pages some of the most important dangers I think we face whenever we use technology to enhance our minds (or for anything else for that matter). We should keep a careful lookout for these. I'm not sure we can do much else at this point.

DANGER #1

Being Manipulated

The big danger from all the information that technology is collecting about us is not that we will lose much of our traditional privacy—I believe that is inevitable in the coming world—but that, because of this, we will be manipulated, by companies or governments, in ways we don't like. But "manipulation" can cut many ways, and much of it we already accept as useful. Are we being manipulated if we are shown only one side of the (e.g., political) picture because the other side lacks the freedom, money, or technological sophistication to present it? Absolutely. But are we being manipulated dangerously if we are offered a product—based on information collected about us—that we truly want? Possibly not.

Will some of our freedom to choose and our ability to control our own lives be compromised by people using technology? Probably. But we should bear in mind that in these cases we are being manipulated not by the technology itself, but by the people using it. Marketers (and sometimes governments) work hard to manipulate us and see this as their job.

One of the latest technology-based manipulation techniques many of these people use is known as "persuasion profiling"—that is, figuring out, from the data collected about us, the best way to persuade each of us individually, based our individual thinking patterns. For example, it appears, according to research, that some of us are persuaded more easily by recommendations, some by popularity, or money savings, some by thoughtful arguments, and some by direct "buy now" messages.[8] What these researchers have found is that our same preferred style can persuade us in multiple domains, and that by adjusting pitches to each of us, they can make us buy more.[9] This principle is already used in political campaigns where different ads—some using humor, some negativity, and some positive messages—are often targeted at separate groups of voters.

We should certainly keep our guard up about people using technological means to persuade us. For one thing, the persuasion is most effective when we don't know it is happening. Movements have already arisen, in Europe for example, to limit what Google and other companies can do in terms of collection and storage. It remains to be seen how effective this will be—they may just be building a Maginot Line[10] that marketers and others with evil intentions can easily go around. But it does reflect growing concern.

DANGER #2

Side Effects, "Second-Order" Effects, and Unintended Consequences

Side effects can be extremely dangerous, and they don't always show up right away. "The effects of technology are not straightforward," says Professor Jeff Hancock of Cornell.[11] Remember Thalidomide? It was prescribed to alleviate pregnant women's morning sickness, but it turned out to cause serious deformation in babies. And although some side effects are tolerable and only occur for a small minority of people ("may cause upset stomach"), others are for more serious ("may, in some rare cases, lead to heart failure").

In Chapter 2, I spoke about the increase in healthy students taking Adderall. There is no disagreement about the drug's power to help these people concentrate, but many are concerned with the drug's side effects, which can include, according to the web site adderallsideeffects.org, "anorexia, dry mouth, chronic thirst, the development of sleeping disorders or generalized difficulty sleeping, chronic headaches or migraines, pain in the stomach, high blood pressure, sudden and unexplained weight loss, mood swings or other emotional changes, nausea with vomiting, sudden dizziness or fainting, a generalized feeling of weakness or tiredness, a sudden spike in heart rate, a higher risk of infections, unexplained fevers, heartburn, chest pains, and a slowing of growth in children." Those who use the drug for an extended period of time may also experience severe withdrawals, periods of depression, and, with extreme abuse, amphetamine psychosis.[12]

Of course one of the most important things to understand about side effects (or any drug effects) is that they are different for different people. Although groups of people may react similarly to the same drug, individual humans react very differently to almost all substances.

Scientists have now learned to test carefully for drug side effects. The U.S. Food and Drug Administration requires up to ten years of carefully controlled, double-blind studies before it approves pharmaceutical drugs. But, importantly, it does so only for approved uses (i.e., the ones listed on the label) and not for any others. "Off-label" use can sometimes lead to side effects that haven't been tested for or studied carefully. (Contrary to what some may think, it is legal in the United States, and in many other countries, to use drugs off label and for doctors to prescribe drug for off-label use.[13]) This often happens.[14] The on-label use of Adderall, for example, is to treat ADHD. Everything else is off label.

"Second-order" effects are a kind of side effect that is, typically, longer term—second-order effects occur when the effect of one cause becomes the cause of another. A first-order effect of building a dam is to create a lake, but second-order effects might include finding, years later, because the region's ecology has changed, fewer salmon are spawning, more people are moving to the area, or the local climate is changing. Since the widespread prescription of antibiotics kills off useful bacteria as well as hostile ones, we now see rising rates of asthma, diabetes, and irritable bowel syndrome as delayed second-order effects.[15] The first-order effect of a central bank's lowering interest rates might be that borrowing becomes cheaper, bringing down commercial interest rates. The second-order effect, though, might be that the increase in real activity increases the money supply, which creates inflation fears and pushes interest rates up.[16]

Both side effects and second-order effects can also be positive. Minoxidil, a vasodilator originally prescribed as a treatment for high blood pressure, safely grew hair when topically applied and became the widely used Rogaine. The development of the automobile and the airplane led to the opening up of many excellent new places to live and more dispersed populations. The development of computers opened up whole new areas of scientific investigation.

When side effects and second-order effects are not positive, we usually refer to them as "unintended consequences." As mind-extending technologies and technology uses increase and develop, digital wisdom demands that we keep a sharp eye out for negative unintended consequences. Much of the world finds cell phones great, for many reasons, but does holding a cell phone to your head over decades cause cancer? The evidence, which to some now appears to be negative, is still emerging, and some effects could be very long term.[17] The World Health Organization, which has put cell phones on its "possibly carcinogenic" risk list, agrees that it is a good idea to be cautious. So why do more people not use earbuds, or the phone's speaker function, rather than constantly holding the phones to their heads? I find doing so digitally wise, and do it myself.

Another potential side effect to be wary of is that changes in our brains, caused by environmental factors (so-called epigenetic changes), may get inherited and affect our thinking and behavior as a species. We currently know relatively little about this, but some scientists are already warning us. Neuroscientist Michael Merzenich, for example, claims that "The brains of our children will be very different from the brains of our ancestors."[18] He fears that things like "years of passive receiving" and "the explosion of pornography"[19] may have long-term deleterious effects. Not all agree, but we should certainly watch out for this, bearing in mind that the effects on different people will not be the same.

DANGER #3

Missing the Inherent Biases in the Technology

A different kind of second-order effect that might lead to unwanted consequences could come from a far less obvious direction: that is, missing, or ignoring, inherent "biases" in the technologies we use.

Marshall McLuhan, writing in the 1950s and 1960s, focused much of his work on technology's (and in particular media technology's) biases, suggesting that such biases can be based on the structure of the media alone, independent of any of its content. His ideas are encapsulated into well-known phrases such as "the medium is the message," and his scholarly discussions of how various communication technologies change our perspective are now classic. Print, for example, McLuhan says, has a bias toward linearity. The introduction of printing, he claims, changed the ways in which people tended to think compared to pre-literate days. Video, in contrast, does not have these same biases—in the sense that it is predominantly visual, it returns us, McLuhan says, to our pre-literate days as humans.

Brilliant and perceptive as McLuhan's ideas are, they are both complex and from a different and earlier time. We should be careful of taking others' interpretation of McLuhan's ideas at face value—people "pull out McLuhan" to support their particular side of almost any media argument. McLuhan's great contribution, I believe, lies not in showing us all the specific media biases—there is still much lively debate going on about exactly what those biases are—but rather in pointing out (and emphasizing) that there are technology-based biases at all.

One observer who has written quite cogently and eloquently about the inherent biases of today's technology is author and teacher Douglas Rushkoff. In his 2010 book *Program or Be Programmed: 10 Commands for a Digital Age,* he considers ten potential biases of computers and technology and what he considers their potential negative consequences. Rushkoff considers the implications of these biases "commandments" for what not to do (he has, of course, ten), and helpfully offers prescriptions.

According to Rushkoff, digital technology has (at least) the following biases:

1. A bias away from continuous time. (Prescription: Don't be always on.)
2. A bias away from the local toward dislocation. (Prescription: Live in person.)
3. A bias toward the discrete. (Prescription: You may choose none of the above.)
4. A bias toward a reduction of complexity. (Prescription: You are never completely right.)
5. A bias toward scaling up. (Prescription: One size does not fit all.)
6. A bias toward depersonalized behavior. (Prescription: Be yourself.)
7. A bias toward social connections and contact. (Prescription: Do not sell your friends.)
8. A bias toward facts and reality, and against fiction and story. (Prescription: Tell the truth.)
9. A bias toward openness. (Prescription: Share, don't steal.)
10. A bias toward those with the capacity to write the code. (Prescription: Program or be programmed.)

Doug's thoughtful and interesting ideas are too complex for me to cover in a few paragraphs. I highly recommend reading Doug's book.[20]

DANGER #4

Forgetting the Past and Its Lessons

Just because we are moving into new, uncharted territory doesn't mean that we can't use the past as a guide. But today, with the speed of technological change accelerating as it is, we have to be much more careful when we do so.

Up until not too long ago, every generation, metaphorically, used to live in and walk through the same forest—most of the major parameters of the earth and of people's lives remained very much the same from one generation to another. The world might change in its details, but it was still basically the same one—with, until quite recently, much less mobility than is currently the case. Most people lived in the same places, lived and worked in the same buildings, and often did the same jobs as their parents.

As a result, we were wise to pass down to our children many of the things we learned from our parents or teachers. Collectively, these pieces of advice became known as "conventional wisdom." Some of it was local, based on where you lived or what you did, but much of it was universal. Stay in school. Learn as much as you can from the past. Master reading, writing, and arithmetic. Keep your job. Do only one thing at a time. Practice makes perfect.

Today the forest is changing rapidly beneath our feet, and as a result, we have to be much more wary of those past lessons than we might have been previously. Digital wisdom consists, in large measure, of figuring out what lessons to keep and which to throw away. And there is great danger in our getting it wrong.

Many music executives (and musicians), for example, thought that—based on the great success of the recording industry—people would always be willing to pay a lot for something as valuable as good music. But they were wrong. As soon as people could get it for free, they did.

Some once thought it was, in every case, wiser to talk face to face (many still do). But first the telephone, then texting, and now widespread telepresence through programs like Skype and high-end conferencing systems have made this conventional wisdom meaningless: In some cases, such as doing business or keeping contact over distance, the old wisdom has been turned upside down—face to face is not always wiser. And in certain instances—such as, for many, a breakup—the wisest thing to do may be to *not* do it physically face to face.

So where do we find the digital wisdom?

One reliable guideline from the past is that people generally tend to overestimate the importance of new technologies in the short term and underestimate their transformational possibilities in the long term.[21]

We are not doing today (as some are fond of pointing out) many things that people predicted we would be doing by this time. We are not flying around in individual vehicles. We are not all jacked in to the Internet. We do not as yet all have implants in our brains. We still cannot literally read each other's minds.

But the technologies to do these things are already invented. And when we do begin doing these things, they will be widespread and affect humankind profoundly.

For example, many readers of the Dick Tracy comic strips in the 1930s, 1940s, and 1950s expected "wrist radios" and televisions to appear very quickly. Those devices took a lot longer than expected, but mobile phones are now owned by two-thirds of the world, those soon will all be smart phones, and straps to attach them to our wrists are already being sold.[22]

Short video is another example. After YouTube's initial period of hype, it appeared (at least in the press) to fade somewhat into the background, eclipsed by newer technologies like Twitter. But over the long term short video will have a profound effect on how people communicate, do things, and learn. The number of short videos online is already more than one billion, and a great many of those are "how-to" videos. For many in our population, video has already almost totally supplanted reading and writing as a way to get information and communicate.

What other lessons from the past is it digitally wise to keep or abandon?

Perhaps one of the most important lesssons relates to collaboration—and, indirectly, to education. It is conventional wisdom to suggest that being able to do something totally on your own is important and something to be cultivated. This is still how we evaluate almost all our young people. But in an age when the isolation booth has been replaced by "phone a friend," and the Internet is more and more available for both collaboration and information, is this still the wisest choice? Business people have generally moved away from the "do everything by yourself" model to a more collaborative model of working. Many educators are now beginning to do so for learning as well. The consequence that some fear, of course, is a decrease in self-reliance. But this may be a digitally wise price to pay.

DANGER #5

Getting the Insource/Outsource Division Wrong

There is no guarantee that, as we outsource more and more of the mind's capabilities to technology and machines (and attempt to keep for ourselves what is important for us to do), we will always get the division right. In fact, it's almost certain that some of the time we won't. There will be things we get wrong, sometimes with unforeseen consequences (such as those the United States experienced when it outsourced more and more manufacturing to low-cost countries, and lost, in the process, much of its manufacturing base).

I thought for a long time that there was no reason in the world *not* to outsource all but the simplest of arithmetical problems from our heads to calculators and computers (much as we outsource keeping track of time to the watches strapped to our wrists or, increasingly, to our cell phones). But Stephen Wolfram convinced me I was not totally right by suggesting face-to-face negotiations, as I discussed, as at least one place where the ability to do quick and accurate mental math can be very useful.

But should we let a single case (which may, as I also noted, soon go away)—or even a couple of cases—influence or change the digital wisdom of a decision to outsource something? One of the central and most difficult problems of humankind's move into the age of digital technology is making the best insource/outsource decisions. "A lot more of our thinking process will be outsourced,"[23] says Wolfram. Digital wisdom suggests thinking through as deeply and carefully as possible—and often re-thinking—what things we retain for our minds to do "in our heads," and what we outsource to the machines, and when.

"Facts" are a great case in point. Facts are still important—as important today as they ever were—for understanding and for backing up arguments. But today we have the Internet, Wikipedia, Wolfram Alpha, and other more-or-less well-curated sources of facts, and all these facts are, as Bill Gates promised us for years they would be, "at our fingertips."[24] Today, if you own an iPhone, the answer to practically any factual question is just a quick request to Siri (the iPhone's voice-activated personal assistant) away—my 7-year-old son now turns to Siri to find definitions for his school vocabulary words on the Internet. And facts will only become faster and easier to find and retrieve in real time as our technological capabilities increase.

Teachers and critics often raise a big red flag about the accuracy of getting our facts in this way, particularly from non-curated sites—as my copyeditor did repeatedly for this book's frequent citations of Wikipedia (all of which I retained). The truth is that, in many cases (and maybe even in most), this is hardly the big issue that those people make it seem. For many of the types of facts people want and need, there is, actually, little question of accuracy and difference of opinion—many have single sources (e.g., the United Nations) and many are dates or occurrences that no one disputes. For example, short of a typo, it would be hard to come up with, from a quick web search, the wrong date that the United States declared its independence from England or the wrong atomic weight of a particular element. Not only is the bulk of "standard" reference facts on the web highly accurate, the web also contains a great many alternative sources for those facts that may be in dispute, such as market shares or death tolls. It has also been pointed out more than once that factual errors can be found even in heavily curated and "expert-based" sources such as the Encyclopedia Britannica. (Since many of those references have moved online, hopefully those errors are now much more frequently updated and corrected as they are found from other sites.)

So are there *any* facts that are "wise" to all retain in our heads? Should we outsource *all* our facts to our technology and teach and learn none? Or is it digitally wiser to decide on a case-by-case basis? Everybody needs, and retains, certain facts—especially related to their daily lives and work—that they use often. Can we learn just whatever facts we need on an individual basis? (This is what we essentially do today, although many more facts may be "taught" to us.)

Where is the digital wisdom here? Are our brains more impoverished when we don't know as many facts, or do we instead free up more space (at least figuratively) leading to brain gain? The truth is that no one knows yet, although many are trying to investigate this. It is a question that is complex to answer because it depends on many variables: who you are, what your training is, and how you are operating.

One digitally wise way we might approach this issue is to consider what could be the unintended consequences of *not* having certain facts in our heads.

That is, what could go wrong if temporarily, for some reason, we couldn't get access to our technological enhancements and got a fact wrong? In some cases, clearly very little or nothing would be affected. In others, though (e.g., the operator of a critical technology not being able to quickly find a particular password or code), there could be major consequences.

Another area in which we might get the insource/outsource division wrong is following processes and procedures. According to Doug Rushkoff, "What's different now . . . is that it's not just lists, dates and recipes that are being stored for us, but entire processes. The processes we used to use for finding a doctor, or a friend, mapping a route, or choosing a restaurant are being replaced machines that may, in fact, do it better. What we lose in the bargain, however, is not just the ability to remember certain facts, but to call upon certain skills. . . . Instead of simply offloading our memories to external hard drives, we're beginning to download our thinking as well."[25]

If this is the case, it raises the important question of whether we are willing and able to be connected to our networks all the time. Consultant Mark Anderson thinks the answer is yes, and he welcomes the coming time when we will all have what he calls AORTA: always-on real-time access. Others like Rushkoff and science fiction writer Vernor Vinge question the wisdom of being always on and recommend either keeping more in our heads (Rushkoff), or on local machines (Vinge),[26] in case the machines become unavailable for some reason. I have already written about the dangers of unnecessary "backup education."[27]

The right balance needs to be struck. Digital wisdom suggests that balance will be a moving target, and that we should review all our decisions about this frequently.

DANGER #6

Letting Our Current Capabilities Atrophy

Underlying many people's fears about technology, or perhaps summing many of them up, is the idea that capabilities that humans once possessed that are, or were, important to us are being lost as machines take over more and more functions. Some suggest that as we communicate more and more online, we lose not just our ability but our *capacity* to relate in person—that it is a trade-off, perhaps even neuron by neuron.[28] It is important to note that such a hypothesis is based only on a few limited and inconclusive experiments and, for the most part, is speculation. But in areas as important as this, speculate we must.

Few people, if any, want their capacities—particularly their mental capacities—to atrophy or decline. The best ways to prevent this are still being discovered. Digital wisdom in this area means staying tuned, keeping well informed, and exercising judgment. One thing is clear: We rarely get better at things that we do *not* do. So digital wisdom suggests that we consciously decide what the important human functions, both physical and mental, that we would like to keep active (and therefore constantly practice) actually are.

DANGER #7

Becoming Addicted and "Amusing Ourselves to Death"

"Addiction to technology" is something that many worry about. But it is important to distinguish between true clinical addiction, where a person becomes totally dependent and incapable of living a healthy life, and "metaphorical" addiction, where a person strongly prefers and does a lot of one type of activity.

Metaphorical addiction to certain things is accepted and used often in the vernacular: "She is addicted to her work, or to golf, or to sweets (or to reading)," we might say. A metaphorical addiction to reading or learning is often even viewed as a positive thing in both children and adults.

Clinical addiction, in contrast, is universally bad and requires help to overcome.

Does metaphorical addiction ever spill over into clinical addiction? Sometimes, perhaps, but rarely. Many think that those who do get physically addicted have particular brain chemistries (based, perhaps, on particular genes or alleles), because the same person often gets addicted to several different things. Psychologists speak of "addictive personalities" and "addictive personality disorder" (or even of clinical addiction as a "brain disease"). Most agree that the destructive addictive behavior is related less to the activity itself and more to other factors, particularly stress. So an "addiction" to the Internet or to games is probably not caused, at its root, by the nature of the technology but rather by other factors in the person's life. (This is different from the way certain types of screen images can sometimes induce nausea.)

But even if it is not "officially" clinical addiction, too much of one thing can be bad. And that includes technology. This is particularly true, some think, of technologies that entertain us. In the 1960s, Neil Postman's book *Amusing Ourselves to Death: Public Discourse in the Age of Show Business* warned of the dangers of television and a future full of mindless entertainment, and of what can result when politics, journalism, education, and even religion become subject to the demands of entertainment. In his introduction, Postman writes, "In [Aldous] Huxley's vision [of the dystopian future in *Brave New World*], no Big Brother is required to deprive people of their autonomy, maturity and history. As he saw it, people will come to love their oppression, to adore the technologies that undo their capacities to think." "As Huxley remarked in *Brave New World Revisited*," Postman goes on to say, "the civil libertarians and rationalists who are ever on the alert to oppose tyranny 'failed to take into account man's almost infinite appetite for distractions.'"[29]

Well-known writers like George Orwell (*1984*) and Ray Bradbury (*Fahrenheit 451*) have posited similar scenarios. Many think that in the digital age, Postman's warnings have taken on even more significance.

Digital wisdom demands that we be on guard against addiction—both clinical and metaphorical—that is, if not caused by, at least abetted by technology. However, to quote *Psychology Today,* "No matter which kind of addiction is meant, it is important to recognize that its cause is not a search for pleasure, and [that] addiction has nothing to do with one's morality or strength of character."[30]

DANGER #8

Becoming "Less Human"?

A meme that has gotten wide press in recent times is the idea of "our"—that is, everyone—becoming "less human" because of technology. I believe those who espouse this idea are mainly just our brooding, intellectual classes (who may, in fact, think of themselves as "more human" than the rest of us). But it is also a concern heard from religious people as well: Those who see our "humanness" as magical, or God given, may find the growing mind-technology symbiosis troubling and even dangerous. If we outsource too much of our mind to technology, their argument goes, what is left?

I personally have little tolerance for this meme and will give it short shrift here. "Human" is a moving target and a target that is different for almost every observer. Whatever we become (or don't become), we are the "humans" of our time. We will have always had, and will likely always have, a great diversity in our species. I have already noted my own optimism and preference for seeing humans as improving—particularly because of our new symbiosis with digital technology.

What I personally believe we are becoming because of technology is not "less human," but, as the title of a 1953 novel by Theodore Sturgeon says, *More Than Human.*

DANGER #9

Annihilation

The most extreme danger, of course, is that technology, and technological enhancement, leads to human annihilation. This is not inconceivable. The best guess of scientists is that a meteor annihilated the dinosaurs, and that there have been not just one but several mass extinctions in the earth's history. We have the technological capability, in warheads that exist, to annihilate humankind almost entirely from the planet and to render the earth unlivable.

Digital wisdom requires that we be truly vigilant about these dangers. Efforts toward nuclear antiproliferation and containment are digitally wise. So is continually scanning the sky for approaching meteorites.

DANGER #10

Machines "Taking Us Over"

There is another technological sense, however, in which "annihilation" is possible—and, some think, even probable. That is machines "taking over" and eliminating us.

A lot of people are afraid of this and consider it a real danger. It may, in fact, be. As we will see in the next chapter, a group of very intelligent scientists believe that the time until machines become more intelligent than humans—and, as a result, "sentient" (although no one is exactly sure what that means)—is now measured not in millennia, but in decades.

Literature and movies are full of dystopian scenarios of humans being taken over by machines, from either our planet or outer space. We seem to enjoy these types of scenarios, perhaps because we regard them, reassuringly, as only fiction. And the possibility can't just be dismissed out of hand, particularly with the speed of technology growth today.

And that brings me to our conclusion. In the final chapter of this book, I will look at a movement called the Singularity that is seriously investigating this possibility and trying to stave off the advance of the machines and technology for human good.

EIGHT

AFTER DIGITAL WISDOM

The Singularity and the Eternally Evolving Human

Let us hope—and assume—that most of us enter the realm of digital wisdom, at least partially, in our own lifetimes, or in those of our children (or perhaps of our children's children). What comes next? Can humans get even wiser?

A growing group of people certainly think so. They form a movement—some call it a community—around something known as "the Singularity." While the term "singularity" is used in science to denote a one-way event, such as the "event horizon" of a black hole, its metaphorical meaning is an event from which there is no turning back.

The event that the Singularity—with a capital S—refers to is the moment, not very far off, supporters claim, when our technology will become as powerful, and even more powerful, than our human brains. The time is near, they say, when artificial intelligence—machine intelligence—will equal, and then surpass, that of humans. This is known as a "strong" artificial intelligence (or "strong AI").

Predicted to come relatively soon (some have said 2029, other predictions vary widely), this new machine capability will lead to even faster technological development, as machines become as capable as humans are of making hypotheses about how to improve themselves, conducting experiments, and controlling, therefore, their own evolution. Because such technology, they claim, will be "sentient"—self-aware and aware of its own needs—in the way humans are, the technology will start to grow, learn, develop, and set and achieve goals on its own, with no human control or intervention. The members of the Singularity community are trying to look hard and carefully at what is likely to happen as a result.

The head guru of the Singularity movement, and the person now most associated with the term (which was originally coined by science fiction writer Vernor Vinge), is Ray Kurzweil, a highly successful and respected engineer and inventor, now turned deep ponderer about the future. Despite what you may think of his ideas—and many find them hard to accept or strongly dispute them—Kurzweil is no wide-eyed new-age kook. He is, rather, a very serious and careful thinker. He has written two important books: *The Age of the Spiritual Machine,* in which he first lays out his theories, and *The Singularity Is Near,* in which he defends them. He has also just released a documentary about the Singularity called *Transcendent Man.* Before getting deeply into this "future stuff," Kurzweil was widely known for his invention of both high-end music synthesizers and readers for the blind. Stevie Wonder is a user of both.

Kurzweil is a particular kind of futurist—not a fantasizer, as many science fiction writers are, but an analyst. He deals in data and makes his predictions based on the data he finds. What Kurzweil and his associates have been analyzing for some time now is the future of technology and how that interacts with humankind.

Kurzweil did not start out worrying about, or predicting, the "big picture" future of humankind and machines. He originally began his analyses to aid in the timing of his company's technological products. As an analyst, he started graphing the rate of progress of various technologies, such as the growth of computing power, and found the growth to be exponential, that is, growing at a rate based on *multiplying* by a constant, rather than just adding a constant. His own data, he found, fit well with what is known as Moore's law, predicting the exponential growth of the number of transistors that can be placed on a computer chip. Intrigued, Kurzweil began graphing other types of technological progress—not just recent advancements, but those in history going all the way back to the iron age, the stone age, and the origins of humankind.

Kurzweil's analyses led him to a huge insight: No matter how far back you go, the progress of technology follows a similar curve, which he calls "the law of exponential returns." Technology's power increases exponentially, doubling faster and faster. In ancient history, when technology was incredibly small, the doublings meant very little or nothing. But gradually over time, they started building up and accelerating enormously.

In his books, Kurzweil provides the graphs he constructed showing the continuous progress of technology since the beginning of humankind, viewed on the long scale (Figure 1).

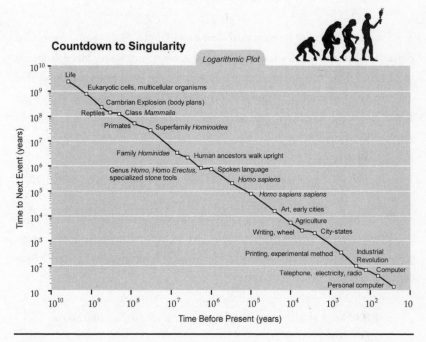

Figure 1

What this shows, he claims, is that technology improvement happens not at the relatively slow and steady pace that we usually associate with change but rather at an exponential rate.

Kurzweil's 2001 essay entitled "The Law of Accelerating Returns"[1] begins as follows:

> An analysis of the history of technology shows that technological change
> is exponential, contrary to the common-sense "intuitive linear" view. So
> we won't experience 100 years of progress in the 21st century—it will be
> more like 20,000 years of progress (at today's rate). The "returns," such
> as chip speed and cost-effectiveness, also increase exponentially. There's

even exponential growth in the rate of exponential growth. Within a few decades, machine intelligence will surpass human intelligence, leading to the Singularity—technological change so rapid and profound it represents a rupture in the fabric of human history. The implications include the merger of biological and nonbiological intelligence, immortal software-based humans, and ultra-high levels of intelligence that expand outward in the universe at the speed of light.

For any of you not familiar with "exponential growth," it is the enormous power behind things like high compound interest rates and Moore's law. It means that if you double something over and over, it takes less and less time for it to grow to enormous proportions. For example, if you start with $100 and it grows at a linear, compounded rate, of say 10 percent per year, you will get the following kind of growth:

100, 110, 121, 132, 145, 160, 176, 194, 213, 236, 259, 285, 314, 345, 380, 418 . . .

Not bad—in 15 years, your money has quadrupled.

But if, instead, that same $100 grows at an *exponential* rate, doubling every year (which can be easily calculated, for those interested, as 2 to the "number of doublings" power), you get:

100, 200, 400, 800, 1600, 3200, 6400, 12800, 25600, 51200, 102400, 204800, 409600, 819200

In only 15 doublings, you are not at $418 but more than $1 million (just a slight difference).

From there it keeps rising faster: With only 15 more doublings (a total of 30), the $100 becomes more than $1 billion. With 10 more doublings (a total of 40), it is more than $1 trillion.

This kind of exponential growth can also be seen by folding a sheet of paper in half over and over—no matter how big it starts, it quickly becomes quite thick and impossible to fold. All this takes is roughly seven foldings—try it for yourself. This is, to many, counterintuitive. "We are not evolved," says Kurzweil, "to think in terms of exponential growth. It's not intuitive. Our built-in predictors are linear. When we're trying to avoid an animal we think the linear prediction of where it's going to be in 20 seconds and what to do about it. That linear forecasting is actually hardwired into our brains."[2] Linear thinking may have been useful once. But it seriously limits our thinking about our future, according to Kurzweil.

Understanding the law of exponential returns—which Kurzweil is careful to point out is not a physical law but rather an empirical observation of how things have worked in the past combined with an assumption that they will continue to work this way in the future—is, Kurzweil believes, the key to understanding how humankind's future with technology will proceed. When the power of something (in this case, technology) *starts* quite large, as it does today, doubling it can accelerate things unbelievably fast, producing gains far beyond our linear expectations.

This ability to now double from what has become an enormous base, Kurzweil believes, is where humans are today. We are just entering what he calls the "payoff" period, where each new doubling is huge, leading to technological progress that is much greater, and faster, than we might otherwise assume. Advances will now happen, he says, at a pace and rate of change humans have a hard time getting their heads around, because humans have never before experienced this pace. (Feel familiar?)

If we look carefully, we can see exponential growth happening around us, says Kurzweil. Gordon Moore saw it in the progress of transistors on a computer chip. It is also why, for example, the human genome was deciphered so quickly, even though it seemed to have a very slow start. Because deciphering the initial small percentage of the genome took a long time, Kurzweil explains, many expected the whole job to take many times as long as that. But with progress proceeding not linearly but exponentially, and with only a few doublings in power needed to get the job done, scientists finished the task in only a couple of years. As Craig Venter noted in Chapter 3, we can now decipher a genome in a couple of hours.

To those to whom the kinds of change he is talking about seem impossible, Kurzweil offers additional evidence—such as self-diagnosing elevators and self-repairing electronics—that the beginnings of this "new world" are already with us today. He predicts that by 2045, the amount of artificial intelligence created (i.e., knowledge and capabilities created solely by machines) will be about a billion times the sum of all the human intelligence that exists today (you can calculate this as 2^{30}).

Given that today we are already working below the level of atoms, at the quantum level, we are, says Kurzweil, close to many big discoveries. Kurzweil answers the critics who say—rightly—that we are still very far from understanding how the brain works with, "Yes, but we are only a few doublings away from having the full picture." This could come very quickly, he thinks. Kurzweil calculates that it will not take that many yearly doublings before the power of our technology is on a par with that of our brains and surpasses them. It could happen, he thinks, in only 30 to 40 years, which is within the lifetime of many of us, and certainly of most of our children. (There are, it should be pointed out, fairly wide disagreements on this date, even among Singulatarians.)

Kurzweil's conclusion (or rather hypothesis) is, as you might guess, a highly controversial one, among both scientists and people in general. Many believe that the human brain is, being biological, much different than any technology humans have created, and we are not even close to its capabilities. Others think there is something "ineffable" in the brain and mind, a "spark" that can never be fully understood, duplicated, or surpassed technologically.

I, for one, wouldn't bet on this last. I think we and our children have to take Kurzweil's ideas very seriously. Not that they will happen tomorrow or the next day. But the chances are good that something like the Singularity will happen—"What humans are good at," suggests author and Singulatarian Vernor Vinge, "is a smaller and smaller subset of what is possible"[3]—and digital wisdom suggests we had better be thinking about it and be as prepared as possible when it does.

Unlike many dystopian thinkers and writers, Kurzweil is essentially optimistic. What the current and future exponential growth in technology is leading to, he believes, is a new, far better era for humankind, far beyond what we have here called "digital wisdom." An appealing element of Kurzweil's vision of the future is that it is not one of machines taking over, but rather of a better human-machine combined future. "It is not," he asserts, "an alien invasion." In fact, Kurzweil refers to this coming time as "the era of Transcendent Man."

The Singularity movement has moved far in developing and promoting its ideas, and Kurzweil's controversial contention is now accepted by a growing number of scientists and others. In addition to his two influential books, Kurzweil has founded a graduate school, Singularity University. He also started an organization known as Singularity Institute, which promotes his ideas by, among other things, holding yearly conferences. Many well-known and well-regarded figures, including Doug Hofstadter, the author of *Gödel, Escher, Bach*; Google director of research Peter Norvig; Stanford AI lab director Sebastian Thrun; MIT professor of robotics Rodney Brooks; CTO of Intel Justin Rattner;

CEO and Founder of Wolfram Research Stephen Wolfram; economist Tyler Cowan; science writer Michael Shirmer; and PayPal founder Peter Thiel, speak at the Singularity conferences. I have now attended two Singularity conferences (called "Singularity Summits"), including the most recent. I can report that there are some very, very smart people in attendance, both speaking and in the audience. Not surprisingly a great many of the attendees—including me—believe some or all of Kurzweil's ideas.

One of Kurzweil and the Singularity movement's main goals—the goal that he and many others believe is possible in the not-too-distant future—is to "reverse engineer" the human brain and, when we understand how it works—which he agrees we don't yet today—build something even better. Many think this is impossible because of the brain's complexity, but Kurzweil is of the opinion that humans already deal with things of equal complexity. "There aren't trillions of separately evolving mechanisms in the brain," he says. "The human genome has 400 billion bytes, but if you compress out the redundant parts, there are only 50 million bytes, half of which, 25 million bytes, describe the brain. That's not too much—it's a level of complexity we can handle." The main issue, he believes, is understanding, which will come. In fact, Kurzweil is far from alone in his attempts to understand the brain—several others are trying to understand and outdo the human brains as well. The Blue Brain project, run by Henry Markham in Lausanne, Switzerland, is just one of many attempts.

Critics dismiss the Singularity's ideas as just "the rapture of the geeks" and see it as a quasi-religious movement, complete with its own eschatology (i.e., end-of-the-world scenario).[4] To many, surpassing the human brain is inconceivable, either because the analogy to a "machine" is wrong or because we don't yet know about critical parts (in which case, Kurzweil says, it will just take longer), or because man is "special" and cannot be surpassed. (This last would be a real stumbling block, if true, but Kurzweil obviously thinks it isn't.)

To other people, though, we are already at the goal: While Kurzweil is busy looking for a "general" (some say "strong") artificial intelligence, encompassing everything the human brain can do, already, in many specific areas, machines and technology far surpass human capabilities. Consultant Mark Anderson, for example, points to our growing ability to send and receive information, including video, at broadband speeds over an always-on network as a kind of "singularity," one that is today available in many places. This is, as he points out, already changing the world's political map. Anderson sees one of the most useful roles of future technology as providing humans with a "personal assistant" (of which the iPhone's current Siri is an early example) whose capabilities go far beyond those of any human assistant.

Kurzweil's view is larger. Although Kurzweil doesn't use the term "digital wisdom," that is, I believe, exactly what the Singularity movement and Institute are trying to find. Their goal is to both understand the future and guide it in positive and wise directions. They believe that that deliberate action ought to be taken to ensure that the Singularity benefits humans. Writes Kurzweil:

> What, then, is the Singularity? It's a future period during which the pace of technological change will be so rapid, its impact so deep, that human life will be irreversibly transformed. Although neither utopian or dystopian, this epoch will transform the concepts we rely on to give meaning to our lives, from our business models to the cycle of human life, including death itself. Understanding the Singularity will alter our perspective on the significance of our past and the ramifications for our future. To truly understand it inherently changes one's view of life in general and one's particular life. I regard someone who understands the Singularity *and who has reflected on its implications for his or her own life* [emphasis mine] as a "singularitarian."[5]

As technology continues to evolve at what is likely to be an exponential pace—however far and fast each of us sees it going—digital wisdom, I believe, will come in focusing not on the technology itself, but on the types and quality of humans' interactions with that technology.

How do we arrange things so that technology doesn't just outpace or even eliminate humans in a totally dystopian scenario, but remains our constant partner, and a tool, however intelligent, for advancing our common species and civilization?

Which brings up an important point about all this mind enlargement and expansion we have been discussing: are we talking figuratively or literally? How literally *should* we take terms like enhancement, augmentation, extension, etc.?

The answer in the future, I believe, is literally. Very literally.

One intriguing possibility is to get humans to "evolve" faster—not just in the metaphorical sense that I have been talking about, but in a true, genetic sense, creating an entirely new species. Some refer to this as "designed evolution." In an online book called *Homo Evolutis,* writers Juan Enriquez and Steve Gullens claim that this is already happening. Scientific advances in biotechnology (including fields like gene therapy, epigenetics, proteomics, and biomics), they argue, along with advances in delivery systems through nanotechnology, are speeding up human evolution. Taking my *Homo sapiens digital* metaphor even further into the future, they claim that humans are already evolving, *scientifically speaking,* into a new species. Not a sub-species, like *Homo sapiens whatever,* but rather a totally new species, which they call *Homo evolutis.* "We are transitioning," they write, "from a hominid that is conscious of its environment into one that drastically shapes its own evolution. Our species alters itself. In other words . . . We are entering a period of hypernatural evolution." Their final claim in the book is that "We [humans] will either adapt and adopt, or like so many others, say 99% of all species, we too will go extinct." A general term often used by people who think like this is "transhumanist."

AFTER THE SINGULARITY?

And what happens *after* the Singularity, or once we become *Homo evolutis* (assuming both happen)? Now we clearly enter the realm of science fiction. But science fiction authors, who have been some of our greatest seers, have been thinking about this for a long time. Their thinking anticipates, and informs, many ideas and concerns of the Singularitarians.

Science fiction author Greg Bear has written about new and different humans in his books *Darwin's Radio* and *Darwin's Children.* These new humans, distinguished by subtle markings on their faces, possess extraordinary powers of the mind. And they are, in Bear's stories, highly discriminated against by "ordinary" humans.

This is, in some sense, the key issue, and the one I want to leave you with.

We all know things are changing rapidly—not just in the United States, but in the whole world. Although life is far from perfect, and many are still struggling, nobody who looks around, almost no matter where they are in the world, can doubt that life is far different, and in many ways better, than it was in the past—even if those observers miss, and regret the loss of, some of the elements of that past.

Most of us understand that technological progress has increased and will not slow down, even as we debate just how fast it is actually progressing. We all see technology making major changes in our lives. And we all feel, to a greater or lesser extent, uncomfortable with, or at least unsettled by, some elements of these changes. I have not met anyone who isn't—including myself.

But I also believe that most people are becoming increasingly comfortable with the fact that we are already a hybrid society of humans and technology, people and computers—even if we argue around the margins of what this means and how to deal with it. We have, as humans, already experienced a great deal of brain gain, compared to our pre-digital days. We are, in many ways, already digitally wise.

The people who are thinking in these new ways about the future, including the proponents of the Singularity, are regarded by many as kooks—a future so extremely different from the present, in which technology plays a far greater role than it does even today, is hard for many to swallow. In the words of Lev Grossman, there is "an intellectual gag reflex that kicks in."[6]

A great deal of the fear, though, has less, I believe, to do with the ideas themselves—most people are in favor of extending human reach, improving our tools, enhancing ourselves, and becoming better people (i.e., after all, the goal of most religion and art)—and more with the ways we have tended to present them.

Most humans value wisdom. They are attracted to it rather than scared of it. Most of us aspire to it.

That is why I have tried to make the conversation about digital wisdom.

While we may be forever defining exactly what digital wisdom is, I hope we can all agree that it is a worthwhile goal.

NOTES

INTRODUCTION

1. "The physiochemical brain does enable the mind in some way we don't understand . . ." "the mind . . . is somehow generated by the physical processes of the brain, . . ." writes leading scientist Michael Gazzaniga, in Michael S. Gazzaniga, *Who's in Charge?: Free Will and the Science of the Brain* (New York: HarperCollins, 2011), 3–4.

2. P. Murabito, F. Rubulotta, and A. Gullo, "Quality Management in the ICU: Understanding the Process and Improving the Art," in *Anesthesia, pain, intensive care, and emergency: Proceedings of the 22nd postgraduate course in critical care medicine, Venice-Mestre, Italy, November 9-11, 2007,* ed. A. Gullo (Milan, Italy: Springer-Verlag Italia, 2008), 345–404.

3. Clive Thompson, "Can Game Theory Predict When Iran Will Get the Bomb?" *The New York Times Magazine,* August 12, 2009, http://www.nytimes.com/2009/08/16/magazine/16Bruce-t.html?pagewanted=all.

4. "Modelling Behaviour: Game Theory in Practice," *The Economist,* September 3, 2011, http://www.economist.com/node/21527025.

5. Stephen J. Blumberg, Julian V. Luke, Nadarajasundaram Ganesh, Michael E. Davern, Michel H. Boudreaux, and Karen Soderberg, "Wireless Substitution: State-level Estimates from the National Health Interview Survey, January 2007–June 2010," National Health Statistics Reports, no. 39, April 20, 2011, http://www.cdc.gov/nchs/data/nhsr/nhsr039.pdf.

6. "21st Century Skills as a Vision for K-12 Education: What Should Schools and Districts Do?" PowerPoint, Partnership for 21st Century Skills, FETC, Orlando, FL, January 25, 2007, slide 12, www.p21.org/storage/documents/FETC%20Orlando.ppt.

7. Described to me by one of my editors.

8. Juan Enriquez and Steve Gullens make this case in *Homo evolutis* (TED Books 2011). Published (only) as a Kindle Single eBook, January 26, 2011.

9. My good friend David Engle calls this the "VUCA."

10. The quote is often given as "The [significant] problems that exist in the world today cannot be solved by the level of thinking that created them." However, that formulation is never given a source and is only "attributed" to Einstein. An actual Einstein quote is, "a new type of thinking is essential if mankind is to survive and move to higher levels," which appeared in "Atomic Education Urged by Einstein," *New York Times,* May 25, 1946, and was later quoted in Michael Amrine, "The Real Problem Is in the Hearts of Man," *The New York Times Magazine,* June 23,

1946. Einstein also is quoted as saying, "Past thinking and methods did not prevent world wars. Future thinking *must* prevent wars."

11. Zynga's first game was published in 2007, its IPO was in 2011. http://en.wikipedia.org/wiki/Zynga.

CHAPTER 1

1. Among writers using these terms are Allen Buchanan, Andy Clark, Howard Rheingold, and Clay Shirkey.

2. David Pogue, "A Parent's Struggle with a Child's iPad Addiction," *The New York Times*, February 24, 2011, http://pogue.blogs.nytimes.com/2011/02/24/a-parents-struggle-with-a-childs-ipad-addiction/.

3. UC Berkeley News Center, "Scientists Use Brain Imaging to Reveal the Movies in Our Mind," September 22, 2011, http://newscenter.berkeley.edu/2011/09/22/brain-movies/; and "Mind Goggling," *The Economist*, October 29, 2011, http://www.economist.com/node/21534748.

4. "'Mind-Reading' Experiment Highlights How Brain Records Memories," March 13, 2009, Wellcome Trust website, http://www.wellcome.ac.uk/News/Media-office/Press-releases/2009/WTX053749.htm.

5. Theodore W Berger, Robert E Hampson, Dong Song, Anushka Goonawardena, Vasilis Z. Marmarelis, and Sam A. Deadwyler, "A Cortical Neural Prothesis for Restoring and Enhancing Memory," *Journal of Neural Engineering* 6, no. 4 (August 2011).

6. Dr. Shaun Jones, personal interview.

7. The Penrose-Hameroff model (orchestrated objective reduction: "Orch OR") suggests that quantum superposition and a form of quantum computation occur in microtubules—cylindrical protein lattices of the cell cytoskeleton within the brain's neurons, http://rsta.royalsocietypublishing.org/content/356/1743/1869.abstract.

8. Dr. David Warner, personal interview.

9. "[The] disagreement about how the human brain differs from other animals, and indeed how the brains of other animals differ from one another, whether it is one of quantity versus quality continues, but the evidence for a truly qualitative difference, a difference in kind, is far more compelling," writes neuroscientist Michael Gazzaniga in his recent book *Who's in Charge?: Free Will and the Science of the Brain* (New York: HarperCollins, 2011).

10. Craig M. Bennett, Crista-Lynn Donovan, Scott Guerin, and Michael Miller, "How Reliable Are the Results from fMRI?" Poster from UC Santa Barbara, 2010, http://prefrontal.org/files/posters/Bennett-Reliability-2010.pdf; and Edward Vul, Christine Harris, Piotr Winkielman, and Harold Pashler, "Puzzlingly High Correlations in fMRI Studies of Emotion, Personality, and Social Cognition," *Perspectives on Psychological Science* 4, no. 3 (2009).

11. Marion Long and Valerie Ross, "Noam Chomsky, the Radical Linguist," *Discover*, November 2011, 66–71.

12. Dr. David Warner, personal interview.

13. Research by Dr. Eleanor McGuire of University College London, http://news.bbc.co.uk/2/hi/677048.stm.

14. S. Hutchinson, L.H. Lee, N. Gaab, G. Schlaug, "Cerebellar Volume of Musicians," *Cereb Cortex.* 9 (September 13, 2003), 943–949. http://www.ncbi.nlm.nih.gov/pubmed/12902393.

15. Daniel Kahneman, *Thinking Fast and Slow* (New York: Farrar, Straus and Giroux, 2011).

16. An example might be a manager of a baseball or football team, who, to make each decision, has to put together everything he knows, from past history to current conditions on the field, to the state of the crowd and each of the players.

17. Kahneman, *op cit.* His list of mental illusions, or biases in our thinking, includes the affective bias, the anchoring effect, the substitution of easier questions for hard ones, our pervasive optimistic bias, the planning fallacy, loss aversion, What You See Is All There Is (WYSIATI), framing, and mistaking the value of sunk costs. Brief explanations of all of these are found at http://en.wikipedia .org/wiki/Thinking,_Fast_and_Slow#Prospect_Theory.

18. Malcolm Gladwell, *Blink: The Power of Thinking Without Thinking* (New York: Little, Brown and Company, 2005).

19. Kahneman refers to these as "System 1" (quicker, more emotional and intuitive) and "System 2" (more deliberate and rational).

20. Pierre Bayard, *How to Talk about Books You Haven't Read,* trans. Jeffery Mehlman (New York: Bloomsbury, 2007).

21. *The Complete Essays of Montaigne,* trans. Donald Frame (Stanford: Stanford University Press, 1957), quoted in Bayard, *How to Talk about Books You Haven't Read.*

22. In his short story "Funes the Memorious," Jorge Luis Borges describes a man crippled by an inability to forget. Borges concludes, in his story, that it is forgetting, not remembering, that is the essence of what makes us human. "To think," Borges writes, "is to forget." For more on this, see Joshua Foer, "Extremes of Human Memory," http://www.mindpowernews.com/ExtremeMemory.htm.

23. Malcolm Gladwell, *Blink: The Power of Thinking Without Thinking* (New York: Little, Brown and Company, 2005); Kahneman, *Thinking Fast and Slow* (New York: Random House, 2011); Nassim Nicholas Taleb, *The Black Swan: The Impact of the Highly Improbable* (New York: Random House, 2007).

24. David Brin, personal interview.

25. "Smarter Than You Think" was the collective title of various articles in *The New York Times,* 2010–2011.

26. Richard Dawkins, *The Blind Watchmaker: Why the Evidence of Evolution Reveals a Universe without Design* (1966; reprint, New York: W. W. Norton and Company, Inc., 1986), 64. Excerpted in Richard Dawkins, "Creation and Natural Selection," *New Scientist* (September 25, 1986), 38, 111.

27. Kurt Anderson, "We Robot," op-ed, *The New York Times,* August 13, 2011.

28. Ray Kurzweil, *The Singularity Is Near* (New York: Viking, 2005), p. 26.

29. A. Clark and D. J. Chalmers, "The Extended Mind," *Analysis* 58 (1998), 7–19, http://consc.net/papers/extended.html.

30. This comment was made by a student during one of my student panels.

31. Devices from Smart Brain Technologies and Emotive Systems allow players to control the action in video games using their minds; NeuroSky is working on another version of the technology. The U.S. Air Force is experimenting with using similar technology to train pilots in hands-off flying. See "Hands Off F-16 Lands Using Lockheed Martin Computer Control Technology," *Satnews Daily,* December 11, 2008, http://www.satnews.com/cgi-bin/story.cgi?number=1057554591.

32. Maslaw's hierarchy is described in the article "Hierarchy of Needs," http://en .wikipedia.org/wiki/Maslow%27s_hierarchy_of_needs.

33. This quote appeared in "Atomic Education Urged by Einstein," *New York Times* May 25, 1946, and was later quoted in Michael Amrine's article, "The Real

Problem Is in the Hearts of Man," *New York Times Magazine,* June 23, 1946. Einstein also is quoted as saying, "Past thinking and methods did not prevent world wars. Future thinking *must* prevent wars." The oft-cited quotation that "The [significant] problems that exist in the world today cannot be solved by the level of thinking that created them" is never given a source and is only "attributed" to Einstein.

34. From Ken Jennings's talk at the 2001 Singularity Summit in New York City.

35. Said by a ten-year-old girl on one of my student panels.

36. "When historian Charles Weiner found pages of Nobel Prize–winning physicist Richard Feynman's notes, he saw it as a 'record' of Feynman's work. Feynman himself, however, insisted that the notes were not a record but the work itself." In Andy Clark, *Supersizing the Mind: Embodiment, Action, and Cognitive Extension* (Oxford: Oxford University Press, 2008).

37. Heard at 2011 Singularity Summit in New York City.

38. Andy Clark, *Supersizing the Mind: Embodiment, Action, and Cognitive Extension* (Oxford: Oxford University Press, 2008).

39. Andy Clark quoted at http://en.wikipedia.org/wiki/Andy_Clark.

40. Andy Clark, personal interview.

41. Ibid.

42. Jason Dechant and Dennis Kowal, "Overview of Developments in Human Performance Enhancement," Institute for Defense Analyses, February 2007 (IDA Document D-3373).

43. Ibid.

44. Jean-Baptiste Pierre Antoine de Monet, Chevalier de la Marck (1744–1829), often known simply as Lamarck, was a French naturalist and an early proponent of the idea that evolution occurred and proceeded in accordance with natural laws. Lamarck is widely remembered for a theory of inheritance of acquired characteristics, called soft inheritance, Lamarckism, or use/disuse theory. See http://en.wikipedia.org/wiki/Jean-Baptiste_Lamarck.

45. Thomas Friedman, *The World Is Flat: A Brief History of the 21st Century* (New York: Farrar, Straus and Giroux, 2005); Thomas Friedman, *Hot, Flat and Crowded: Why We Need a Green Revolution—And How It Can Renew America* (New York: Farrar, Straus and Giroux, 2008).

46. Kevin Kelly, *What Technology Wants* (New York: Viking/Penguin, 2010).

47. Interview with Kevin Kelly in *The Economist,* October 2, 2010.

48. Charles Duhigg, "Psst, You in Aisle 5," *The New York Times Magazine,* February 19, 2012, 30.

49. I heard Mark Bauerlein say those words in a private class setting.

CHAPTER 2

1. H. Greeley, B. Sahakian, J. Harris, R. C. Kessler, M. Gazzaniga, P. Campbell, and M. J. Farah, "Toward Responsible Use of Cognitive-Enhancing Drugs by the Healthy," *Nature* 456 (2008), 702–705, http://www.nature.com/nature/journal/vaop/ncurrent/full/456702a.html.

2. Professor Hank Greeley, personal interview.

3. Some question whether pharmacological enhancements are "digital." I believe they are in the sense that without modern digital technologies most of the drugs would not have been found.

4. Anahad O'Connor, "A.D.H.D. Drug Shortage Has Patients Scrambling," *The New York Times,* December 31, 2011.

5. *Oxford English Dictionary,* 2nd. ed., s.v. "wisdom," definition 1a.

6. Robert Nozick, *The Examined Life: Philosophical Meditations* (New York: Simon & Schuster-Touchstone,1990).

7. Aristotle, *Nicomachean Ethics,* cited in Barry Schwartz and Kenneth Sharpe, *Practical Wisdom: The Right Way to Do the Right Thing* (New York: Riverhead Books, 2010).

8. Barry Schwartz and Kenneth Sharpe, *Practical Wisdom: The Right Way to Do the Right Thing* (New York: Riverhead Books, 2010).

9. Professor Hank Greely, personal interview.

10. Howard Gardner, *Intelligence Reframed: Multiple Intelligences for the 21st Century* (New York: Basic Books, 2000).

11. I am indebted to Jim Tracy, headmaster at Cushing Academy, for this thought.

12. Neil Postman, *Amusing Ourselves to Death: Public Discourse in the Age of Show Business* (New York: Penguin, 1986).

13. W. L. Whitters and P. Jones-Whitter, *Human Sexuality—A Biological Perspective* (New York: Van Nostrand, 1980). Rats in Skinner boxes with metal electrodes implanted into their nucleus accumbens will repeatedly press a lever that activates this region and will do so in preference over food and water, eventually dying from exhaustion.

14. Larry Summers, personal conversation at *The New York Times*'s Schools for Tomorrow Conference, September 22, 2011.

15. Professor Hank Greely, personal interview. See also Henry T. Greely, "Remarks on Human Biological Enhancement," in *Kansas Law Review* 56 (2008).

16. Henry T. Greely, "Remarks on Human Biological Enhancement," *Kansas Law Review,* 56 (2008), 1139–1157.

17. Ibid.

18. Schwartz and Sharpe, *Practical Wisdom,* 5. People possessing *phronesis* were called by Aristotle *phronemoi* (ibid., 12).

19. CYA means "Covering your ass."

20. Schwartz and Sharpe, *Practical Wisdom,* 10.

21. Denise Grady, "Despite Safety Worries, Work on Deadly Flu to Be Released," *The New York Times,* February 17, 2012, http://www.nytimes.com/2012/02/18/health/details-of-bird-flu-research-will-be-released.html?_r=1&scp=1&sq=H5N1%20bird%20flu%20virus%20publish&st=cse.

22. Jaron Lanier, *You Are Not a Gadget* (New York: Alfred A. Knopf, 2010).

23. The technology of Twitter "back channels" in lectures now often allows both.

24. Mark Anderson, personal communication.

25. David Brin interviewed in *Wired* magazine, Sheldon Teitelbaum, "Privacy Is History—Get Over It," *Wired* 4, no. 2 (1996), http://www.wired.com/wired/archive/4.02/brin.html.

26. Ibid.

27. William Powers, *Hamlet's Blackberry: A Practical Philosophy for Building a Good Life in the Digital Age* (New York: HarperCollins, 2010),11 (Kindle version).

28. Also see Carl Honoré, *In Praise of Slowness: How A Worldwide Movement Is Challenging the Cult of Speed* (New York: HarperCollins, 2004).

29. Daniel Kahneman's book, *Thinking Fast and Slow* is about all of these biases in our thinking. See Chapter 1, Note 16.

30. The studies were conducted by Elizabeth Lorch, a psychologist at Amherst College, and cited in Malcolm Gladwell, *The Tipping Point: How Little Things Can Make a Big Difference* (New York: Little, Brown & Company, 2000), 101.

31. David Staryer and Jason M. Watson, "Supertaskers and the Multitasking Brain," *Scientific American Mind* (March/April 2012), 22.

32. Dr. Michael Merzenich, personal interview.
33. Dr. Adam Russell, personal interview.
34. John Bruer, "Education and the Brain: A Bridge Too Far," *Educational Researcher* 26 (8), 4–16.
35. It was stated to me, for example, by eminent neuroscientist Dr. Michael Merzenich, in a personal interview.
36. I heard Dr. Conrad Wolfram make this point in a lecture.
37. Dr. Stephen Wolfram, personal interview.
38. Michael Nielsen, *Reinventing Discovery* (Princeton: Princeton University Press, 2011), 5.
39. For more on this, see "The Science behind Foldit," http://fold.it/portal/info /science.
40. Dr. Dave Warner, personal interview.
41. Edward Westhead, former professor of Biochemistry at the University of Massachusetts at Amherst, personal communication.
42. Noted by Bill Clinton in his autobiography, *My Life* (New York: Knopf, 2004).
43. Gary Small and Gigi Vorgan, *iBrain: Surviving the Technological Alteration of the Modern Mind* (New York: HarperCollins, 2008).
44. Tim Kreider, "In Praise of Not Knowing," op-ed, *The New York Times,* June 18, 2011, http://www.nytimes.com/2011/06/19/opinion/19Kreider.html.
45. Isaac Asimov, *iRobot.* First published by Gnome Press in 1950. Available free online at http://www.firstload.com/?uniq=6904f985795c82c2&log=47382&fn=i+ robot+pdf+free
46. "Three Laws of Robotics," http://en.wikipedia.org/wiki/Three_Laws_of_Robotics.
47. Dr. Michael Merzenich, personal interview.

CHAPTER 3

1. Dr. Stephen Wolfram, personal interview.
2. Gordon Bell and Jim Gemmell, *Your Life Uploaded: The Digital Way to Better Memory, Health and Productivity* (New York: Plume, 2010).
3. Robert Niebergall, Paul S. Khayat, Stefan Treue, and Julio C. Martinez-Trujillo, "Multifocal Attention Filters Targets from Distracters within and beyond Primate MT Neurons' Receptive Field Boundaries," *Neuron* 72, no. 6 (December 22, 2011), 1067, cited in "We Are Natural Born Multitaskers" *Science Daily,* December 21, 2011.
4. Many are online. Search "tapes for relaxation" on Google.
5. The web site for this game is http://www.wilddivine.com/servlet/-strse-72/ The-Passage-OEM/Detail.
6. Jason Dechant and Dennis Kowal, "Overview of Developments in Human Performance Enhancement," Institute for Defense Analyses, February 2007 (IDA Document D-3373).
7. Ibid.
8. Ibid.
9. Ibid.
10. David L. Strayer and Jason M. Watson, "Top Multitaskers Help Explain How Brain Juggles Thoughts," *Scientific American Mind* (February 16, 2012).
11. You can see IBM's marketing for these virtual worlds at http://domino.research .ibm.com/comm/research_projects.nsf/pages/virtualworlds.index.html/$FILE /ebo_brochure_100207.pdf.
12. "Azeroth" is the name of the virtual world in the game World of Warcraft.

13. Dechant and Kowal, "Overview of Developments in Human Performance Enhancement."

14. Ibid.

15. Wizcom Reading Pen, http://www.wizcomtech.com/eng/catalog/a/readingpen2/.

16. There are many statistics cited on the Internet, but few reliable sources. Brent Armstrong cites the American Booksellers Association as saying that 58 percent of American adults never read a book after high school (http://www.brentd armstrong.com/get-smarter/). Other web sites repeat this, but I have not found this statistic from the American Booksellers Association.

17. This statistic can be found at http://www.intellectualtakeout.org/library/literacy /functional-illiteracy-and-literacy-problems-america.

18. One such estimate is at http://answers.yahoo.com/question/index?qid=2008021 2121243AAmtWFP.

19. Einstein is reported to have said, "A scientific theory should be as simple as possible, but no simpler." Some report this as "Things should be . . ."

20. Harriet Alexander, "10 Famous Telegrams," *The Telegraph*, November 4, 2009, http://www.telegraph.co.uk/news/uknews/6494297/Ten-famous-telegrams.html.

21. Larry Smarr, "Quantified Health: Towards Digitally-Enabled Genomic Medicine: A 10-Year Detective Story of Quantifying My Body," *Strategic News Service Newsletter* 14, no. 36 (September 26, 2011).

22. For more on Jawbone wristband (UP), Fitbit pedometer, and Exergen temporal scanner, see Farhad Manjoo, "A Dashboard for Your Body," *New York Times*, August 4, 2011, http://www.nytimes.com/2011/08/04/garden/gadgets-to-track-your-health -home-tech.html; also see Randall Stross, "Tracking Vital Signs, Without the Wires," *New York Times*, September 4, 2011, http://www.nytimes.com/2011/09/04/technol- ogy/wireless-medical-monitoring-might-untether-patients.html; and Brad Stone, "Jawbone's Wristband Heart Monitor," Bloomberg Businessweek, November 3, 2011, http://www.businessweek.com/magazine/jawbones-wristband-health-mon- itor-11022011html?chan=rss_topEmailedStories_ssi_5.

23. Mark Anderson, *Strategic News Service Newsletter* 14, no. 36 (September 26, 2011).

24. Thomas Goetz, "Why Doctors Need to Embrace Their Digital Future Now," *Wired* (February 2012), http://www.wired.com/magazine/2012/01/st_topolqa/.

25. These are cancer-causing nuclear mutations, mitochondrial mutations, intracel- lular aggregates such as atherosclerosis, extracellular aggregates such as the plaque in Alzheimer's, cell loss, cell senescence, and extracellular crosslinks. See http:// en.wikipedia.org/wiki/Aubrey_de_Grey.

26. "Stephen Coles," http://en.wikipedia.org/wiki/L._Stephen_Coles.

27. Genescient web site, http://www.genescient.com/.

28. Tony Candela, "An Oral History Interview With Ray Kurzweil," American Foundation for the Blind, November 12, 2004, http://www.afb.org/section .aspx?FolderID=2&SectionID=4&TopicID=456&SubTopicID=231&Document ID=5447.

29. Thomas Goetz, "Harnessing the Power of Feedback Loops," *Wired* (July 2011), http://www.wired.com/magazine/2011/06/ff_feedbackloop/all/1. A feedback loop involves four steps: Evidence, or data collection; Relevance, or proving the infor- mation collected to the individual in a useful context; Consequence, where the information illuminates one or more paths ahead; and Action, a moment when the individual can recalibrate a behavior, make a choice, and act. Then that action is measured, and the feedback loop can run once more, every action stimulating new behaviors that inch us closer to our goals.

30. Ibid.
31. Ibid.
32. "Psychiatry—Therapist-Free Therapy: Cognitive-Bias Modification May Put the Psychiatrist's Couch Out of Business," *The Economist*, March 3, 2011.
33. Ibid.
34. "Reading the Brain: Mind-Goggling," *The Economist*, October 29, 2011.
35. Shinji Nishimoto, An T. Vu, Thomas Naselaris, Yuval Benjamini, Bin Yu, and Jack L. Gallant, "Reconstructing Visual Experiences from Brain Activity Evoked by Natural Movies," *Current Biology*, 21, no. 19 (September 22, 2011), 1641–1646.
36. Tom M. Mitchell et al., "Predicting Human Brain Activity Associated with the Meanings of Nouns," *Science* 320, no. 5880 (May 30, 2008), 1191–1195, http://www.sciencemag.org/content/320/5880/1191.abstract.
37. Christopher James, personal interview.
38. Alexander J. Doud, John P. Lucas, Marc T. Pisansky, and Bin He, "Continuous Three-Dimensional Control of a Virtual Helicopter Using a Motor Imagery Based Brain-Computer Interface," *Public Library of Science*, October 2011. PLoS ONE 6, no. 10, e26322. doi:10.1371/journal.pone.0026322.
39. Benedict Carey, "Memory Implant Gives Rats Sharper Recollection," *The New York Times*, June 17, 2011, http://www.nytimes.com/2011/06/17/science/17memory.html.
40. K. Warwick, M. Gasson, B. Hutt, I. Goodhew, P. Kyberd, H. Schulzrinne, and X. Wu, "Thought Communication and Control: A First Step Using Radiotelegraphy," *IEE Proceedings on Communications* 151, no. 3 (2004), 185–189.
41. "Kevin Warwick," http://en.wikipedia.org/wiki/Kevin_Warwick.
42. "The Evolution of Generosity: Welcome, Stranger," *The Economist*, July 30, 2011, http://www.economist.com/node/21524698.
43. "Guilt, Cooperation Linked by Neural Network: Why People Choose to Cooperate Rather Than Act Selfishly," *ScienceDaily*, May 11, 2011, http://www.sciencedaily.com/releases/2011/05/110511131126.htm.
44. Ibid.
45. "The Evolution of Generosity." *The Economist*, July 30, 2011, http://www.economist.com/node/21524698.
46. "Stanford Opens Seven New Online Courses for Enrollment (Free)," Open Culture, November 18, 2011, http://www.openculture.com/2011/11/seven_new_stanford_courses.html; Open Courseware, . http://ocw.mit.edu/index.htm.
47. Dr. Ralph Chatham, formerly with DARPA, personal communication.
48. "Lying Is Exposed by Micro-Expressions We Can't Control," University at Buffalo News Release, May 5, 2006, http://www.buffalo.edu/news/fast-execute.cgi/article-page.html?article=79300009.
49. Anne Eisenberg, "Software That Listens for Lies," *The New York Times*, December 4, 2011, http://www.nytimes.com/2011/12/04/business/lie-detection-software-parses-the-human-voice.html.
50. Ibid.
51. Ibid.
52. "Decoding the Psychology of Trading," *Financial Times*, July 16, 2010, http://www.ft.com/cms/s/0/7332e44a-9109-11df-b297-00144feab49a.html#axzz1oXTjAFc8.
53. "The Future of Armour: The Armour Strikes Back," *The Economist*, June 2, 2011, http://www.economist.com/node/18750636.
54. Danielle Dellorto, "WHO: Cell Phone Use Can Increase Possible Cancer Risk," CNN, May 31, 2011, http://www.cnn.com/2011/HEALTH/05/31/who.cell.phones/index.html.

55. Jamie Beckland, "How to Use Geolocation in Your Marketing Initiatives," April 14, 2011, http://www.socialmediaexaminer.com/how-to-use-geolocation-in-your-marketing-initiatives/.

56. Thomas L. Friedman, "This Is Just the Start," *The New York Times,* March 1, 2011, http://www.nytimes.com/2011/03/02/opinion/02friedman.html.

57. Faiza Saleh Ambah, "In Bahrain, Democracy Activists Regret Easing of U.S. Pressure," Washington Post Foreign Service, November 27, 2006, http://www.bahrainrights.org/en/node/785.

58. WeBIRD, "Bird Song App Identifies Feathered Friends by Tweets," University of Wisconsin Madison News, October 11, 2011, http://www.news.wisc.edu/19882; Leafsnap, http://leafsnap.com/; and StarWalk: Bob Tedeschi, "When You Wish Upon a Star, Now You Can Call It by Name," *The New York Times,* April 28, 2010, http://www.nytimes.com/2010/04/29/technology/personaltech/29smart.html.

59. Bruce Feiler, "Our Plugged-in Summer," *The New York Times,* August 14, 2011, http://www.nytimes.com/2011/08/14/fashion/this-life-a-plugged-in-summer.html?pagewanted=all.

60. Emma Marris, Peter Kareiva, Joseph Mascaro, and Erle C. Ellis, "Hope in the Age of Man," op-ed, *The New York Times,* December 7, 2011, http://www.nytimes.com/2011/12/08/opinion/the-age-of-man-is-not-a-disaster.html?_r=1&scp=1&sq=Anthropocene%20December%208,%202011&st=cse.

61. Chris Anderson, "The End of Theory: The Data Deluge Makes the Scientific Method Obsolete," *Wired* 16, no. 7 (2008).

62. See Craig Venter's TED talk at http://www.ted.com/talks/craig_venter_on_dna_and_the_sea.html.

63. Ibid.

64. Wolfram Alpha, http://www.wolframalpha.com/.

65. Dr. Stephen Wolfram, personal interview.

66. "News From the Future: Your GPS Data Sold to Cops for Speed Traps," http://blog.makezine.com/2011/05/04/news-from-the-future-your-gps-data-sold-to-cops-for-speed-traps/; "You're Not So Anonymous: Medical Data Sold to Analytics Firms May Be Used to Track Identities," http://news.harvard.edu/gazette/story/2011/10/you%E2%80%99re-not-so-anonymous/; and Geoffrey A. Fowler and Emily Steel, "Facebook Says User Data Sold to Broker," *The Wall Street Journal,* October 31, 2010, http://online.wsj.com/article/SB10001424052748704477904575586690450505642-search.html.

67. Patricia Cohen, "Digital Keys for Unlocking the Humanities' Riches," *The New York Times,* November 16, 2010.

68. Patricia Cohen, "Giving Literature Virtual Life," *The New York Times,* November 16, 2010.

69. Patricia Cohen, "Analyzing Literature by Words and Numbers," *The New York Times,* December 3, 2010.

70. Ned Stafford, "Analytical Techniques Employed in Art Forgery Case," Royal Society of Chemistry, September 7, 2011, http://www.rsc.org/chemistryworld/News/2011/September/07091101.asp; and Patricia Munter, "Uncovering Art Forgery Using Analytical Chemistry," PowerPoint presentation, University of Pennsylvania Master of Chemistry Education Program, 2011, http://www.sas.upenn.edu/~patann/ImagesforPresentation-Munter.ppt.

71. Ibid.

72. "Art Criticism and Computers: Painting by Numbers," *The Economist,* July 30, 2011, http://www.economist.com/node/21524699.

73. Ibid.

74. Patricia Cohen, "Analyzing Literature by Words and Numbers."

75. Patricia Cohen, "Digital Keys for Unlocking the Humanities' Riches."

76. Guy Gugliotta, "Deciphering Old Texts, One Woozy, Curvy Word at a Time," *The New York Times*, March 29, 2011, http://www.nytimes.com/2011/03/29/science/29recaptcha.html.

77. Martin K. Foys, who is analyzing the Bayeux tapestry. Quoted in Cohen, "Digital Keys for Unlocking the Humanities' Riches."

78. Patricia Cohen, "Scholars Recruit Public for Project," *The New York Times*, December 27, 2010.

79. See it at http://www.youtube.com/watch?v=L5akbOKGSFM.

80. http://www.npr.org/blogs/deceptivecadence/2012/01/02/144482863/double-blind-violin-test-can-you-pick-the-strad.

81. Cited on the Internet Movie Database at http://www.imdb.com/title/tt0086879/quotes.

82. Dr. Stephen Wolfram, personal conversation.

83. Patricia Cohen, "In 500 Billion Words, a New Window on Culture," *The New York Times*, December 16, 2010.

84. Ibid.

85. David Carr, "Steve Jobs Reigned in a Kingdom of Altered Landscapes," *The New York Times*, August 29, 2011.

86. Kenton Powell, "The New Venture Capital," *Bloomberg BusinessWeek*, October 24, 2011.

87. "Kickstarter," http://en.wikipedia.org/wiki/Kickstarter.

88. Ben Sisario, "Google Opens a Digital Music Store," *The New York Times*, November 17, 2011, http://mediadecoder.blogs.nytimes.com/2011/11/16/google-opens-a-digital-music-store/.

89. Brad Stone, "Hotel Tonight, a Last-Minute Travel App," *Bloomberg Businessweek*, November 17, 2011, http://www.businessweek.com/magazine/hotel-tonight-a-lastminute-travel-app-11172011.html.

90. Ira Boudway, "Hyperink: A Content Farm That Grows Books," *Bloomberg BusinessWeek*, October 31, 2011, http://www.businessweek.com/magazine/hyperink-a-content-farm-that-grows-books-10272011.html.

91. Brad Stone, "Amazon's Bezos Fuels Tablet Wars With a $199 Kindle," *Bloomberg Businessweek*, October 3, 2011, http://www.bloomberg.com/news/2011-09-28/bezos-portrays-pocket-sized-fire-as-service-not-tablet-in-ipad-challenge.html.

92. Ibid.

93. Ibid.

94. Quoted in David Carr, "Steve Jobs Reigned in a Kingdom of Altered Landscapes," *The New York Times*, August 11, 2011.

95. Ibid.

96. Ben Sisario, "Site to Resell Digital Files has Critics," *The New York Times*, November 15, 2011.

97. "Mechanical Turk," http://en.wikipedia.org/wiki/Amazon_Mechanical_Turk.

98. Brian Stelter, "Embattled Netflix Kills Plan to Split Up Services," *The New York Times*, October 11, 2011, available at http://articles.boston.com/2011-10-11/business/30267353_1_netflix-stock-steve-swasey-netflix-spokesman.

99. "Velcro," http://en.wikipedia.org/wiki/Velcro.

100. "Silk from the Sea: No Sow's Ear," *The Economist*, November 19, 2011, http://www.economist.com/node/21538659.

101. Janice Karin, "Bone-Setting Glue," The Future of Things web site, November 11, 2009, http://thefutureofthings.com/news/8345/bone-setting-glue.html.

102. "Robots: Zoobotics," *The Economist,* July 7, 2011, http://www.economist.com/node/18925855.
103. Modha quoted in Steve Lohr, "Creating Artificial Intelligence Based on the Real Thing," *The New York Times,* December 6, 2011.
104. Kelly quoted in ibid.
105. Ibid.
106. Diane Ackerman, "Evolution's Gold Standard," op-ed, *The New York Times,* August 9, 2011.
107. Sherry Turkle at Family Safety Council Conference, Washington, D.C., 2011.
108. http://www.seeklyrics.com/lyrics/Jimmy-Buffett/Changes-In-Latitudes-Changes-In-Attitudes.html; http://www.youtube.com/watch?v=IpsTRbJKoa0.
109. Kahneman, *Thinking Fast and Slow.*
110. Ibid.
111. Nassim Nicholas Taleb, *The Black Swan: The Impact of the Highly Improbable* (New York: Random House, 2007).
112. John C. Beck and Mitchell Wade, *Got Game: How the Gamer Generation Is Reshaping Business Forever* (Cambridge: Harvard Business School Press, 2004).
113. Steven Johnson, *Everything Bad Is Good for You* (New York: Penguin, 2005).
114. Pentagon Office of Readiness and Training, personal interview.
115. Ray Kurzweil, "From Eliza to Watson to Passing the Turing Test," Singularity Summit 2011, http://www.youtube.com/watch?v=WPqjYrLhDnk&list=UU1zny_jKmgnEbQitfPgAlxg&index=2&feature=plcp.
116. "White Coat, Stethoscope, . . . iPad?" *Yale Alumni Magazine,* September/October 2011, http://www.yalealumnimagazine.com/issues/2011_09/lv_ipads.html.
117. Dr. Shaun Jones, personal interview.
118. Personal interview with Pentagon Office of Readiness and Training.
119. You can read more about this at http://www.usread.com/flight587/coverups_n_foulups/summ.html.
120. Nassim Nicholas Taleb, *The Black Swan: The Impact of the Highly Improbable* (New York: Random House, 2007).
121. Lev Grossman, "The Singularity," *Time,* February 21, 2011, p. 44.
122. Annat Katz, posted May 2, 2011, http://www.allmyfaves.com/blog/music/wolfram-tones-beautiful-music-created-by-algorithms/.
123. Ibid.
124. Semmelhack quoted in Nick Bilton, "An Interactive Exhibit for About $30," *The New York Times,* March 16, 2011, http://www.nytimes.com/2011/03/17/arts/design/arduinos-provide-interactive-exhibits-for-about-30.html.
125. Jason Silva quote at http://www.youtube.com/watch?v=vsuuJ7pa_D0.
126. Steve Lohr, "New Ways to Exploit Raw Data May Bring Surge of Innovation, a Study Says," *The New York Times,* May 13, 2011.
127. James Manyika, Michael Chui, Brad Brown, Jacques Bughin, Richard Dobbs, Charles Roxburgh, and Angela Hung Byers, "Big Data: The Next Frontier for Innovation, Competition, and Productivity" McKinsey Global Institute, May 2011, http://www.mckinsey.com/Insights/MGI/Research/Technology_and_Innovation/Big_data_The_next_frontier_for_innovation.
128. http://radar.oreilly.com/2011/01/what-is-hadoop.html.
129. Richard Adhikari, "Big Data, Big Open Source Tools," LinuxInsider, February 25, 2011, http://www.technewsworld.com/story/71945.html.
130. Quote from Qmarkets, Company Wide Innovation page, http://innovation.qmarkets.net/innovation-management/customer-challenges/innovation-process.

131. Steve Lohr, "With a Learner Model, Start-ups Reach Further Afield," *The New York Times,* December 5, 2011, http://www.nytimes.com/2011/12/06/science/lean-start-ups-reach-beyond-silicon-valleys-turf.html?pagewanted=all.

132. Ibid.

133. I heard game developer Chris Crawford say this at one of the first Game Developers' Conferences.

134. Dean Takahashi, "The Sims Celebrates 125 Million Games Sold across 10 Years," VentureBeat, February 3, 2010, http://venturebeat.com/2010/02/03/the-sims-celebrates-125-million-games-sold-across-10-years/.

135. "Print Me a Stradivarius: How a New Manufacturing Technology Will Change the World," *The Economist,* February 10, 2011.

136. Ibid.

137. "Frank Gehry," http://en.wikipedia.org/wiki/Frank_Gehry

138. "3D Printing: The Shape of Things to Come," *The Economist,* December 10, 2011, http://www.economist.com/node/21541382.

139. "Printing Body Parts–Making a Bit of Me," *The Economist,* February 18, 2010, http://www.economist.com/node/21004902.

140. Arduino web site, http://www.arduino.cc/.

141. Mindstorms web site, http://mindstorms.lego.com/en-us/Default.aspx.

142. Aggregative Contingent Estimation Program web site, http://www.iarpa.gov/. The ACE program manager is Jason Matheny.

143. Chris Velazco, "Android Still Most Popular Smartphone OS, iOS Holds Steady in Second Place," TechCruch.com, November 3, 2011, http://techcrunch.com/2011/11/03/android-still-most-popular-os-ios-holds-steady-in-second-place/.

144. Tim Gower's Polymath project is discussed in Michael Nielsen, *Reinventing Discovery: The New Era of Networked Science* (Princeton: Princeton University Press, 2011).

145. Ibid.

146. Ibid.

147. "Planetary-Scale Intelligence," talk given by Alexander Wissner-Gross, 2011 Singularity Summit, New York, NY.

148. (2^{40}).

149. Marc Prensky, "Programming Is the New Literacy," Edutopia.com, January 13, 2008, http://www.edutopia.org/programming.

CHAPTER 4

1. Catalog of the Hammacher-Schlemmer company, spring 2012, http://hammacher.com.

2. The video can be viewed at http://www.youtube.com/watch?v=L5akbOKGSFM.

3. David Pogue, *The World According to Twitter* (New York: Black Dog and Leventhal Publishers, Inc., 2009).

4. Sarah Kessler, "How Twitter Tracks the Spread of Flu in Real Time," Mashable.com, October 19, 2011, http://mashable.com/2011/10/19/twitter-track-h1n1/.

5. Matt Richtel, "For Multitaskers, Multiple Monitors Improve Office Efficiency," *The New York Times,* February 7, 2012, http://www.nytimes.com/2012/02/08/technology/for-multitaskers-multiple-monitors-improve-office-efficiency.html?pagewanted=all.

6. Nassim Nicholas Taleb, *The Black Swan: The Impact of the Highly Improbable* (New York: Random House, 2007). Taleb argues that spreadsheets encourage linear projections, which rarely reflect the real world and are rarely accurate, but, using the spreadsheet, are very easy to make.

7. Natural language searching is using full sentences, such as "what was the population of New York City in 2012" rather than just key words.

8. Ruben Van Ryan, "Murdoch $580 Million My Space Buy a 'Huge Mistake,'" Gizmaestro.com, October 21, 2011, http://gizmaestro.com/22/10/2011/media/murdoch-580-million-myspace-buy-a-huge-mistake/.

9. Philip Evans and Thomas S. Wurster, *Blown to Bits: How the New Economics of Information Transforms Strategy* (Cambridge: Harvard Business School Press, 1999).

CHAPTER 5

1. Jon Russell, "Fuelled by Emerging Markets, Facebook Set to Hit 1 Billion Users in August," thenextweb.com, January 12, 2012, http://thenextweb.com/facebook/2012/01/12/fuelled-by-emerging-markets-facebook-set-to-hit-1-billion-users-in-august/.

2. According to the Entertainment Software Association (ESA), women age 18 or older represent a significantly greater portion of the game-playing population (37 percent) than boys age 17 or younger (13 percent), http://www.theesa.com/facts/pdfs/ESA_EF_2011.pdf.

3. An RSS feeder is a software program, often built into a web browser, that allows a user to subscribe to online news feeds and blogs and receive updates automatically as they are published.

4. A listserv is a software group one can subscribe to that enables an email from anyone in the group to go automatically to all members. These are very useful for sharing ideas within a community. Features in Facebook and Google Plus (and other services) can also be used for this purpose.

5. "I like both for different reasons, but I spend a lot more time on youtube than watching tv," posted by sepiasunrise, http://www.youtube.com/all_comments?v=wGDDxWX2zqc&page=1.

6. Interview with Julie Evans, Agency for Instructional Technology, AIT.net, April 4, 2012, http://www.ait.net/technos/e-zine/interviews/julie_evans.php.

7. "Shaquille O'Neal's All-Star Twitter Coach," in *Bloomberg Businessweek,* October 27, 2011.

8. Ryan Kim, "4 in 10 U.S. phones are now smartphones," Gigaom.com, September 1, 2011, http://gigaom.com/2011/09/01/four-in-ten-u-s-phones-are-now-smartphones/.

9. Hashtags are simple codes beginning with a hash mark (such as #egypt) that one adds to tweets. In addition to the tweet going to all one's followers, it gets sent to a particular list that any Twitter user can browse. People create, share, and use hashtags for many activities, from political activism to sharing opinions during a lecture.

10. http://www.dickssportinggoods.com/product/index.jsp?productId=3708316&010=SKU-6401619&003=3933188&camp=CSE:GoogleBase:3708316&camp=CSE:GoogleBase:3708316; http://www.amazon.com/SFO-Medical-Handheld-Diagnostic-Electrodes/dp/B003K9OTYQ.

11. Samantha Murphy, "E-filing Becomes the New Normal," *Tech News Daily,* March 26, 2011, http://www.msnbc.msn.com/id/42275764/ns/technology_and_science-tech_and_gadgets/t/tax-season-e-filing-becomes-new-normal/.

12. Mark Anderson, consultant and publisher of the *Strategic News Service* newsletter, remarked, "Our greatest untapped resource is our unused computer cycles" at his annual Future in Review conference in 2004.

13. Bharat Mediratta as told to Julie Bick, "The Google Way: Give Engineers Room," *The New York Times,* October 21, 2007.

14. Mark Anderson, Strategic News Service Newsletter, February 24, 2011.
15. "Shaquille O'Neal's All-Star Twitter Coach," in *Bloomberg Businessweek,* October 27, 2011. The coach is Amy Jo Martin.
16. David Segal,"What They Don't Teach Law Students: Lawyering," *The New York Times,* November 19, 2011, http://www.nytimes.com/2011/11/20/business/after-law -school-associates-learn-to-be-lawyers.html?scp=4&sq=legal%20training&st=cse.
17. "Printing Body Parts—Making a Bit of Me," *The Economist,* February 18, 2010, http://www.economist.com/node/15543683.
18. Marc Prensky, "In the 21st-Century University, Let's Ban (Paper) Books," *The Chronicle of Higher Education,* November 13, 2011, http://chronicle.com/article /In-the-21st-Century/129744/.
19. Jonathan Shaw "The Humanities, Digitized," *Harvard Magazine,* May–June 2012, http://harvardmagazine.com/2012/05/the-humanities-digitized.
20. Ibid.
21. A cute example of a synthespian is found in the 2002 movie, *S1m0ne,* starring Al Pacino. See http://www.imdb.com/title/tt0258153/.
22. "Uncanny Valley," http://en.wikipedia.org/wiki/Uncanny_valley.

CHAPTER 6

1. Marc Prensky, "Digital Natives, Digital Immigrants: A New Way to Look at Ourselves and Our Kids," *On the Horizon* (MCB University Press, Vol. 9 No. 5, October 2001), http://www.marcprensky.com/writing/Prensky%20-%20Digital %20Natives,%20Digital%20Immigrants%20-%20Part1.pdf.
2. Marc Prensky, *From Digital Natives to Digital Wisdom: Hopeful Essays for 21st Century Learning* (New York: Corwin, 2012).
3. "Video Game Statistics/Video Game Industry States," Grabstats.com, http://grab stats.com/statcategorymain.asp?StatCatID=13.
4. Said by one of the participants in a student panel accompanying one of my talks.
5. "Cyber-English" classes were created by New York City teacher Ted Nellin, www. tnellen.com/cybereng/.
6. Kevin Kelly, *What Technology Wants* (New York: Viking/Penguin, 2010).
7. Howard Rheingold, *Tools for Thought: The History and Future of Mind Amplifiers* (Boston: MIT Press, 2000); and *Net Smart: How to Thrive Online* (Cambridge: MIT Press, 2012).
8. "What Is Collective Intelligence and What Will We Do About It?" transcript of remarks by Thomas W. Malone at the official launch of the MIT Center for Collective Intelligence, October 13, 2006, http://cci.mit.edu/about/malone launchremarks.html.
9. Zoran Popovic, personal interview.
10. See James Paul Gee, *What Videogames Have to Teach Us about Learning and Literacy* (New York: Palgrave MacMillan, 2003); Jane McGonigal, *Reality Is Broken* (New York: Penguin Press, 2011); and Marc Prensky: *Don't Bother Me, Mom, I'm Learning* (St. Paul, MN: Paragon House, 2005).

CHAPTER 7

1. Octavia Estelle Butler (1947–2006) was a Hugo and Nebula award-winning Afro-American science fiction writer, the first science fiction writer to receive a Macarthur Foundation "genius" grant.

2. Nicolas Carr, "Is Google Making Us Stupid?: What the Internet Is Doing to Our Brains," *The Atlantic,* July/August 2008, http://www.theatlantic.com/magazine/archive/2008/07/is-google-making-us-stupid/6868/.

3. "Changes in Young Adulthood," Massachusetts Institute of Technology, http://hrweb.mit.edu/worklife/youngadult/changes.html.

4. "Two billion years ago, our ancestors were microbes; a half-billion years ago, fish, a hundred million years ago, something like mice; then million years ago, arboreal apes; and a million years ago, proto-humans puzzling out the taming of fire. Our evolutionary lineage is marked by mastery of change. In our time, the pace is quickening." Carl Sagan, *Pale Blue Dot: A Vision of the Human Future in Space* (New York: Random House, 1994), 332.

5. See James Paul Gee, *What Videogames Have to Teach Us about Learning and Literacy* (New York: Palgrave Macmillan, 2003); Jane McGonigal, *Reality Is Broken* (New York: Penguin Press, 2011); and Marc Prensky, *Don't Bother Me, Mom, I'm Learning* (St. Paul, MN: Paragon House, 2005).

6. http://novascone.com/first-human-cyborg-neil-harbisson.html http://articles.cnn.com/2002-03-22/tech/human.cyborg_1_cyborg-nerve-signals?_s=PM:TECH.

7. "No Killer App: The Moral Panic about Video Games Is Subsiding," *The Economist,* December 10, 2011.

8. You can find much of this research at http://www.persuasion-profiling.com/downloads/.

9. Eli Pariser, "Welcome to the Brave New World of Persuasion Profiling," *Wired,* May 2011, http://www.wired.com/magazine/2011/04/st_essay_persuasion_profiling/.

10. The Maginot Line was a set of fortifications built by France on the border with Germany after World War I that, at the start of World War II, the Germans simply went around.

11. Georg Lowery, "Technology Changes Our Brains But Doesn't Lead to Idiocy," Cornell University Chronicle Online, February 23, 2011, http://www.news.cornell.edu/stories/Feb11/HancockOneDayU.html.

12. For more on side effects, see http://adderallsideeffects.org/.

13. "Off-Label Use," http://en.wikipedia.org/wiki/Off-label_use.

14. For more on off-label drugs and cancer treatment, see http://www.cancer.org/Treatment/TreatmentsandSideEffects/TreatmentTypes/Chemotherapy/off-label-drug-use.

15. "Gut Instinct," *The Economist,* September 3, 2011, http://www.economist.com/node/21528214.

16. This useful example is offered here: http://www.wilmott.com/messageview.cfm?catid=8&threadid=69364.

17. "Worrying about Wireless," *The Economist,* September 3, 2011, http://www.economist.com/node/21527022.

18. Dr. Michael Merzenich, personal interview.

19. Ibid.

20. Douglas Rushkoff, *Program or Be Programmed: 10 Commands for the Digital Age* (New York: O/R Books, 2010).

21. I do not know who was the first to note this—I first heard it from Paul Saffo.

22. You can buy them on Amazon at http://www.amazon.com/s/?ie=UTF8&keywords=iphone+wrist+band&tag=googhydr-20&index=aps&hvadid=6217946367&hvpos=1t2&hvexid=&hvnetw=g&hvrand=642772452205753046&hvpone=&hvpt wo=&hvqmt=b&ref=pd_sl_8ddlg89raq_b.

23. Stephen Wolfram, personal interview.

24. "Information at Your Fingertips" was the title of Bill Gates's keynote speech at the COMDEX convention in Las Vegas in November 1990.
25. Douglas Rushkoff, *Program or Be Programmed*, Amazon Kindle e-book location: 375, 381.
26. Vernor Vinge, personal interview.
27. Marc Prensky, "Backup Education?" in *From Digital Natives to Digital Wisdom* (Corwin, 2012), http://www.marcprensky.com/writing/Prensky-Backup_Education-EdTech-1-08.pdf
28. Small and Vorgan, *iBrain*.
29. Ibid.
30. "Addiction," http://www.psychologytoday.com/basics/addiction.

CHAPTER 8

1. "Accelerating Change," http://en.wikipedia.org/wiki/Accelerating_change#cite_note-6.
2. From remarks by Raymond Kurzweil at the 2011 Singularity Summit in New York. Kurzweil's remarks can be viewed at http://www.youtube.com/watch?v=WPqjYrLhDnk&list=UU1zny_jKmgnEbQitfPgAlxg&index=2&feature=plcp.
3. Vernor Vinge, personal interview.
4. Jaron Lanier, *You Are Not a Gadget* (New York: Alfred A. Knopf, 2010), 18, 178.
5. "Singularitarianism," http://en.wikipedia.org/wiki/Singularitarianism#cite_note-Kurzweil_2005-0.
6. Lev Grossman, "The Singularity," *Time*, February 21, 2011, p. 44.

INDEX

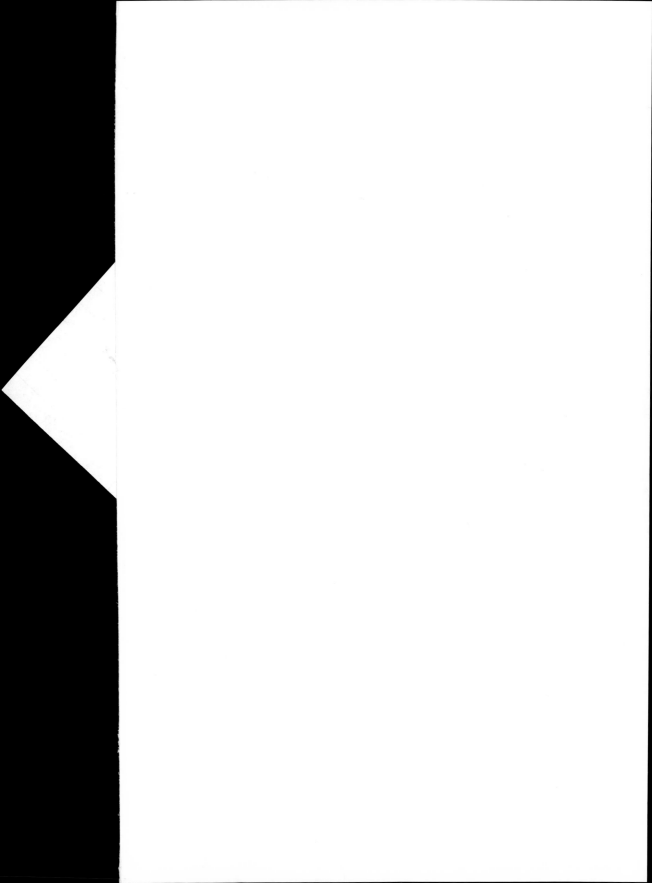

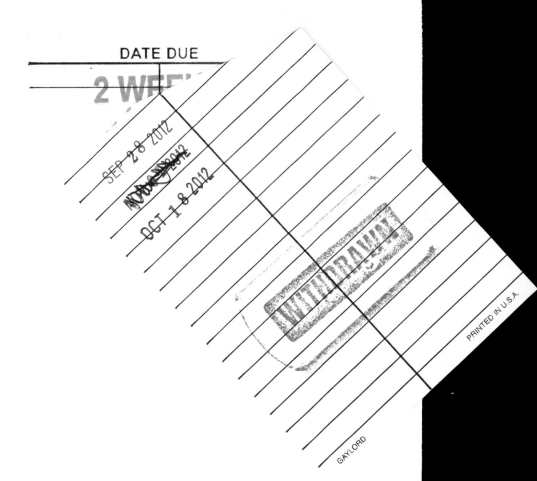